DECENTRALIZATION:
MANAGERIAL AMBIGUITY BY DESIGN

DECENTRALIZATION:
Managerial ambiguity by design

by

Richard F. Vancil

with the assistance of
Lee E. Buddrus

A research study and report prepared for the
FINANCIAL EXECUTIVES RESEARCH FOUNDATION

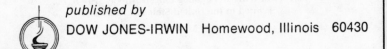

published by
DOW JONES-IRWIN   Homewood, Illinois   60430

Decentralization: Managerial
Ambiguity by Design

Copyright 1978 and 1979

Financial Executives Research Foundation
633 Third Avenue, New York, N.Y. 10017

International Standard Book Number   0-910586-32-2 (hardbound)
International Standard Book Number   0-910586-33-0 (paperbound)

Library of Congress Catalog Card Number   79–51782
Printed in the United States of America

M 1015

1 2 3 4 5 6 7 8 9 0 K 6 5 4 3 2 1 0 9

PROJECT ADVISORY COMMITTEE

About the authors

Richard F. Vancil is Lovett-Learned Professor of Business Administration at Harvard Business School. He received his B.S. from Northwestern University in 1953 and his M.B.A. (1955) and D.B.A. (1960) from Harvard University. He joined the HBS Faculty as an Instructor in 1958, and was appointed Professor in 1968.

Professor Vancil's professional interests are in the broad field of management systems, focusing particularly on resource allocation systems and measurement systems. He is an author, coauthor, or editor of more than 20 books and monographs, most recently, *Strategic Planning Systems* (1977). He has also contributed more than a dozen articles to *Harvard Business Review*.

Mr. Vancil is active as a management consultant to large industrial corporations. In 1964, he founded Management Analysis Center, Inc., a management consulting firm, and serves as chairman of its board of directors. He is also a director of Connecticut General Insurance Company.

Lee E. Buddrus was an Associate at Management Analysis Center, Inc., during 1973–77, and was the primary research assistant on this study. He received his B.A. from Rice University in 1970, an M.E.E. from Rice University in 1971, and an M.B.A. from the Harvard Business School in 1973. Mr. Buddrus is currently employed by Acme Engineering & Manufacturing Corp. in Muskogee, Oklahoma.

Foreword

In 1965, the Financial Executives Research Foundation (FERF) published the most widely read book bearing our imprint—*Divisional Performance: Measurement and Control* by David Solomons. In a commercial edition published by Richard D. Irwin, Inc., it is still in print.

One reason for the success of Solomon's study is the pervasive use of divisional "profit centers" in U.S. industrial firms. The trend was still emerging in the early 1960s when Solomons began his work and he most probably contributed to the adoption of that form of organization.

In late 1973, the Trustees of the Foundation decided to commission a new study on the same topic, but with somewhat broader scope. The original prospectus for a study tentatively titled "Decentralization" read in part as follows:

> Profit centers and decentralized management have become almost a hallmark of the American business organization. The underlying philosophy is that authority and responsibility should be parallel and that in a complex business the authority and responsibility must inevitably be delegated. This principle is valid—but only up to the point that there is a conflict with the principle that overall management should optimize overall performance.
>
> * * * * *
>
> It is suggested that a research project be considered which would explore the various methods employed by companies to administer a diversified, multiplant operation; to evaluate the performance of the divisional management; to motivate the divisional management; and to decide the product lines to be expanded as well as those to be discontinued.
>
> This research would include such areas as interdivisional pricing; establishing "arms-length" transactions between divisions; and the allocation of common costs and expenses. In the course of conducting this research, the subjectivity and variety of methods would be studied and the relative merits of various methods under various conditions would be analyzed.

The above concepts are incorporated in this new study. Part One contains the theory of decentralized management: Why decentralize? How much? The philosophical, physical, and systemic methods necessary to achieve decentralization are discussed in Part Two. Questionnaires were distributed to measure the extent of business diversification, profit center manager autonomy, and the realism of the profit measurement in use. The result is an index to measure the profit center manager's perception of his autonomy plus an index of his functional authority over operating activities.

The Foundation's Trustees are pleased that Dow Jones-Irwin has contracted with FERF for the publishing rights to this new study, thus assuring a wider availability than is possible through our normal channels.

The Foundation's Trustees express their appreciation to Richard Vancil and his research team from the Management Analysis Center, to the hundreds of executives who responded to the mail questionnaires, and to the Project Steering Committee.

Kenneth S. Axelson, President
Financial Executives Research Foundation

Acknowledgments

A researcher whose project stretches over six years from conception to publication has time to accept a lot of help from his friends—and I certainly did in this case. The best way to acknowledge all those contributors is to proceed in roughly chronological order.

The idea for a study on "Decentralization" was originated by the Trustees of the Financial Executives Research Foundation (FERF), but the scope of the study (the "initial hypothesis" in Chapter One) was significantly influenced by three colleagues at Harvard Business School: Joseph L. Bower, Charles J. Christenson, and Jay Lorsch. In the early 1970s, the four of us were looking for opportunities to explore the relationships among strategy, structure, and management systems. Without their advice and encouragement, this study would have been narrowly focused on profit center measurement systems.

The sponsorship by FERF provided three resources that were even more valuable than the research funds. First, the response to a long and complex questionnaire by nearly 300 financial executives produced the rich data base presented in Part Two of this book. Second, the Steering Committee chaired by Paul Rizzo proved to be invaluable. They were unbelievably patient, encouraging me to extend my thinking rather than scolding me for an unending series of missed deadlines. Finally, Ben Makela, FERF's Director of Research, succeeded in cheerfully managing both me and the committee in such a way that nobody got mad at anybody.

Staff support during the first years of the study was provided by a group of consultants at Management Analysis Center, Inc. (MAC). Paul J. Stonich was the Senior Vice President in charge of that staff, and also made important substantive contributions. Lee E. Buddrus was the MAC associate who finally delivered a clean and accessible data base—and then produced and digested mountains of computer analyses.

In mid-1977, Harvard Business School became a cosponsor of the study, providing both computer facilities and access to a broad group of academic colleagues. Professors Richard S. Rosenbloom and Stephen P. Bradley, Director and Associate Director, respectively, of the Division of Research, understood the potential which, at that point, was still latent in the study and agreed to support it. Support of a more tangible sort was contributed by four doctoral candidates who subsequently became collaborators in writing up the detailed findings. The sections written by Paul C. Browne, Judith B. Kamm, Richard G. Linowes, and Srinivasan Umapathy are separately identified in Part Two.

Finally, two prepublication editions of the manuscript were produced, in January and July 1978, and were widely circulated for critical comment. Special thanks are due to Robert N. Anthony, my teacher, mentor, and colleague for over 25 years, for his detailed and penetrating critique. At the risk of omitting someone, I would also like to acknowledge the comments offered by Professors Stephen A. Allen III, Cornelius J. Casey, Jr., Charles J. Christenson, W. W. Cooper, Peter Lorange, Kenneth A. Merchant, Richard S. Rosenbloom, Richard P. Rumelt, Malcolm S. Salter, Vijay Sathe, Arthur Schleifer, Jr., and Renato Tagiuri. Over 200 M.B.A. and executive students also read the manuscript and made many suggestions for improvement. Most recently, only six weeks ago, the study was discussed in the Faculty Workship on Research in Administration, and the result was a nontrivial revision. It is clearly time to put this book to press because there seems to be no end to the opportunity for modifying it.

To all of these people, in some sense the collective "we" who speak in the pages that follow, I am immensely grateful. My secretary during the entire project, Marianne D'Amico, also gave tireless and cheerful support. But, of course, I accept personal responsibility for the final result of all these efforts.

July 1979   **Richard F. Vancil**

Contents

Conceptual backdrop. Scope and methodology: *Product line diversification. Functional independence of profit centers. Profit center measurement practices. Perceived autonomy of profit center managers. Design of this book: Part one: A theory of decentralized management.   Part two: Detailed findings and analyses.*

PART ONE
A THEORY OF DECENTRALIZED MANAGEMENT

The philosophy of decentralization: *Elements of the philosophy. Implementing decentralization.* Responsibility and authority: *Efficiency and adaptability. The implicit matrix in a decentralized firm.* The strategy of decentralization.

Patterns of functional authority: *Functional authority in diversified firms. Functional authority of profit center managers.* Patterns of perceived autonomy: *Autonomy: The corporate perspective. Perceived autonomy of profit center managers.* The authority/autonomy relationship.

Decentralization and management systems: *Strategy formulation and implementation. Purposes of management systems.* Measurement systems: *Characteristics of financial measurement systems. Purposes of financial measurement systems. Limitations of profit measurement systems.* Reward systems: *Rewards and measurement. Bonuses and autonomy.*

Chapter 5: The interdependence of profit center managers:
Responsibility and control **99**

Financial responsibility of profit center managers: *Patterns of cost responsibility. Patterns of asset responsibility. Responsibility and autonomy.* Control of shared resources: *Cost assignment practices. Control and autonomy.*

Chapter 6: A theory of decentralized management **121**

The profit center manager. Corporate managers: *Organizational climate. Autonomy and decision-making processes.*

PART TWO
DETAILED FINDINGS AND ANALYSES

Chapter 1

Introduction

THIS STUDY is an attempt to understand and explain how decentralized firms are managed. Nearly all large U.S. manufacturing corporations are decentralized in the sense that corporate managers have segmented their enterprises into business units in order to hold a subordinate manager accountable for the performance of each line of business. These subordinates, typically called "division general managers" or some such title, are responsible—more or less—for all aspects of the performance of their businesses. The critical characteristic that defines a decentralized firm is that the subordinate manager is responsible for the financial performance, including the profitability, of "his" or "her" business. In this book, we will refer to such managers, whatever their precise title, as "profit center managers."*

As initially conceived, this study was intended to focus on how "profit" is calculated for profit centers in decentralized firms. The sponsors—and the researchers—believed that the profit center measurement system was a tool of central importance in the management of decentralized firms. We wanted to gather empirical data on this topic and make it available to corporate financial executives who are responsible for designing these measurement systems.

As events turned out, however, the broad approach that we adopted for our survey ultimately led to a sharp downward revision in our appraisal of the importance of measurement systems. They are important, of course, but less important than such primary factors as "authority" and "autonomy." The result, we hope, is a study that will be of value to a far broader group of executives than we initially

---

* For convenience of expression, the singular masculine pronoun will be used frequently in this book but is intended to refer to individual managers of either sex.

1

expected. We now view this study as aimed primarily at general managers, both corporate and divisional, in decentralized firms. While we offer no prescriptions about *how* to manage such firms, we do provide a focal point and a set of operational definitions that may help such managers gain a new perspective on the issues inherent in the interrelated concepts of authority, autonomy, responsibility, and control.

Decentralized firms are commonly referred to as employing the "divisional" form of organization, in contrast to centralized firms which employ the "functional" form. This organizational dichotomy between centralization and decentralization, while simplistic, is a useful starting point for our analysis. Corporate managers in almost any firm with more than a few dozen employees must subdivide their managerial tasks. Prior to such a subdivision, all business decisions are made "centrally," i.e., by the corporate manager(s). An evolutionary first step for a growing firm is for the corporate managers to retain the authority for "important" (cross-functional) decisions and to delegate authority for the management of the principal operating functions such as research, manufacturing, distribution, sales, and administration. Subordinate "functional managers" are then held accountable for the performance, really the technical management, of their operating functions.

The differences between functional and divisional organizations, between delegating technical authority and decentralizing the responsibility for business profits, are explored more fully in Chapter 2. For the moment, we shall simply assert that decentralization introduces great complexity into the managerial task. Business executives will have no difficulty accepting that assertion, and the primary reason for the complexity has been succinctly expressed by one of their peers. In 1920, Alfred P. Sloan prepared an organization study for General Motors, even then one of the largest organizations of its day, as it grappled with the problem of how to organize itself:

> The basis upon which this study has been made is founded upon two principles, which are stated as follows:
>
> 1. The responsibility attached to the chief executive of each operation shall in no way be limited. Each such organization headed by its chief executive shall be complete in every necessary function and enable(d) to exercise its full initiative and logical development.
>
> 2. Certain central organization functions are absolutely essential to the logical development and proper control of the Corporation's activities.[1]

---

[1] Alfred P. Sloan, Jr., *My Years with General Motors* (Garden City, N.Y.: Doubleday, 1964), p. 52.

In his book, published 40 years later, Mr. Sloan commented as follows:

> . . . Looking back on the text of the two basic principles, after all these years, I am amused to see that the language is contradictory, and that its very contradiction is the crux of the matter. In point 1, I maximize decentralization of divisional operations in the words "shall in no way be limited." In point 2, I proceed to limit the responsibility of divisional chief executives in the expression "proper control." The language of organization has always suffered some want of words to express the true facts and circumstances of human interaction. One usually asserts one aspect or another of it at different times, such as the absolute independence of the part, and again the need of coordination, and again the concept of the whole with a guiding center. Interaction, however, is the thing, and with some reservation about the language and details I still stand on the fundamentals of what I wrote in the study. Its basic principles are in touch with the central problem of management as I have known it to this day.[2]

That comment is the genesis for the subtitle of this book, "Managerial Ambiguity by Design." In contrast to the clean lines of functional authority in a centralized organization, decentralization produces contradictory, ambiguous roles for profit center managers—and intentionally so. Surely such ambiguity is to be avoided, unless it is judged to be the only way to cope with the managerial problems caused by sheer size (as in General Motors in 1920) or by a bewildering diversity in the range of businesses in which the corporation is engaged. Yet, the first finding to emerge from our study is that decentralization is *the* most common organizational mode in U.S. manufacturing corporations today, not only in large diversified firms but also in relatively homogeneous businesses with sales of $100 million or less. The benefits of managing ambiguity are apparently worth the costs, and a better understanding of how that ambiguity is managed would seem to be worth the effort.

Given the pervasiveness of decentralization in the United States, one might expect that a vast literature on the subject would already exist. There is admittedly no shortage of books about management, written by business executives, business philosophers, and academic researchers. The academics, in particular, have become increasingly prolific during the last two decades, conducting myriads of empirical studies to explore how managers interact in business organizations and to identify the factors that appear to influence their behavior. The striking aspect of nearly all of these studies is that their data are drawn from relatively low organizational levels. Those studies that are

---

[2] Ibid., pp. 52−53.

concerned with "top management" usually draw their data from functional organizations, either in centralized firms or, more frequently, in divisions of decentralized firms where the profit center manager also, typically, has functional subordinates. With the exception of a handful or so of studies, there is a paucity of empirical research aimed explicitly at exploring the relationships between corporate managers and profit center managers in decentralized firms.

This study addresses that target, approaching it from the point of view of both levels of general managers. The central focus is on the "autonomy" of the profit center manager, trying to identify the principal factors that affect his perceived "freedom to take action" in the face of the ambiguous relationships in a decentralized firm. The most important factors appear to be (1) the design of the assignment pattern of physical resources among profit center managers, and (2) the design of management systems intended to influence the behavior of those managers.

Corporate managers are the architects of both of these interrelated designs, and this study may be useful to them in providing an explicit framework for their thinking as they continually review and modify those designs. Profit center managers, who live in that managerial structure, may find that this study helps them understand both why their autonomy is inevitably constrained and how to cope with the resulting ambiguity. Finally, because the definition of "profit" that is used to measure the financial performance of profit center managers does influence the behavior of those managers, we are confident that this study will be useful for corporate financial executives. As a member of the corporate management team, it is the chief financial officer who carries primary responsibility for ensuring that the design of the profit center measurement system is consistent with the degree of decentralization which his firm is trying to achieve.

CONCEPTUAL BACKDROP

This study is a direct descendant of an earlier book by David Solomons, *Divisional Performance: Measurement and Control,* and it is no accident that it is sponsored by the same research foundation.[3] As Solomons described his efforts:

> The purpose of this study is to investigate the financial relations existing between the central management of a divisionalized company and the

---

[3] Financial Executives Research Foundation, New York, 1965.

management of its several divisions; and, as a result of such investigation, to arrive at recommendations which would make for the more effective coordination and control of divisional operations in accordance with the objectives of the corporation.

. . . Twenty-five companies . . . participated in it. All of them were visited, a number of them both at head office and at divisional level, and I was able to talk freely with their financial executives.

It was not my objective simply to make a survey of existing practices, for which purpose a much broader coverage by questionnaire would have been more suitable. Rather, I wanted to uncover the pros and cons of different practices, and then to form my own judgment about their relative merits.[4]

Solomons' book was a major contribution to the literature of decentralization, along several dimensions. He did identify and discuss the pros and cons of different measurement practices. He also attempted to prescribe the most appropriate measurement practice under a defined set of circumstances. But perhaps most importantly, he recognized and highlighted the fact that those circumstances, a "genuine division," did not always hold:

The more difficult it is, in a particular situation, effectively to measure divisional performance by the profit test, the more circumscribed is divisional freedom of decision-making likely to be. The difficulty is likely to arise whenever a division's affairs cannot be sufficient   disentangled from other parts of the business. Ultimately, a point is reached when the "division" loses the right to be regarded as a genuine division at all. But because of the many gradations encountered in the amount of autonomy enjoyed by divisions of different companies—a subject to which we return later—no attempt will be made to define just where this point lies.[5]

When he did return to that point later, Solomons illustrated it with several examples and concluded that, "nothing is to be achieved by a system of fictitious profit responsibility . . . which cannot be achieved without it." (p. 164)

Divisional interdependence, particularly the transfer of goods and services from one division to another, was clearly one of the major problems of profit center measurement. Solomons also identified the other major issue: the division of operating responsibility between the corporate headquarters and the divisions, which he termed the "au-

---

[4] Ibid, p. ix.
[5] Ibid., p. 9.

tonomy" of the division general manager. He cited the data from a 1962 survey by a business magazine reporting the rank of the manager who had the authority to make nine different types of profit decisions. From his analysis of those data, he concluded:

> The picture is one of great diversity. But out of the diversity another pattern emerges; there is a large group consisting of about three-quarters of the companies divided between those who give most of the decision-making power to the division manager and those who give it to a corporate vice president. This "split down the middle" does bring into clear focus the difference of opinion which exists about the merits of divisional autonomy.[6]

For Solomons, a "genuine division" was one which was relatively independent of other divisions and for which the division general manager had substantial operating autonomy from corporate headquarters, such that the measurement of profit responsibility was "realistic."

A second major contribution to our knowledge about decentralization was the work done by Joseph L. Bower on *Managing the Resource Allocation Process.*[7] Bower did an intensive clinical study of a large decentralized firm and found that the decision-making process engaged in by corporate and profit center managers was importantly affected by what he defined as the "structural context":

> . . . The formal organization (with associated definitions of managers' jobs), the system of information and control used to measure performance of the business, and the systems used to measure and reward performance of managers.

> . . . The role of structural context is that it shapes the purposive manager's definition of business problems by directing, delimiting, and coloring his focus and perception; it determines the priorities which the various demands on him are given. Structural context has this role because it is the principal way in which the purposive manager learns about the goals of the corporation.

> Structural context is particularly important because all of its elements are subject to control by top management. Thus, management has in its hands the levers that influence behavior of managers many levels below the top of the hierarchical organization. What is necessary in order to prescribe for managers is a view of what constitutes desirable behavior. With such a view, it would be possible to reason what structural forms are likely to generate that behavior.[8]

---

[6] Ibid., pp. 17–19.

[7] Boston: Division of Research, Graduate School of Business Administration, Harvard University, 1970.

[8] Ibid., pp. 71–73.

The third important empirical study on decentralization is the work of Lorsch and Allen, *Managing Diversity and Interdependence.*[9] They studied corporate headquarters units and 22 divisional top management groups in six firms. An abstract of the final chapter of their book described the scope and thrust of their work as follows:

> It is argued that the tendency to treat the issues covered by the study as simply a problem of centralization versus decentralization of authority has often obscured a much more complex management task: to build an organization which can help managers develop the patterns of perception, information exchange, and decision making necessary to cope effectively with the unique patterns of diversity and interdependence faced by their firm. Specific attention is devoted to how structural choices, the design of measurement and reward systems, and on-going management behavior can be systematically used to achieve an effective balance between the internal workings of a multidivisional firm and the external realities of its environment.

These three studies prepared, respectively, by an academic interested in management accounting, a scholar in the field of corporate strategy, and a pair of behavioral scientists, are all addressed to the same phenomenon. Each of these studies, however, was grounded in a relatively limited quantity of empirical data. The research opportunity that we perceived was to synthesize the suggestive conclusions of those three studies into an initial conceptual framework which would facilitate further exploration into the management of decentralized firms. To accomplish this, we decided to conduct a large-scale survey to gather data about (1) the interdependencies among profit centers in a sample of decentralized firms, (2) the perception of the profit center managers in those firms about the extent of their autonomy, and (3) the practices followed by those firms in the design of their profit center measurement systems. We also hoped to establish an independent variable which would explain why the variations in interdependencies, autonomy, and measurement systems existed. The hypothesized interrelationships between these variables are shown graphically in Figure 1–1.

The relationships expressed in Figure 1–1 were not, we thought, controversial. We were confident that, among corporations that had defined internal profit centers, there were wide variations in the extent of business diversity. We decided to use business diversity as a measure of the independent variable reflecting the corporation's diversification strategy. We believed that in highly diverse firms the autonomy of the profit center manager would be high, primarily

Figure 1–1
Decentralization: Initial hypothesis

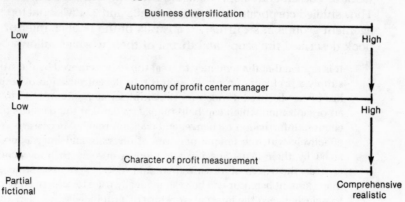

because the corporate managers in such companies would lack the expertise to make detailed decisions for each of their various businesses. Further, in highly diverse firms, fewer decisions would need to be made at the corporate level because the individual profit centers would be relatively independent of each other, thus allowing broad delegation of authority to each profit center manager. On the other hand, in relatively undiversified firms, corporate management's expertise would be sufficient to allow them to intervene in decisions which might impact on several interdependent profit centers, thus reducing the autonomy of an individual profit center manager. Finally, we believed that we would observe wide variations in the character of the "profit" calculated for profit centers. In some firms, we expected to find a very realistic calculation, in the sense that it included all the costs and revenues that might be found on the income statement of an independent corporation. At the other extreme, we expected to find some situations where the "profit" was fictional, either because it included only a part of the costs attributable to the business or because the costs so included were assigned in an arbitrary fashion.

We did not set out to "prove" these relationships in some rigorous academic manner. Rather, we sought to gather data which would permit us to develop measures of each of these variables. We hoped to use the instrument of a questionnaire to measure the extent of business diversification, the extent of the autonomy of a profit center manager, and the realism of the profit measurement system in use. Summary measurements along these three dimensions would permit us to demonstrate whether or not the autonomy of a profit center manager was relatively low in companies that were not very diversified and that the profit measurement system in such a situation was not very realistic.

The data we obtained turned out to be richer than we expected, with the result that we were able to develop not only an index to measure a profit center manager's perception of his autonomy but also an index of his functional authority over operating activities. The character of the measurement system was also subdivided into two variables: (1) an index of the comprehensiveness of a profit center manager's financial responsibility for the resources consumed or employed in his or her business, and (2) an index of the accuracy with which those resources are accounted for, reflecting the manager's control over resource consumption or utilization. Putting all those pieces together, as summarized finally in Chapter 6, has led us to an enriched theory about how decentralized firms are managed.

SCOPE AND METHODOLOGY

We conducted a large-scale, two-stage direct mail survey focused on the domestic profit centers of U.S. manufacturing firms. A profit center was defined as "any fairly independent organizational unit, accountable separately for its performance, for which some measure of profit is determined periodically." The questionnaires used in this survey are reproduced in Part Two, Section H, which also includes a list of those respondents who allowed us to disclose that they participated.

The use of profit centers is also fairly common in financial institutions, public utilities, transportation companies, and retail and wholesale distribution chains. We chose not to include such corporations in our sample, because there are fewer large firms in these sectors and also because the use of profit centers by such firms is relatively newer and less well established than in manufacturing firms. The focus on *domestic* profit centers of manufacturing firms was intended to avoid the measurement complications that might be introduced by considerations of differing income tax rates in various countries and of fluctuations in foreign currency exchange rates.

The first questionnaire (the "structural" questionnaire) was mailed to the senior member of the Financial Executives Institute (FEI) located in the corporate office of 684 manufacturing firms. A total of 313 questionnaires, 46 percent, were returned, of which only 17 stated that their company did not have two or more domestic profit centers. The fact that 296 respondents, 95 percent of the total, did have profit centers suggests that the use of profit centers is pervasive in U.S. manufacturing firms. Suggestive evidence that profit centers are less widely used in other types of firms is presented in Part Two, Section A.

The structural questionnaire was not mailed to a random sample of FEI members. Instead, the sample was weighted to include a relatively higher proportion of the larger manufacturing corporations while still ensuring an adequate representation among smaller firms. In order to keep the structural questionnaire short, we did not ask the financial executives to provide demographic data about their companies but only to include a copy of their most recent annual report. Most respondents did so, and we were able to glean the desired information from that document. For those who failed to provide such data, we requested it in the second stage mailing, although we did not receive a 100-percent response rate. Nevertheless, for most of the 291 respondents that completed usable questionnaires, we do have data on four demographic characteristics: sales revenue, net income as a percent of sales, net income as a percent of investment, and ten-year compound growth rate in earnings per share. As might be expected, the size and performance of the respondents was well dispersed across each of these variables. The detailed distribution of responses for each demographic variable are presented in Part Two, Section A.

Product line diversification

While the primary focus of the structural questionnaire was on profit center operations and measurement practices, the respondents were also asked to answer a series of questions about the diversity of their firms' product lines. Other researchers have attempted to measure diversification in a variety of ways, but most of these are mechanistic, such as tabulating the number of 2- or 3-digit SIC codes in which the corporation has a significant volume of sales. We chose, instead, a categorization scheme developed by Richard P. Rumelt and presented in his book, *Strategy, Structure and Economic Performance.*[10] The four major diversification categories, and the distribution of our sample across them, is shown in Figure 1–2.

---

[10] Boston: Division of Research, Graduate School of Business Administration, Harvard University, 1974. The classification scheme was originated by Leonard Wrigley and described in "Divisional Autonomy and Diversification," unpublished doctoral dissertation, Harvard Business School, 1970.

Figure 1–2
Diversification strategy of 291 U.S. manufacturing companies

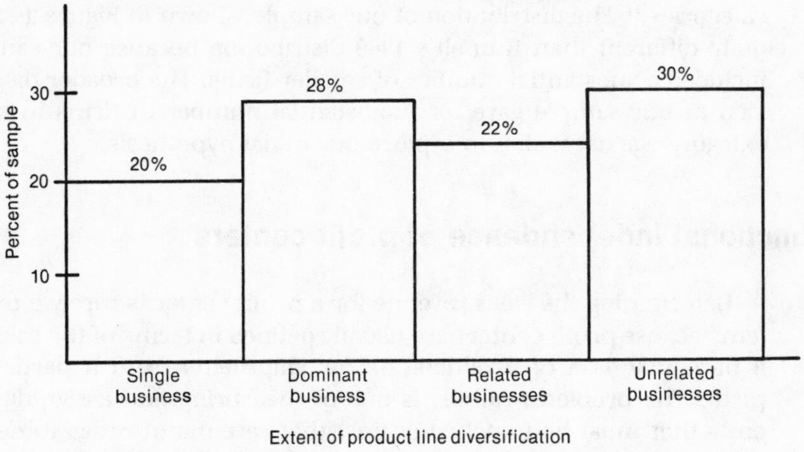

Extent of product line diversification

Source: Part Two, Exhibit A–3.

The primary virtue of Rumelt's classification scheme is that it attempts to capture the underlying strategy of the firm regarding business diversification. Briefly defined (see Part Two, Section A for more details), the categories are:

1. *Single business.* This company obtains more than 95 percent of its sales revenue from the "production and marketing of a single product/service or a line of closely related products/services." This category also includes many vertically integrated firms.
2. *Dominant business.* This company has a core product line like that of a single business, but it accounts for between 70 percent and 95 percent of total sales revenues.
3. *Related businesses.* This company derives 70 percent or more of its revenues from a group of "somehow related businesses." The questionnaire contained several examples to assist the respondent in deciding whether or not the company fell into this category.
4. *Unrelated businesses.* This company does not have a single product line nor a set of related businesses which account for as much as 70 percent of total sales revenues. This category includes most conglomerates that have grown through a series of acquisitions.

Rumelt's study documented that, over time, many firms tend to evolve from a single business to one that is more diversified. He estimated that in 1949 nearly 70 percent of the 500 largest industrial firms were in either the single business or dominant business category, and that by 1969 only 35 percent of the 500 largest firms were in those two categories.[11] The distribution of our sample, shown in Figure 1–2, is quite different than Rumelt's 1969 distribution because our sample included a substantial number of smaller firms. The broader dispersion in our sample gave us a substantial number of firms in each category against which to explore our initial hypothesis.

Functional independence of profit centers

Determining the sales revenue for a profit center is rarely a problem because profit centers are usually defined in terms of the sales of a particular line of products and/or shipments from a particular plant. The problem, rather, is one of measuring and assigning the costs that must be matched against that revenue in order to determine the amount of "profit" earned by the profit center. Figure 1–3 is an overview of the data that we gathered on the incurrence of costs by, or assignment of costs to, profit centers.

Figure 1–3
Major elements of costs assigned to a typical profit center

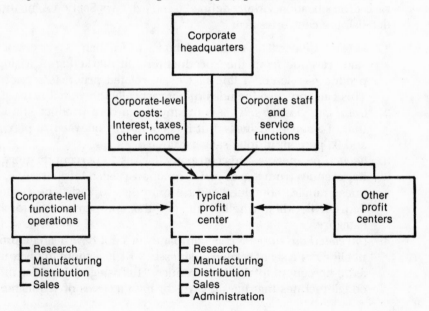

---

[11] Ibid., pp. 50–51.

The conventional manufacturing firm is involved in five major functional activities: research, manufacturing, distribution, sales, and administration, although the relative importance of each function would depend upon the nature of the business. A "typical" profit center in such a firm might be more or less self-contained in terms of performing each of these functions in the generation of its sales revenue. Theoretically, a profit center could be completely self-contained, meaning that it had no transactions with other operating units in the corporation and received no services from the corporate headquarters. Legal subsidiaries, particularly if less than 100 percent-owned, might meet this test, but our survey was restricted to profit centers which were not separate legal entities. Unincorporated profit centers are never completely independent, at least in our sample of 291 firms.

The typical profit center does have a variety of transactions with other units in the corporation. Research may be done in a central research laboratory; a corporate manufacturing facility may supply raw materials or components to several profit centers; there may be a central warehouse and distribution activity serving several profit centers; or a field sales force may be run from the corporate level to serve several profit centers. It is also common for profit centers within the same corporation to deal with each other, transferring goods or services, or sharing joint facilities.

Some of the administrative services required to run a manufacturing firm are usually performed at the corporate level, to a greater or lesser extent. We defined a dozen major categories of such services, including electronic data processing, general marketing services, industrial relations, purchasing, etc. Finally, there are two items, interest expense and income taxes, which are only incurred at the corporate level but which might be construed as payments made on behalf of the unincorporated profit centers.

We gathered two types of data about each of these items. First, we ascertained the extent to which a typical profit center was self-contained in terms of the five functional activities. If the profit center was not totally self-sufficient on any function, we then inquired as to whether the costs that were incurred by other units in its behalf were assigned to the profit center and, if so, how the cost assignment was calculated. These two types of data provided a rich description of both profit center operating interdependencies and profit center measurement practices.

Our measure of the extent of profit center independence for each of the five functional activities is relatively crude. Our structural questionnaire was long and complex; assuming that our respondents were knowledgeable about their companies, we wanted them to be able to complete the form without leaving their desks in a search for detailed information. So, for example, we asked whether the company had "a common domestic sales force which sells products for more than one profit center." If so, we then asked "What percent of *total* domestic corporate sales is handled by the common sales force?" In responding to the second question, each respondent was asked to check one of four boxes, 1–30 percent; 30–70 percent; 70–99 percent; or all. Using those answers, we could then calculate a rough measure of the degree of independence of a typical profit center in relation to the sales function: if there were no common sales force, the profit center was 100 percent independent; if all corporate sales were handled by a common sales force, the profit center was 0 percent independent. The three intermediate values were scored at the midpoint of each range: 15 percent, 50 percent, or 85 percent. The results for each of the five functions are displayed in Figure 1–4.

Figure 1–4
Degree of independence of a typical profit center

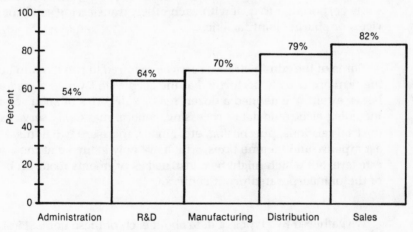

Mean percent of function
performed within typical profit center

Sources: Part Two, Exhibits C–23, D–13.

The main message in Figure 1–4 is that profit centers are essentially customer-focused. The percentage shown for each function is the mean for all respondents who answered the necessary questions (detailed data are shown in Section C). The pattern is clear: as the activity to be performed gets closer to the ultimate customer, a typical profit center is more self-sufficient in performing that activity. Profit centers are less independent in the research function (64 percent) than they are in the sales function (82 percent).

As described in detail in Chapter 3, these data, even though crude, were sufficient to permit us to prepare a summary index of profit center independence that appears to be a major factor that influences a profit center manager's perception of his or her autonomy.

Profit center measurement practices

An example of one type of data we gathered on profit center measurement practices is shown in Figure 1−5; Sections B, C, and D in Part Two present the full array of such data.

More than three quarters of the companies in our sample said that they transferred goods between profit centers to a greater or lesser extent. The cost assignment methods used by these companies, commonly called transfer prices, vary widely. We offered the respondent a choice of ten specific transfer pricing policies plus an opportunity to define the method used in his or her company as either "full manufacturing cost plus some other defined profit," "some other market price," or "some other method." It should be noted that the most common response was that the price was negotiated between profit center managers, which is more properly regarded as a transfer pricing process rather than a transfer pricing formula. Subsequently, we grouped the data for analytical purposes as shown in the last column of Figure 1− 5. In terms of the four major transfer pricing methods (cost, cost plus, negotiated, and market) there is still a substantial divergence of practice across the companies in our sample. One surprise in these data is that only 5 percent of the respondents transfer goods at variable cost, despite the fact that this policy is commonly prescribed in much of the literature on transfer pricing.

The choice of a cost assignment method can affect the ability of a profit center manager to "control" the resources consumed or employed on behalf of his or her business. Some firms assign the costs of corporate research activities to profit centers as a proration based on sales; others assign the costs using project accounting to determine the costs incurred for each profit center. In the latter case, profit center managers are in a better position to influence the amount of corporate research that is performed in their behalf than if the former method were used.

Figure 1–5
Transfer pricing methods

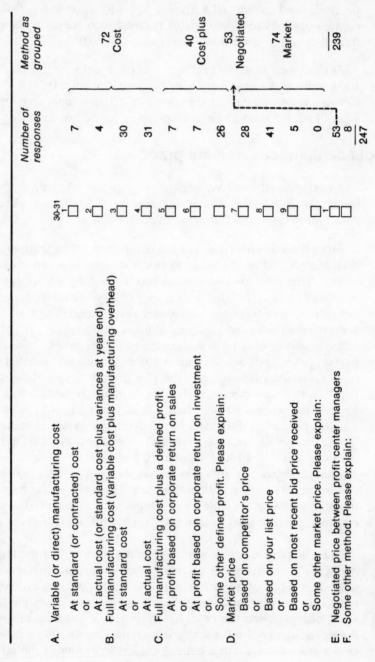

		Number of responses	Method as grouped
A.	Variable (or direct) manufacturing cost		
	At standard (or contracted) cost	7	
	or		
	At actual cost (or standard cost plus variances at year end)	4	
B.	Full manufacturing cost (variable cost plus manufacturing overhead)		72 Cost
	At standard cost	30	
	or		
	At actual cost	31	
C.	Full manufacturing cost plus a defined profit		
	At profit based on corporate return on sales	7	
	or		40 Cost plus
	At profit based on corporate return on investment	7	
	or		
	Some other defined profit. Please explain:	26	
D.	Market price		53 Negotiated
	Based on competitor's price	28	
	or		
	Based on your list price	41	74 Market
	or		
	Based on most recent bid price received	5	
	or		
	Some other market price. Please explain:	0	
E.	Negotiated price between profit center managers	53	
F.	Some other method. Please explain:	8	
		247	239

Source: Part Two, Exhibit B–10.

We obtained one additional type of data about cost assignment practices. As noted in Figure 1–4, profit centers are least independent in the functions of administration and research; in many firms, a significant portion of these activities is performed by corporate-level units for the benefit of some or all of the profit centers. An important decision in the design of a profit center measurement system is whether or not to assign these costs to the profit centers, and our survey shows that practices vary in this regard. In terms of our initial hypothesis, failure to assign these costs affects the financial responsibility of a profit center manager, resulting in a profit measurement which is "partial" and less "comprehensive" than if the costs were assigned.

Finally, we also collected data about measurement practices regarding the assets employed by or on behalf of a typical profit center: whether the investment is calculated, which assets are included, and how the asset values are ascertained. The full array of these data are displayed in Part Two, Section G.

Using these data on cost and asset assignments and assignment methods, we constructed several indices to describe the financial responsibility and the management control of costs and assets for the profit center managers in each firm. As reported in Sections E and G of Part Two, the indices we prepared did not correlate with the other primary variables of diversity, independence, and autonomy. On a disaggregated basis, we did find that measurement practices do have an effect on the profit center manager's perception of his autonomy, and these findings are reported in Chapter 5.

Perceived autonomy of profit center managers

The second stage of the survey (the "autonomy" questionnaire) solicited responses from profit center managers in the 291 companies that responded to the structural questionnaire. The packet that we sent to each initial respondent included a tabulation of the results of the first-stage survey and requested his further assistance in the second stage. We provided three autonomy questionnaires (see Part Two, Section F) and asked that one be sent to each of three "typical" profit center managers in the corporation. The autonomy questionnaire was designed to be completed in about ten minutes, and an envelope was provided so that the respondent could return it directly to us rather than to the corporate financial executive.

Of the 873 autonomy questionnaires distributed we received 317 usable responses, a response rate of 36 percent. We had expected that the response rate might be low, both because the financial executive might be reluctant to make such a request of profit center managers and because those managers would have less interest in the research project than would a member of FEI.

The autonomy questionnaire listed 20 "actions which could have an impact on the performance of your profit center." We told the managers that we were "interested in the extent of your influence in determining what action is taken," and asked them to check one of five decision-making categories for each type of action. The responses, of course, are not objective facts but represent the manager's perception of his or her influence. We wanted to obtain three responses from each corporation so we could average the results and diminish the likelihood that the perceptions of an individual respondent were not "typical" for his or her corporation. The 317 autonomy respondents represented 124 corporations, and 12 of those were single respondents from a corporation. For most of our analyses, we eliminated those respondents and used the average of the score for the two or three respondents from 112 corporations. Averaging did have the effect of reducing the dispersion of responses slightly, but we believe that it improved the quality of the resulting data.

The autonomy questionnaire solicited two additional pieces of data. We asked the profit center managers for their perception of the "fairness" of the profit measurement system and asked them to comment on the "flaws" and "imperfections" in the system. These data are displayed in Part Two, Section F and discussed in Chapter 4. We also asked the profit center managers for information about the bonus system in their firm: how large their bonus was as a percentage of their salary and how, if at all, the size of their bonus was related to the financial performance of their profit center. The bonus index we constructed from these data does correlate with the managers' perceived autonomy but, as discussed in Chapter 4, we do not believe that this necessarily implies a cause and effect relationship.

DESIGN OF THIS BOOK

This study, then, consists of a large amount of empirical data from which we have attempted to synthesize a practical theory of how decentralized firms are managed. The unique feature of such firms is the existence of a second layer of general managers—profit center managers—each responsible for the profitable performance of a defined business. If a theory of decentralized management is to have operational value for practicing executives, it must focus on the role of the profit center manager in the decision-making process.

One way of phrasing the central issue faced by corporate managers in decentralized firms is: How much autonomy—freedom to take action on their own initiative—should profit center managers have? The answer, of course, is "it depends," or, more precisely, "the proper amount, considering the specific circumstances at this point in time." As a practical matter, the question as stated is unanswerable, even by the corporate managers of a particular firm who are the architects of its decentralization.

A more useful statement of the central issue is: How do corporate managers affect a profit center manager's perception of his or her autonomy such that, at any point in time, he or she knows whether or not to act independently? The answer to this more complex question is, "there are a number of ways," and that is what this book is all about.

A profit center manager's role is ambiguous because corporate managers cannot precisely define his intended autonomy in a manner that covers all circumstances, and because his perceived autonomy changes in response to the continuing stream of signals that he receives from corporate managers. The subtitle of this book, "Managerial Ambiguity by Design," is itself ambiguous. Using "design" as a noun, it is the intent of corporate managers to put a profit center manager into a role in which his responsibility exceeds his authority by an unspecified amount. Using "design" as a verb, corporate managers create a set of management systems to aid themselves and their subordinates in coping with an ever changing task. This book is about design in the latter sense, seeking to identify, understand, and interrelate those elements of management systems that significantly affect the role of the profit center manager.

Part One: A theory of decentralized management

In order to avoid swamping the reader in a mass of statistical detail, the book is divided into two parts. Part One, the next five chapters, takes the reader through the conceptual development of a theory of decentralized management, drawing on the underlying data only in summary form or for occasional specific examples. This part is written for the managerial audience, focusing on the design issues that they must grapple with from time to time as the degree of decentralization in a firm ebbs and flows episodically as environmental conditions change. These major issues are identified and addressed briefly in the next few paragraphs.

Two of those issues—Why decentralize? and How much?—have major implications for the design of management systems. As discussed in Chapter 2, the creation of a layer of profit center managers is the primary way that corporate managers express their managerial philosophy and their strategy for the firm. Corporate strategy may conveniently be divided into two parts: diversification strategy (how many lines of business to engage in) and business strategy (how to compete within each line of business). Both types of strategic choice affect the way a decentralized firm is managed. In particular, the definition of business strategy usually involves the definition and selection of market segments and, frequently, the appointment of a profit center manager to be responsible for each segment. Thus, the business strategy (number of market segments) converts the "How much decentralization?" issue into a more operational question: "How many profit centers should we have?" That question, of course, is answered only temporally; the redefinition of profit centers, either subdividing some or consolidating others, can and does happen occasionally.

Against that strategic backdrop, the broad issue for the management of a decentralized firm is: How is decentralization achieved? Our answer is tripartite: philosophically, physically, and systemically. Of these, the managerial philosophy of decentralization is both the most important and the most difficult to describe with any precision. Chapter 2 attempts this, nevertheless, using mushy words like climate, culture, and style. Corporate managers design formal processes for strategic planning, budgeting, and reviewing performance as a way of scheduling a certain amount of direct contact with each profit center manager. The way that corporate managers behave in these settings—and in informal day-to-day encounters—provides a steady stream of current, subtle messages from which a profit center manager can continually recalibrate the extent of his or her autonomy.

Physical decentralization is a second major action which corporate managers take in order to express the intended autonomy that they are trying to imbue in each profit center manager. Chapter 3 examines the physical structure of U.S. manufacturing firms in a way never attempted before. The core issue here for corporate managers is the trade-off between efficiency (from the economies of scale that are possible in centralized functional activities such as manufacturing or research) and adaptability (from the enhanced market responsiveness that is possible when profit center managers have their own plants, labs, and so forth). More specifically, corporate managers must decide on the extent to which each functional activity should be disaggregated and, if so, the profit center manager to which each separate pool of physical resources should be assigned. The data from our surveys demonstrate that the physical custody of corporate resources, which we define as the functional authority of a profit center manager, has a major impact on his or her perceived autonomy to take independent action.

Management systems also have an important, but clearly tertiary, effect on a profit center manager's perception of his autonomy. Chapter 4 etches a broad perspective for these systems, and then focuses on the central role played by the accounting system that is used to measure the financial performance of profit center managers. The bonus system that most companies use to reward good performance involves two familiar managerial issues: How large should the bonus be, as a percent of salary? and How closely should the size of the bonus be tied to current financial performance? Our data show that there is a strong relationship between the answers to these design questions and the perceived autonomy of a profit center manager.

The primary function of a profit center measurement system, however, is to define the financial responsibility of a profit center manager. Chapter 5 addresses the two major issues inherent in the design of this system: (1) Should costs that are incurred in other operating units for the benefit of a profit center be assigned to the profit center?; and (2) If so, how should the amount of assigned costs be determined? Stated somewhat more crisply, the issues for corporate managers are: (1) What do you want a profit center manager to worry about? (he can't pay attention to costs that are not assigned) and (2) How much do you want him to worry? (the method of cost assignment may give him more or less direct control over the amount of costs charged to him). Corporate managers answer these questions in a manner consistent with their intended autonomy for each profit center manager, and the answers are effective in influencing his behavior as measured by his perceived autonomy to take action.

Finally, these issues and concerns are summarized and interrelated in Chapter 6. The diagram in Figure 6−3 is, in effect, a graphic table of contents of Part One of this book, and the reader might usefully examine it now before proceeding. The impatient reader may even prefer to read Chapter 6 next, and then return to the intervening chapters for a more full-blown definition and discussion of the major concepts.

Part Two: Detailed findings and analyses

The second part of this book presents the detailed findings from our surveys and our analyses of those data. Part Two is designed to serve both executive and academic readers. Executives may use it as a sort of reference book, a catalog of management practices in decentralized firms. Scholars will find that Part Two contains the detailed information that they need to form an independent judgment on the value of this study, and to appraise the potential utility of the instruments that we have developed for their own research in the future. Sections E, F, and G explain how the summary variables have been constructed and report the statistical significance of the relationships we have found.

The findings presented in Part Two are of two sorts. First, we have a large array of factual, descriptive data about profit center operations and profit center measurement, organized to facilitate their access by the reader. Part Two is divided into eight sections, each with its own table of contents and a brief opening summary pointing out some of the more interesting information it contains. These descriptive data will have intrinsic interest for many students of management— executives or academics—and we recommend that the reader spend a few minutes becoming familiar with the storehouse of information that Part Two contains.

The second sort of findings are the relationships that we discovered (or found did not exist) among the various types of descriptive data. We have not searched blindly for such relationships, but we have attempted to explore all the reasonably likely pairs of data where we thought that a relationship might exist. All of these analytical probes are cataloged in Part Two and, where an apparent relationship does exist, the data are presented in cross-tabulated form along with our brief interpretive comment of the probable meaning of the relationship.

For further information, the reader is referred to the Introduction to Part Two.

PART ONE

A THEORY OF DECENTRALIZED MANAGEMENT

Decentralization: Why, how, and how much

DECENTRALIZATION is the primary organizational philosophy in U.S. manufacturing corporations today. Julius Caesar gave great power to the local commanders of his far-flung legions—geographic decentralization—out of necessity in an age of primitive communications. Du Pont's motives in the early years of this century, and General Electric's at mid-century, were quite different. It is not inaccurate to say that managerial decentralization—the measured, intentional distribution of responsibility for the financial performance of a segment of the enterprise—was invented in the United States.

If decentralization was a managerial invention in 1920, it was an articulated philosophy by 1950, a reorganizational trend by 1960, and a universal practice by 1970. Today, the issue for a manufacturing corporation of any size is not whether it should decentralize, but how much. This chapter addresses that issue; but before we can confront it directly, we must understand why corporate managers decide to decentralize and how that decision is implemented. The questions of "how" and "how much" are tightly interrelated, but the question of "why" is importantly a matter of managerial philosophy. Dealing with that matter first, we will examine the underlying rationale for decentralization, identifying the major economic and social forces that cause companies to decentralize and probing the elements of the managerial philosophy that decentralization entails.

25

THE PHILOSOPHY OF DECENTRALIZATION

The primary force motivating the adoption of managerial decentralization is economic; more specifically, the economics of the managerial task, and the effect that the quality of managerial decisions has on the economic performance of the firm. The steady, massive growth of the U.S. economy in the last 100 years created great opportunities for business corporations. As such firms grew in size and complexity, it became almost mandatory for their top managers to restructure the division of their work in order to reap the benefits inherent in their current size and to capitalize on future opportunities.

Alfred D. Chandler, Jr., in his definitive work on the evolution of the decentralized form of organization, stated the problem succinctly:

> The lack of time, of information, and of psychological commitment to an overall entrepreneurial viewpoint were not necessarily serious handicaps if the company's basic activities remained stable, that is, if its sources of raw materials and supplies, its manufacturing technology, its markets, and the nature of its products and product lines stayed relatively unchanged. But when further expansion into new functions, into new geographical areas, or into new product lines greatly increased all types of administrative decisions, then the executives in the central office became overworked and their administrative performance less efficient. These increasing pressures, in turn, created the need for the building or adoption of the multidivisional structure with its general office and autonomous operating divisions.[1]

Chandler's basic thesis is that structure follows strategy, that the organizational structure of a firm is altered so that it will be effective in implementing the strategy that the firm is pursuing. But he also recognizes the interrelationship between strategy and structure:

> . . . Once the new type of structure became known, as it did during the 1930s, its availability undoubtedly encouraged many enterprises to embark on a strategy of diversification, for the ability to maintain administrative control through such an organizational framework greatly reduced the risks of this new type of expansion.[2]

Thus, we might say that the adoption of the decentralized form of organization has fed on itself. The originators of the concept, Du Pont and General Motors, invented it out of necessity. Their businesses had

---

[1] Alfred D. Chandler, Jr., *Strategy and Structure: Chapters in the History of the Industrial Enterprise* (Cambridge, Mass.: The M.I.T. Press, 1962), p. 297. Reprinted by the permission of the MIT Press.

[2] Ibid., p. 394.

great potential for growth, and they wanted to improve corporate performance by improving the quality of managerial decisions. Later, other corporate managers, who had constrained the growth of their business in order to keep it manageable, realized that they could seize on new opportunities for diversification and, by decentralizing, maintain managerial effectiveness.

There is a second important force that motivates managerial decentralization and it is not economic but social; more specifically, the professionalization of management. Here, we mean more than the simple fact that most corporate managers today are paid employees rather than owner-managers. Rather, we refer to the fact that, over the last several decades, hundreds of thousands of young men and women have taken formal training to equip themselves to assume managerial positions. In 1977 alone, over 40,000 masters' degrees in the fields of business and management were conferred by U.S. universities.

There are several aspects of this rather startling fact. First, no corporate manager would deliberately assign substantial responsibility to an incompetent subordinate. The simple availability of a pool of trained potential managers made decentralization more feasible in the 1960s than it was in the 1930s. Second, the last several decades have witnessed a rapid increase in sophistication of the technology of management, due both to the increasing size and complexity of modern business corporations and to the research done by the faculties of the institutions that are granting all those degrees. One result has been a dramatic increase in the amount of managerial work that *ought* to be done if the top managers of large corporations are to fulfill their responsibilities in a professional way. Finally, there are the aspirations of those young potential managers themselves: they are well-trained, there is a lot of work to be done, and they are eager to have a piece of the action. Senior managers, knowing that they must respond to those ambitions if they are to keep their best young people, seek ways to delegate authority and assign responsibility and the answer is called decentralization.

Elements of the philosophy

For whatever combination of these economic and social forces, the *concept* of decentralization has been appealing to the top managers of many corporations. But immediately two questions arise: If we do decentralize, what are we trying to accomplish? And, how must we change our behavior and the behavior of our subordinates? Answering these questions requires the development of a managerial philosophy which is both understood and shared by managers at several levels in the corporate hierarchy.

Philosophy is not the natural language of hard-nosed business managers. But effective decentralization requires an articulation of the intent behind this method of corporate governance. We are fortunate in having two extensive first-person statements of this philosophy: Alfred P. Sloan, Jr.'s, autobiography, *My Years with General Motors*,[3] describing his invention of decentralization in the 1920s, and a series of lectures by Ralph J. Cordiner,[4] expressing what he was attempting to accomplish as he introduced decentralization into the General Electric Company in the early 1950s.

Sloan and Cordiner faced quite different organizational problems, but both men realized that their already large companies were blessed with a favorable economic environment that would permit rapid and sustained growth. Their task was to organize their firms so that management facilitated such growth rather than constrained it. For Sloan, this meant rationalizing the collection of independent automotive manufacturers that his predecessor, Willie Durant, had brought under the General Motors' corporate umbrella through a series of acquisitions and mergers. Sloan's problem was too much decentralization; he had to figure out how to gain some control over the entrepreneurial barons who were still running "their" companies. Sloan's question of "how much?" was really "how much to centralize?" For Cordiner, the managerial task was to dismantle the monolithic functional organization that General Electric had become in order to create more centers of initiative that would capitalize on the opportunities in a burgeoning market.

In such radically different circumstances, a careful comparative analysis of what these two men say about their experiences sheds considerable light on the philosophy of managing a decentralized firm. As we attempted to synthesize the comments of Cordiner and Sloan, we discerned three broad elements of such a philosophy that they clearly share. These are identified below, and illustrated with liberal quotations from the two men.

---

[3] Garden City, New York: Doubleday, 1964. © 1963 by Alfred P. Sloan, Jr. Reprinted by the permission of the Harold Matson Company, Inc.

[4] *New Frontiers for Professional Managers* (New York: McGraw-Hill, 1956). © 1956 by McGraw-Hill Book Company. A more detailed description of the reorganization of General Electric is presented by Ronald G. Greenwood in *Managerial Decentralization* (Lexington, Mass.: Lexington Books, 1974).

Stratification of managerial work. The primary benefit from decentralization lies in its potential for improving the quality of managerial decisions. Chandler stated that decentralization was a success in the four companies he studied because:

> . . . It clearly removed the executives responsible for the destiny of the entire enterprise from the more routine operational activities and so gave them the time, information, and even psychological commitment for long-term planning and appraisal. Conversely, it placed the responsibility and the necessary authority for the operational administration in the hands of the general managers of the multifunction divisions. (p. 309)

The basic concept is simplicity itself, but putting that concept into action in a large organization is not quite so straightforward. Sloan's recognition that "contradiction is the crux of the matter" was cited earlier in Chapter 1. He wanted to achieve a division of managerial labor, but he also realized that the division of labor could not be precisely defined:

> . . . The actual forms of organization that were to evolve in the future under a new administration—what exactly, for example, would remain a divisional responsibility and what would be coordinated, and what would be policy and what would be administration—could not be deduced by a process of logic. . . . (p. 55)

Sloan recognized that the resolution of this problem would evolve over time and that, in fact, the problem can never be resolved once and for all. Instead, a *continuing process* is required to deal with this fundamental problem of decentralized management:

> Our management policy decisions are arrived at by discussions in the governing committees and policy groups. These were not the creation of a single inspired moment, but the result of a long process of development in dealing with a fundamental problem of management, that of placing responsibility for policy in the hands of those best able both to make the decisions and to assume the responsibility. To a certain extent this involves a contradiction. On the one hand, those best able to assume responsibility must have broad business perspective oriented toward the interest of the shareholder. On the other hand, those best qualified to make specific decisions must be close to the actual operation of the business. (p. 343)

As president of General Electric in the early 1950s, Ralph Cordiner was faced with a quite different business situation in a different era. He, too, recognized the need for local authority:

> . . . Unless we could put the responsibility and authority for decision making closer in each case to the scene of the problem, where complete understanding and prompt action are possible, the Company would not be able to compete with the hundreds of nimble competitors who were, as they say, able to turn on a dime. (pp. 45–46)

But at the same time, Cordiner warned:

> There is a need for some practical instruments to assure that local decisions will recognize and advance the interests of the Company as a whole, rather than work at cross-purposes with the rest of the organization. (p. 76)

Cordiner defined these practical instruments as a fundamental part of his managerial philosophy:

> . . . Decentralization rests on the need to have general business objectives, organization structure, relationships, policies, and measurements known, understood, and followed; but realizing that definition of policies does not necessarily mean uniformity of methods of executing such policies in decentralized operations. (p. 51)

Cordiner's conclusion, near the end of his lectures, is not much different from Sloan's. The division of managerial authority can never be described with sufficient detail; effective decentralization requires a shared understanding of the concept on the part of all the managers involved:

> However, beyond such formal means as common objectives, policies, and nomenclature, the integration of a decentralized company requires an active understanding and acceptance of the concept of deliberate and voluntary teamwork. The concepts of teamwork, integration, and balanced effort need to prevail or the company can drift inevitably toward recentralization. Hence the Company's managers, in order to preserve their freedom of decision making, need deeply to learn the habits of voluntary teamwork in the interests of the enterprise as a whole. (p. 78)

These comments by Sloan and Cordiner make clear that they were trying to achieve a redistribution of managerial authority, while recognizing the limits of precision by which such authority could be defined. The concepts of authority and responsibility are interrelated and slippery, and we shall turn our attention to them shortly. For the moment, the main point is that both Sloan and Cordiner believed that decentralization could be effective only if the managers shared a philosophy about what they were trying to achieve and were willing to work together over time toward that objective.

Leadership and organizational culture. A second, closely related element in the philosophy of decentralization concerns the need to change the style of executive leadership and, in fact, the culture of the organization itself. Sloan was able to develop the practice of "selling" major proposals at General Motors:

> The role of the division managers is an important one in our continuing efforts to maintain both efficiency and adaptability. These managers make almost all of the divisional operating decisions, subject, however, to some important qualifications. Their decisions must be consistent with the corporation's general policies; the results of the division's operations must be reported to the central management; and the division officers must "sell" central management on any substantial changes in operating policies and be open to suggestions from the general officers.

> The practice of selling major proposals is an important feature of General Motors' management. . . . It assures that any basic decision is made only after thorough consideration by all parties concerned. (p. 433)

Again, here is a concept that sounds good in theory, but is difficult to put into practice, as Sloan himself freely admits:

> . . . There is a strong temptation for the leading officers to make decisions themselves without the sometimes onerous process of discussion, which involves selling your ideas to others. This group will not always make a better decision than any particular member would make; there is even the possibility of some averaging down. But in General Motors I think the record shows that we have averaged up. . . . (p. 435)

This leadership issue is essentially one of self-restraint rather than abdication of responsibility. We may be sure that no executive had any doubt about who had the ultimate authority at General Motors while Sloan was its president:

> Decentralization or not, an industrial corporation is not the mildest form of organization in society. I never minimized the administrative power of the chief executive officer in principle when I occupied that position. I simply exercised that power with discretion; I got better results by selling my ideas than by telling people what to do. Yet the power to act must be located in the chief executive officer. (p. 54)

Cordiner, talking about exactly the same leadership issue, calls it leading by persuasion:

> Another major challenge posed by the decentralization philosophy is the challenge to lead by persuasion rather than command. This is inherent in the very idea of decentralization.

> In this situation, the manager's work is to lead others by drawing out
> their ideas, their special knowledge, and their efforts. Since self-
> discipline rather than boss-discipline is the hallmark of a decentralized
> organization, the manager resorts to command only in emergencies
> where he must admit temporary failure to make the situation and the
> necessary course of action self-evident. To the degree that the contribu-
> tions of every individual are made voluntarily and are self-disciplined,
> the manager is leading by persuasion rather than command. (p. 16)

Recognizing that this style of management requires the development of competent subordinate managers, Cordiner also talks about
the organizational climate necessary for the development of such
executives:

> . . . Growth—or lack of growth—of strong leaders and self-reliant indi-
> viduals depends a great deal on what we call "managerial climate." This
> "tone" or "atmosphere" in an organization can be subjected to analysis
> and a certain degree of measurement. Furthermore, the manager and
> the individuals in the components can do specific things to improve the
> climate, so that men will develop faster and work will be done more
> effectively and enthusiastically. (p. 72)

Finally, like Sloan, Cordiner recognized that the most difficult
change in behavior is that required of him and his corporate
managers:

> Decentralization requires confidence that associates in decentralized
> positions will have the capacity to make sound decisions in the majority
> of cases, and such confidence starts at the executive level. Unless the
> president and all the other officers have a deep personal conviction and
> an active desire to decentralize full decision-making responsibility and
> authority, actual decentralization will never take place. The officers
> must set an example in the art of full delegation. (pp. 50–51)

Leading subordinates by persuasion or requiring subordinates to
sell their ideas at a higher level are two sides of the same coin. One
who must "sell" a proposal clearly lacks the unilateral authority to
adopt it. But if one succeeds in selling it, who is responsible for the
results? The seller is, of course, and that is the basic mechanism by
which a manager is led to accept responsibility that exceeds direct
authority. Cordiner may use the phrase "full decision-making responsibility and authority," but, as we shall see later, the two are
rarely equivalent.

Institutionalized management. The third element in the philosophy of decentralization that we discerned from our study of Sloan

and Cordiner is clearly intertwined with the first two. This element might be termed the "depersonalization of management," but we prefer the more positive idea of attempting to institutionalize a form of professional management that is capable of reproducing itself.

Sloan presents the General Motors philosophy by contrasting two types of executives:

> . . . Mr. Durant had been able to operate the corporation in his own way, as the saying goes, "by the seat of his pants." The new administration was made up of men with very different ideas about business administration. They desired a highly rational and objective mode of operation. (p. 52)

> . . . General Motors is not the appropriate organization for purely intuitive executives, but it provides a favorable environment for capable and rational men. In some organizations, in order to tap the potentialities of a genius, it is necessary to build around him and tailor the organization to his temperament. General Motors on the whole is not such an organization. . . . (pp. 433 – 34)

Cordiner, talking about the work of managers, expressed a similar thought:

> . . . The work had to be made more manageable so that it could be understood and carried out by people of normally available energy and intelligence, thus leaving no requirement for the so-called indispensable man. (p. 46)

Cordiner made it clear that the kind of managers that he wanted at General Electric were team players:

> . . . There is no question but that decentralization can set up powerful centrifugal forces that could pull a company apart. We have had to discourage managers from pre-empting, through squatters' rights, everything they could see. They had been suppressed by strong hands, and the power and authority given to them under decentralization was raw meat. Maybe they were "overtrained" because they sometimes became so independent that they wanted neither advice nor restrictions in the interests of the whole Company. I am greatly concerned when a man talks about "my organization," "my division," or "my men," for all of us are just passing by. (p. 76)

We have quoted at length from Sloan and Cordiner because it is clear that each man had a strong and cohesive philosophy about decentralized management, and believed that a broadly shared understanding of that philosophy within their corporations was essential if decentralization was to be effective. Decentralization requires more than a philosophy, of course, and we turn now to an examination of the actions that must be taken once corporate managers have made the decision to decentralize the management of the firm.

Implementing decentralization

Aware of the benefits to be obtained from decentralization, and the pitfalls to be avoided, how is effective decentralization achieved? The first answer to that question must be that there is no single approach that is universally applicable. This point was so important to Sloan and Cordiner that they both referred to it as their "thesis." First, Sloan:

> . . . It has been a thesis of this book that good management rests on a reconciliation of centralization and decentralization, or "decentralization with coordinated control."
>
> Each of the conflicting elements brought together in this concept has its unique results in the operation of a business. From decentralization we get initiative, responsibility, development of personnel, decisions close to the facts, flexibility—in short, all the qualities necessary for an organization to adapt to new conditions. From coordination we get efficiencies and economies. It must be apparent that coordinated decentralization is not an easy concept to apply. There is no hard and fast rule for sorting out the various responsibilities and the best way to assign them. The balance which is struck between corporate and divisional responsibility varies according to what is being decided, the circumstances of the time, past experience, and the temperaments and skills of the executives involved. (p. 429)

Then, Cordiner:

> . . . If I have any thesis, it is that each company should study, for itself, the particular conditions that will determine its future, and out of such detailed study should evolve a philosophy and structure that is fully appropriate for an individual company. . . . (p. 41)

Despite these caveats, we aspire in this study to say something more definitive and operationally useful about how decentralization can be achieved. In broad terms, corporations achieve a decentralization of authority and responsibility in three ways: philosophically, physically, and systemically. Of these, instilling a philosophy of decentralization across an organization, as Sloan and Cordiner have described, is surely the most important and the most difficult to achieve. In this section we have dealt extensively with the philosophy of decentralization in recognition of its importance, but Cordiner also points out the need for a "structure that is fully appropriate," and it is to this topic that we now turn.

RESPONSIBILITY AND AUTHORITY

It is useful to think about the management structure of an organization along two broad dimensions. One is conceptual. Ask any manager to describe the structure of his firm, and he will usually start by sketching an organization chart to depict the progressive division of responsibilities among the hierarchy of managers of which he is a part. We will refer to that conceptualization as the "responsibility structure" of the firm, defining responsibility as *the set of corporate activities with which a manager is concerned and for which he is held accountable.* The responsibility structure is the centerpiece for a broad set of management systems, policies, and procedures which are designed to support and reinforce the distribution of responsibilities shown on the chart. A more complete discussion of these management systems will be presented in Chapter 4.

The other dimension, so obvious and tangible that it is often overlooked, is physical. The typical business corporation owns an array of physical resources: offices, laboratories, manufacturing plants, and warehouses, and all of these facilities are inhabited by another physical resource of the firm, its employees. At the lowest organizational level in almost every corporation, these resources are grouped into small functional pools that can usually be identified geographically: the sales office in Wichita, or the casting shop in Building 12. These pools are the fundamental building blocks upon which corporate managers erect a managerial hierarchy that reaches from the lowest operating level to the chief executive officer. We will refer to that hierarchy as the "authority structure" of the firm, defining authority as *the set of corporate resources under the custody of a manager and for which he has the power to decide how the resources are utilized.*

The distinction between responsibility and authority can be confusing, because in many situations—particularly at relatively low managerial levels—there is no significant difference between a manager's concern for a set of activities and his or her custody of a set of resources. The distinction is also irrelevant for the chief executive officer—his responsibility and authority are equivalent. But for managers in between the highest and lowest levels there can be an important difference between custody and concern, between the power to control physical resources and the accountability for results that is usually measured in financial terms.

The distinction between the responsibility structure and the authority structure shall be explored at some length because it seems useful in helping us to deal with both the question of how to achieve decentralization and the tougher question of how much decentralization is "appropriate." One of the first things to observe is that the organizational bedrock, the lowest level in the authority structure, is physical and changes very slowly over time. Corporate reorganizations may come and go without changing the lowest level authority structure at all.

Consider the hypothetical example of a manufacturing company with 20 plants scattered across the country. If the company is functionally organized, the manager of the plant in, say, St. Louis reports to a superior who is a part of a hierarchy for managing the manufacturing function that reaches all the way up to the chief executive of the corporation. If that company decides to decentralize by creating a set of division general managers, each responsible for a defined set of product lines, the old functional hierarchies may be disbanded in favor of the new divisional organization. But there will still be a manager responsible for the St. Louis plant whose authority over the activities in that plant will not be affected. That plant manager may now report to a different boss, a division general manager, and the activities within the plant may be somewhat different than they were before, but the plant manager's authority to direct those activities is likely to be unchanged.

Efficiency and adaptability

The last quote from Sloan cited above identified two "conflicting elements" that must be managed by any business corporation. On the one hand, there is the need for "efficiency," the need to ensure that resources are not wasted in manufacturing a product of specified quality as economically as possible. At the same time, corporate managers must be concerned with the "adaptability" of their organization in a competitive marketplace, the need to ensure that existing products can be sold profitably, and that their line of products is modified and extended to match or anticipate changes in the needs of their customers. The issue is not either/or, but how to achieve both.

Corporate managers deal with that issue in their design of the responsibility structure for the firm. In broadest terms, a choice must be made among three basic forms of organization: (1) a centralized, functional organization, (2) a decentralized, divisional organization, and (3) an emerging, mixed form called a matrix organization.[5] The sequence in which these forms are listed reflects not only the chronology of the development of newer forms but also a progression in the complexity of the form of organization; matrix organizations are considerably more complex than functional ones. Let us briefly examine the functional and matrix forms, and then we will return to our analysis of the divisional form of organization.

Functional organizations.   There are two primary virtues of the functional form of organization. First, the responsibility structure and the authority structure are in complete alignment. The manager of that St. Louis plant feels no conflict between his responsibility and his authority for the relatively small pool of resources that he manages, and the same situation exists for his counterpart at corporate headquarters, the vice president for manufacturing. That top-level functional manager is responsible for manufacturing all the products sold by the firm, and he has direct line authority over the large pool of resources necessary to get that job done.

Second, a functional organization has the potential for great efficiency, a potential that is created by the close alignment of responsibility and authority within each functional activity. Efficiency can frequently be measured in terms of the quantity of inputs required to produce one unit of output, and functional managers—from the top to the bottom of their hierarchy—focus on finding more efficient ways of combining inputs to produce the specified output. As a general statement, the larger the total pool of resources, the more efficiently they can be managed because of economies of scale. These economies, in part, result from physical technology: the ability to construct and use the output from the most efficiently sized manufacturing plant, for example. But economies also result from management technology, honing the specialization of effort on both the factory floor (i.e., special-purpose equipment) and in supporting activities (i.e., centralized production scheduling).

The disadvantage of a functional organization, from the point of view of the corporate president, is that it may work too well. The

---

[5] As a practical matter, many corporations use a combination of these forms of organization. For example, as the tobacco companies diversified over the last decade or two, several of them went through an organizational phase in which functional executives in the tobacco business reported to the chief executive at the same time that divisional general managers for the newly acquired product lines reported to the same chief executive. Also, in some decentralized corporations, the divisions may be organized in matrix form.

danger in this form of organization is that his principal subordinates become too identified with their functional bailiwick, striving for ever greater efficiency, leaving no one but the president to worry about the adaptability of the enterprise to changes in its environment. The president is the only executive who can look dispassionately at the interrelationships among the functional activities; the only one who can view the business as a whole and worry about how to make the whole greater than the sum of its functional parts; and the only one who can resolve the inevitable conflicts that arise among his functional subordinates.

The classic example of functional conflict in many businesses occurs between manufacturing and sales. The sales manager wants a broad line of innovative new products, and quick delivery to customers. This makes the most efficient use of his sales force because it reduces the likelihood of losing orders to competitors. The plant manager would like to manufacture a few items in long production runs and have a comfortable backlog of orders. The efficiency of his plant can be optimized under these conditions. The conflicting objectives of these two managers frequently focuses on the finished goods inventory which serves as a buffer between the two functions. On that issue both managers can agree: the larger the inventory, the better. But who is responsible for the capital tied up in inventory? Assigning that responsibility to one manager would infringe on the authority of the other. It is not unusual for the president to retain responsibility for the inventory, managing it as best he or she can in a manner that satisfies neither subordinate completely, and thus perpetuates the conflict.

Managing a business requires a concern for both efficiency and adaptability. Efficiency thrives on repetitiveness; adaptability almost always means change. The two goals are in conflict, and the trade-offs between them cannot be resolved by some precise managerial calculus. Change is made in the face of uncertainty, and, before the fact, the results are always ambiguous.[6] In a functional organization, the president retains both the responsibility and the authority for making these difficult business decisions. Managerial ambiguity is lodged at the top of the organization, thus permitting functional managers to pursue their quest for efficiency with a single-minded determination.

---

[6] Webster's first definition of this adjective is "Doubtful or uncertain especially from obscurity or indistinctness," *Webster's New Collegiate Dictionary* (Springfield, Mass.: G. & C. Merriam Company, 1976).

Matrix organizations. A radically different form of organization is the matrix structure. This form was developed by large corporations in the aerospace industry beginning in the early 1960s. Those companies, then functionally organized, found themselves plagued with cost and schedule overruns on government contracts because each functional manager was responsible for only a phase of the project and no single manager was responsible for the total performance on the contract. The initial means for coping with this problem was to appoint a "project manager" for each major contract. His job was to work laterally across the functional hierarchies that made up the formal organization, trying to ensure that each functional department performed its tasks within the time and budget constraints, coordinating the various functional activities required for the project, and handling all relationships with the customer, the government contracting officer. The structure was initially conceived of as a grid, with functional managers across the top, and a temporary overlay of project managers down the side. The evolution of this form of organization has been studied and documented by Davis and Lawrence, and their conceptualization of a "mature matrix" tips that grid onto one end in the form of a diamond-shaped organization as shown in Figure 2−1.[7]

The advantage of the matrix organization is that it retains the existing functional structure, with its focus on the efficient management of inputs, and adds a new set of managers who are concerned with the outputs of the organization. A managerial focus on outputs captures the central idea in Sloan's concern for adaptability, although project managers in the aerospace industry have a much more restricted sphere of responsibility than division general managers in a decentralized firm. The designers of the matrix organization did not, of course, invent the idea of a managerial focus on outputs; the divisional form of organization was well-established in the 1960s and, in its adaptation into the matrix organization, project managers were conceived of as "mini-general managers."[8]

A matrix organization designed to achieve both efficiency and adaptability, a simultaneous managerial focus on both inputs and outputs, is extremely complex. The primary cause of this complexity, as suggested in Figure 2−1, is the interdependencies that exist between the managers on the two arms of the matrix. A disadvantage of this struc-

---

[7] Stanley M. Davis and Paul R. Lawrence, *Matrix* (Reading, Mass.: Addison-Wesley, 1977), p. 22.

[8] Ibid., p. 41.

Figure 2–1
Example of a matrix design

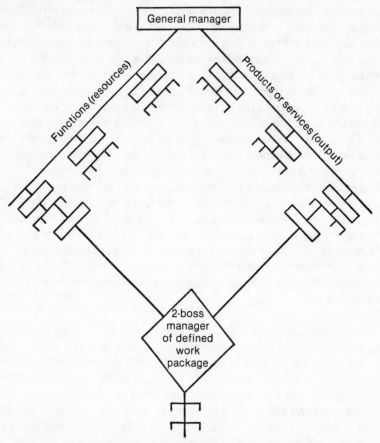

General manager

Functions (resources)

Products or services (output)

2-boss
manager
of defined
work
package

Source: Davis/Lawrence, MATRIX, © 1977, Addison-Wesley, Reading, Massachusettes. Fig. 2.1. Reprinted with permission.

ture is that there will still be conflicts between the two types of managers that will have to be resolved by the general manager. It is feasible for the general manager to play that role when the set of products or services is relatively homogeneous, as in an aerospace company or within a division in a decentralized firm. The matrix structure is less likely to work—or to be needed—as a corporate form of organization when the diversity of products and services is fairly broad.

But the intent of the matrix structure is to provide a mechanism by which most conflicts between the management of inputs and outputs can be resolved at a relatively low level in the organization. A central figure in this structure is what Davis and Lawrence call the "two-boss manager." The authority structure is still intact—that manager still has the power to direct the activities to be performed by his or her small pool of resources—but the responsibility structure has been intentionally bifurcated. This job is the very definition of ambiguous, that is, "capable of being understood in two or more possible senses,"[9] because the two-boss manager must simultaneously manage for both efficiency and adaptability. Ambiguity is pervasive in a matrix organization, but a lot of it rests at the bottom.

The implicit matrix in a decentralized firm

The divisional form of organization used by decentralized firms is perhaps best viewed as a very adaptable structure that can be designed to bridge the entire gap between a pure functional organization on the one hand and a mature matrix organization on the other. Stated another way, based on the 291 manufacturing corporations that we sampled, there is no workable way to define a "pure" divisional form of organization. Sloan and Cordiner have defined it conceptually, but their thesis is that the specific design must be "appropriate" to the circumstances in each individual company. We are now in a position, however, to be somewhat more explicit about how that appropriate design is achieved; at least, we can identify the design decisions that corporate managers must make.

The easiest way to make those design decisions explicit is to continue the hypothetical example of a functionally organized manufacturing firm that has decided to decentralize. To keep the example simple, we will assume that it is perfectly obvious that three product divisions should be established, and that the general manager of each division will report to the corporate president and will be responsible for the profitability of a line of products. The implementation of this decision to decentralize requires top management to deal with two broad types of organizational design issues:

1. To what extent, if at all, should each of the existing functional hierarchies be disaggregated?
2. If the partial or complete disaggregation of a functional activity is desirable, to which of the profit center managers should each pool of physical resources be assigned?

Those questions cannot be answered simply at the policy level, and cannot be dealt with sequentially; for each function they must be resolved simultaneously and in very specific detail.

---

[9] *Webster's New Collegiate Dictionary*, definition 2.

The decision to decentralize does not automatically mean that the existing centralized functions must immediately be disaggregated. In fact, at the initiation of decentralization a major force that constrains disaggregation is purely physical. The responsibility structure of the firm may be changed immediately and, literally, with the stroke of a pen. The lowest-level authority structure, involving dozens or hundreds of pools of physical resources, can also be changed but only more slowly. Even if physical disaggregation is feasible, corporate management must still determine whether or not such a disaggregation is desirable. Many decentralized corporations have answered that question in the negative, for some functions at least.

Nearly 17 percent of the companies in our survey, for example, have decided to retain the research and development function as a totally centralized corporate activity, and only a little over 47 percent of our companies have completely decentralized the research function into their profit centers. On the other hand, only 6 percent of the companies in our sample continue to maintain a completely centralized sales function in their corporations, while nearly 70 percent have completely disbanded the corporate sales activity. For both of these functions, and for others, the issue is not one of all or nothing; nearly 58 percent of the companies do some research as a corporate functional activity, with the remainder being performed within the profit centers, and 31 percent of the companies have a corporate sales force that performs part, but not all, of the selling function for its profit centers.

These data demonstrate that corporate managers can exercise great discretion in deciding whether, and to what extent, each of the operating functions should remain centralized or should be disaggregated. Disaggregation can best be thought of as a decision to reassign functional authority. Our hypothetical company still has that St. Louis plant, and if the manufacturing function is not disaggregated, the plant manager will continue to report to a corporate vice president for manufacturing. Disaggregation would mean a change in the responsibility structure of the firm, in that the plant manager will now report to one of the profit center managers. That profit center manager, thereby, assumes responsibility for the efficient management of the St. Louis plant, relying on his functional subordinate, the plant manager, to achieve that goal. For the 20 plants owned by this hypothetical company, each of the plant managers must be assigned to report to a higher level executive who will hold him responsible for his performance. Some of those plant managers may still report to a corporate vice president for manufacturing, while the others will be assigned to one of the three new profit center managers.

In designing a new, decentralized responsibility structure, corporate managers must make a decision about *each* plant and, more generally, about each pool of physical resources which make up the underlying authority structure of the firm. Assuming that the plants have been operating as a part of an integrated manufacturing activity, realigning them into a new responsibility structure can pose difficult choices. Some of the plants, let us assume, process materials and produce components which are used in all of the products sold by the company. Responsibility for these plants might be retained by the functional manager responsible for manufacturing at the corporate level. Other plants, fortunately, manufacture only a single end product and it is natural to assign them to the profit center manager responsible for that product line. Unfortunately, the remaining plants do not fit neatly into either of the first two categories; they are physical resources that are needed by more than one profit center but not by all of the profit centers in the firm.

Plants in this third category may exist for a variety of reasons. For example, one plant uses a specialized technology to manufacture a variety of products, some of which are sold by two of the new profit centers. Another plant produces only a single product line, but at an intermediate stage it manufactures components which are then shipped to another plant for incorporation into a product line sold by a different profit center. Whatever the cause, these plants exist and their managers must report to higher executives. Corporate managers do not make these assignment decisions arbitrarily; but if no better rationale exists, the plant may be assigned to the profit center manager whose products require the largest share of the capacity of a particular plant.

Plants such as these are not rare; 85 percent of the companies in our survey are organized in such a manner that manufactured products are transferred between profit centers. Nor is this interdependence among profit centers limited to the manufacturing function. Seventy percent of our sample companies have joint facilities (plants, offices, etc.) which are shared by two or more profit centers, and in more than 50 percent of the companies one profit center may perform administrative services on behalf of another.

Once this entire set of organizational design decisions has been made, it is then possible to stand back and survey the resulting patterns of responsibility and authority that emerge. An attempt to describe that pattern for the manufacturing function in our hypothetical firm is shown in Figure 2–2. In this example, we have assumed that the total manufacturing costs amount to $400 million per year,

Figure 2–2
The implicit matrix in a decentralized firm (manufacturing costs, in $ millions)

The business responsibility structure (managing outputs for adaptability)	The functional authority structure (managing inputs for efficiency)				Total manufacturing costs
	Corporate manufacturing services	Profit center 1	Profit center 2	Profit center 3	
Profit center 1	25	60	10	5	100
Profit center 2	60	—	85	5	150
Profit center 3	75	—	5	70	150
Total manufacturing costs	160	60	100	80	400
Number of plants	8	3	5	4	20

and that each of the 20 plants incurs $20 million of these costs. This simple numerical example will help to clarify the concepts of "business responsibility" for a product line or market segment and "functional authority" for a pool of physical resources.

Figure 2–2 can be read both vertically and horizontally, and we will discuss it in that sequence. As shown at the bottom of Figure 2–2, eight of the plants have been retained in a centralized manufacturing function reporting to a corporate vice president. The outputs of those plants are transferred to the three profit centers in the amounts shown in that column. The three plants now assigned to the manager of Profit Center 1 are dedicated to his product line; no products are transferred to the other profit centers. Profit Centers 2 and 3 do transfer a minor part of their output to each of the other profit centers, but most of the capacity is used "locally," that is, to manufacture products for the line of business that the profit center manager is responsible for.

Looking horizontally across Figure 2–2, we see that the total manufacturing costs of the products that the manager of Profit Center 1 sells in the competitive marketplace amount to $100 million. Of these costs, $60 million are incurred in that center's three plants, $25 million in corporate plants, and the balance in plants run by the other two profit centers. Each of the three profit centers provides nearly half or more of its manufacturing requirements, and draws the remainder from plants run by two or three other managers.

The intent of this rather complex set of relationships is twofold. First, the entire $400 million must be spent efficiently. The functional authority of each of the four managers across the top of Figure 2–2 is conveyed by having physical custody of a defined set of corporate resources. Functional authority can be measured by the costs incurred to operate those resources. A manager with functional authority is responsible (concerned and accountable) for the efficient utilization of the physical resources under his custody. Second, the entire $400 million must also be spent adaptively, to use Sloan's term. The business responsibility of the three profit center managers shown at the left of each row in Figure 2–2 is defined in terms of market segments or product lines. Business responsibility can be measured by the revenues received from the sale of those products minus the costs incurred to generate those revenues. A manager with business responsibility has access to the corporate resources that are needed in order to generate revenues and is responsible (concerned and accountable) for the profitable utilization of those resources.

The primary message in Figure 2–2, however, is that each profit center manager really plays two distinct managerial roles: he is both a functional manager and a business manager. As a functional manager, his role appears to be quite straightforward: his responsibility (set of concerns) and authority (custody of resources) are equivalent. As a business manager, his situation is more complex. He does have physical custody of some of the resources needed to manufacture and sell his products, but he must also use resources that are physically located either in other profit centers or in a corporate functional unit. When a profit center manager wants to make a change that will improve the adaptability of his products in their competitive environment, he must persuade other managers, who have functional authority over the resources that will be affected, to modify their operating routines in order to accommodate the proposed change. The profit center manager's responsibility for adaptability is clear, but his responsibility exceeds his authority to effect change.

Looking again at the "straightforward" functional role of the profit center manager, we now see that it, too, is fuzzy. Some of his physical resources are also used to meet the needs of other profit center managers, and a unilateral action that would improve operational efficiency cannot be taken without recognizing the impact that that action might have on the activities of other profit center managers. Further, he must attempt to accommodate changes proposed by other profit center managers even though those changes may not contribute to the efficient utilization of his resources.

Viewed in this way, profit center managers must cope with the conflicting needs of efficiency and adaptability in much the same sense that the president of a functionally organized company does. But the profit center manager faces a double ambiguity in his job. He must propose changes in the way that he runs his business even though the results, before the fact, are uncertain and ambiguous. And, analogously to a "two-boss manager" in a matrix organization, he can conceive of his job as two tasks: managing inputs for efficiency and managing outputs for adaptability.[10] Somebody has to manage ambiguity in every business corporation. In the functionally organized firm, the ambiguity is at the top; in the mature matrix organization, the ambiguity is at the bottom—and also at the top. The effect of decentralization—and the intent of it—in the divisional form of organization, is to place most of the ambiguity on the shoulders of the profit center managers.

Once corporate managers decide to decentralize their firm, the primary implementation device is the design of a new responsibility structure. A myriad of organizational design decisions must be made as the responsibility for the physical resources of the corporation is reassigned, in part at least, to the new profit center managers. This is "how" decentralization is achieved. We turn now to the question of "how much" decentralization is "appropriate" for the firm.

THE STRATEGY OF DECENTRALIZATION

The issue of how much decentralization is appropriate can be more sharply cast as a pragmatic decision on organization design: how many profit centers should we have? For some companies the

---

[10] For further discussion of this point, see Stephen A. Allen, "Organizational Choices and General Management Influence Networks in Divisionalized Companies," *Academy of Management Journal,* September 1978. "The basic organizational choices identified in this paper are the same as those involved in a two-dimensional matrix organized along functional and business lines. . . . Matrix organizations do not seem to involve dimensions of organizational choice different from those encountered in the divisional form. . . ."

answer to that question may be obvious, as we assumed it was for our hypothetical company above, but in most companies that question deserves careful thought. The answer to that question can simplify, or greatly complicate, the new responsibility structure for a firm, and many companies decide that simplicity is not a sufficient virtue unto itself, for reasons that we will now explore.

Some profit centers are "natural," as in the case of an independent business which has been acquired and merged into a larger firm. Even then, although it would be feasible to treat that business as an independent profit center, if part of the motivation for the acquisition was to obtain operating synergy, it will be necessary to create inter-dependencies with other operating units in the firm. As a result, the responsibility and authority of that profit center manager will turn out to be quite different than that of his predecessor who was president of an independent company.

Nevertheless, the concept of a natural profit center, a "genuine" profit center in Solomons' terms, deserves exploration. Such an operating unit has two important characteristics. First, a natural profit center can be defined in terms of a pool of physical resources that are solely dedicated to the design, manufacture, and sale of its line of products. Second, and far more important, a natural profit center can also be defined in terms of the external market that its products are intended to serve. The success of General Motors in overcoming Ford's early lead in the automobile business was due, in large part, to a recognition by Sloan and his colleagues that the market for automobiles in the United States was not one market but several. In order to implement its strategy of market segmentation, General Motors needed to retain an externally focused marketing orientation on the part of some of its managers. Sloan achieved that by creating profit centers and by charging each profit center manager with the responsibility for creating and continually adapting a line of automobiles that would appeal to his assigned market segment.

The profit centers that Sloan established were not "natural" in terms of independent physical resources—the operating efficiencies to be obtained in the large-scale manufacture of automobiles were too great to ignore—but the market definition for each profit center was sufficient to permit each profit center manager to understand the scope of his responsibility. As a more general statement, during the late 1950s and early 1960s corporate managers in a great many U.S. manufacturing companies suddenly realized that they were manufacturing-oriented when they should have been more marketing-oriented. Theodore Levitt contributed to the trend with his prize-winning article on "Marketing Myopia,"[11] and by observing cryptically in a later article that "the customer consumes not things, but expected benefits . . . not quarter-inch drills, but quarter-inch holes."[12] Corporate managers began asking themselves, "What business are we really in?", then developing an explicit marketing strategy, and finally adopting a divisional form of organization in order to decentralize the responsibility for pursuing those markets.

Corporate strategy is the overriding factor in determining the number of profit centers in a decentralized firm. It is useful to distinguish between two aspects of corporate strategy: diversification strategy and business strategy. The companies in our survey vary greatly in the extent to which they have diversified into multiple lines of business. As reported in Chapter 1, our sample spans a spectrum from Single Business firms to those engaged in a number of Unrelated Businesses. It is not surprising that the latter type of firm will decentralize the responsibility for serving each of its markets. And, as we shall see in the next chapter, profit center managers in highly diversified firms are less interdependent in terms of physical resources than their counterparts in less diversified firms. It is somewhat more surprising that firms engaged in a single line of business may also decide to decentralize the responsibility for segments of that business. Decentralization by a Single Business firm rests on the business strategy that it is pursuing in its competitive environment.

As an example of how business strategy determines the number of profit centers to be found in a decentralized firm, let us take the case of a large-scale manufacturer of home appliances.[13] It is engaged in a single line of business, but has decentralized its operations into six profit centers. Three of these are "product" profit centers, one each for laundry equipment, refrigerators, and electric stoves. The other three are "manufacturing" profit centers, one each for electric motors, gears and transmissions, and chrome products. All six profit center managers are expected to earn a profit by designing, manufacturing, and selling their respective lines of consumer products or industrial components. The profit centers are highly interdependent, however, with 70 percent of the sales of the manufacturing profit centers being made to the product profit centers. The managers of

[11] *Harvard Business Review,* July–August, 1960, p. 45.

[12] Theodore Levitt, "The Morality(?) of Advertising," *Harvard Business Review,* July–August, 1970, p. 91.

[13] General Appliance Corporation case number 6-160-003, Harvard Business School.

the product profit centers are not required to purchase components from the manufacturing profit centers, but when they do the price is negotiated between the two profit center managers just as it would be negotiated between an independent buyer and seller. Nevertheless, interdivisional squabbles over transfer prices are frequent and sometimes bitter.

A different responsibility structure might easily be adopted to reduce or eliminate these problems. The plants that manufacture industrial components could be treated as a corporate functional activity, and the corporate functional manager held responsible for the efficient manufacture of components for the product profit centers. The product profit center managers would be required to obtain components from the corporate facilities, and all such transfers would be valued at standard manufacturing cost or some variation thereof. The reason that this company has six profit centers rather than three—or none—is that corporate management conceives of the firm as being engaged in six distinct and competitive lines of business. The manager of the refrigerator division competes for a profitable market share against other companies that manufacture refrigerators, some of whom buy their electric motors from independent suppliers. Similarly, the manager of the electric motor division competes for profitable market share against other manufacturers of electric motors, some of whom do not have captive end-product divisions. The competitive environment demonstrates that it is possible to operate profitably in all six markets, and the business strategy of this firm is to do just that. The fact that only 30 percent of the output of the manufacturing divisions is sold to outside customers does *not* mean that the company "really" earns a profit only on outside sales; both corporate and divisional managers believe that the profit on inside sales is just as real because it is a profit that would otherwise have been earned by an outside supplier.

In such a situation, of course, there is no "real" truth. The internal profits in this case are real because the managers believe in their strategy. An identical firm whose managers decide to pursue a strictly consumer-oriented strategy might believe that "profits" on manufactured components are really fictitious.

The business strategy of a Single Business firm may be viewed as a determination by corporate managers of how to compete in their industry and in how many segments. For each segment thus chosen, a profit center manager must be named in order to assign responsibility for the evolving adaptation of a line of products designed for that

market. In this sense, the responsibility structure of any firm is designed to implement its strategy, both its diversification strategy as to
the number of lines of businesses in which to engage and, within each
line, the business strategy that is adopted to compete successfully in
selected market segments.

How do corporate managers implement their decision to decentralize? Surely, the answer is, "Carefully." The lowest authority structure, those functional building blocks, are like tiles in a mosaic. Those
tiles must now be rearranged, each piece carefully placed, to form a
new pattern—a new responsibility structure—that has coherence and
strength. If that structure is strong, in the sense that it is firmly
grounded on the foundation of an explicit corporate strategy, then the
new profit center managers will understand the scope and intent of
their responsibilities and can attack those tasks with drive and
initiative.

Chapter 3

The independence of profit center managers: Authority and autonomy

IN CHAPTER 2 we looked at decentralization from a corporate perspective, trying to understand why corporate managers decide to decentralize the management of their firm and how they implement that decision. Now we will adopt a different point of view: the profit center manager and how he plays his ambiguous role in a decentralized firm. Accepting the responsibility structure that has been created in each of our sample firms, we shall explore in this chapter how the design of that structure affects the profit center manager's "autonomy," which we define as *his perception* of his power to initiate change and his ability to influence events.

Initiative is what a profit center manager's job is all about: He is responsible for a "business," usually defined in terms of a market with a number of competitors. His first—and continual—job is to figure out what needs to be done to make his business more successful than it is at this moment. Then, whatever the necessary action is, his job is to make it happen, either by redirecting the utilization of the resources at his disposal, if they are sufficient or, if not, by influencing the utilization of resources that are managed by other executives in his firm.

Unless a profit center manager can "make it happen"—at least some of the time—his responsibility is a sham; he is an idea man, not a general manager. Thus, it is important that he have a pool of physical resources at his disposal—"functional authority" as defined in the preceding chapter, and in every firm in our sample he does have such authority to a greater or lesser extent. The importance of that authority lies in the fact that, for those resources at least, the profit center manager has relatively little difficulty in redirecting their utilization in order to effect a change that he thinks is desirable. All he has to do is convince himself, and to make sure that his change does not impact the operations of other units in the firm. Making change happen when the necessary resources are managed by someone else is a more complex process. The profit center manager must learn to master that process of negotiation and influence because, again for every firm in our sample, he or she never has functional authority over all the resources that are needed to accomplish the task.

This chapter seeks to deepen our understanding of how a profit center manager is able to make substantive, profit-oriented improvements in the operation of his business, even though he is part of a larger decentralized corporation with a complex responsibility structure. Our survey yielded data which provide a richer description of the authority structure of such firms than has heretofore been available. We shall present these data in the next section, explaining as best we can why the patterns of functional authority vary so widely across the firms in our sample. The following section will then present data provided by a sample of profit center managers in a subset of these firms, data reflecting their perceptions of the extent of their autonomy. Here, again, we will see variations across the range of firms in our sample, and will attempt to explain them.

The final section then examines the relationship between the profit center manager's functional authority and his perceived autonomy. This relationship documents the importance of the design of the responsibility structure in a decentralized firm: A profit center manager with substantial functional authority has, thereby, substantial "physical independence" from other operating units in the firm. In such a circumstance, the profit center manager also has substantial "perceived independence" which is represented by his sense of enhanced initiative and influence concerning actions that will affect the performance of his profit center.

PATTERNS OF FUNCTIONAL AUTHORITY

The importance of functional authority can perhaps best be demonstrated by an anecdote. A rapidly growing manufacturer of computer systems, with sales in excess of $500 million, had established a dozen profit centers. Each profit center manager was assigned a segment of the market and charged with the responsibility of designing a range of computer systems that could be sold profitably in that market. Because of the substantial economies of scale, however, the manufacturing function was completely centralized, headed by a vice president for manufacturing who reported to the president. The company manufactured many of its major components in a number of plants that were scattered around the world. The output of these plants was shipped to the various assembly plants, which purchased other components as necessary and assembled them into complete computer systems for shipment to customers. The assembly plant where the following event occurred manufactured computer systems for the markets served by three of the profit center managers, typifying a common problem in many decentralized manufacturing firms.

Because of its rapid growth, the company had frequent need to raise new funds in the capital markets. Several dozen of the top managers in the firm believed that maintaining a steady growth in earnings per share was crucial if the company were to continue raising funds for its growth, a belief that was reinforced by their participation in an extremely favorable restricted stock option plan. Many of the "old-timers" in this relatively young company were paper millionaires. One result of this continual need to report record earnings was to introduce a pronounced seasonal cycle in the company's pattern of sales; shipments to customers in the third month of each fiscal quarter were always substantially greater—sometimes twice as high—as shipments in the first month of the next fiscal quarter. The reason for this was simple. As the end of each quarter approached, the assembly plants began to scramble, trying to complete and ship as many systems as possible so that the company could report higher profits for that quarter.

The normal operating procedure for the interface between the profit center managers and the manager of the assembly plant was straightforward. When a customer order was received, the profit center manager would contact the assembly plant for a delivery date and, if the customer accepted that date, a production order would then be placed with the assembly plant. The assembly plant would then put that order into its production schedule and order the necessary components from both internal and independent suppliers. But consider the following example: Order 1 requires components A and B, while Order 2, scheduled for delivery two weeks later than Order 1, requires components B and C. Component A for Order 1 has not arrived on time, although component B has been received. Meanwhile, component C for Order 2 has arrived earlier than scheduled.

The assembly plant manager, trying to ship as much as possible during the last month of the quarter, does the natural thing; having one unit of component B on hand, he uses it to complete Order 2 and ship it. Then when component A does arrive, the completion of Order 1 must be delayed until the unit of component B for Order 2 is received. The assembly plant manager, responsible for using his plant efficiently to maximize the value of shipments during the quarter, has met his objective. But the profit center managers, responsible for keeping their customers happy and for showing that they contributed their share to the current quarter's profits, are extremely frustrated.

One solution to this problem would be to develop an elaborate (computerized!) inventory control system which would identify each component with the customer order, or at least the product line, for which it had been ordered. This company, however, found a simpler solution that could be implemented immediately. One bay in the assembly plant housed the inventory of component parts, the inventory that had taken on almost symbolic value as the cause of the interdependency among the three profit center managers. The solution was to use simple chicken-wire fences, erected overnight, to partition the bay into three holding areas, one each to hold the component inventory that "belonged" to each profit center manager.

This example is not offered as a model of good managerial practice. It was, in fact, inefficient because theoretically a single inventory pool can eliminate the redundant safety stocks in three smaller pools. But this is a compelling example of the kernel of truth in the old adage that "possession is nine tenths of the law." Just as ownership of assets is a primary source of power in a society built on the concept of private property, so physical custody of resources is a primary source of authority in a decentralized firm. Cordiner was quoted earlier as disdaining the use of possessive pronouns, but profit center managers use them all the time. A profit center manager would not disagree that he is "only passing by," but in the meantime he doesn't want you to forget that he has "his" inventory, "his" lab, or "his" plant.

Functional authority in diversified firms

The diversification strategy of a firm, the number of lines of business in which it is engaged, has a major impact on the functional authority of a profit center manager. Figure 3 − 1 presents data which illustrates how the firms in our sample have decided one of the orga-

Figure 3–1
Diversification strategy and corporate-level operating functions

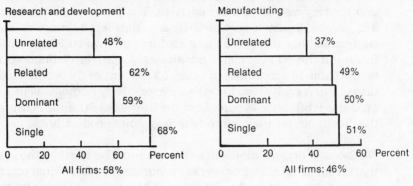

Research and development

Unrelated	48%
Related	62%
Dominant	59%
Single	68%

0   20   40   60   Percent
All firms: 58%

Manufacturing

Unrelated	37%
Related	49%
Dominant	50%
Single	51%

0   20   40   60   Percent
All firms: 46%

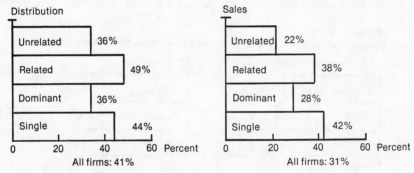

Distribution

Unrelated	36%
Related	49%
Dominant	36%
Single	44%

0   20   40   60   Percent
All firms: 41%

Sales

Unrelated	22%
Related	38%
Dominant	28%
Single	42%

0   20   40   60   Percent
All firms: 31%

Sources: Part Two, Exhibits C–1, C–10.

Percentage of 291 firms with a corporate-level operating function serving two or more profit centers

nizational design issues discussed in Chapter 2: Should each centralized operating function be dismembered so that the individual building blocks within it can be assigned to a profit center manager? Some companies answer yes to that question while others, shown in Figure 3–1 answer, "no, at least not completely."

The trade-off in that decision involves balancing more efficiency against more adaptability, and Figure 3–1 illustrates two aspects of that trade-off. First, ignoring the effects of diversification strategy, the efficiencies that can be achieved through large-scale activities are apparently greatest for the research and development function and least for the sales function, with manufacturing and distribution falling in between. More than half the companies in our sample have a central research lab, even though that means that each profit center manager will not necessarily have "his" or "her" own lab. Second, diversification strategy also affects this decision. The patterns shown in Figure 3–1 do not display a neat progression from less to more diversified companies, but there is a clear distinction between Single Business firms and those in Unrelated Businesses. Again, the distinctions must be traceable to economies of scale; 68 percent of the Single Business firms have a central lab to serve their relatively homogeneous line of products while only 48 percent of the Unrelated Businesses firms find that desirable for their more heterogeneous product lines.

A second organizational design issue must be faced by those firms that decide to retain some sort of corporate-level functional unit: How much of that functional activity should be performed in the corporate unit and how much in the profit centers? Figure 3–2 displays how the firms in our sample have answered that question. The patterns

Figure 3–2
Diversification strategy and magnitude of corporate-level operations

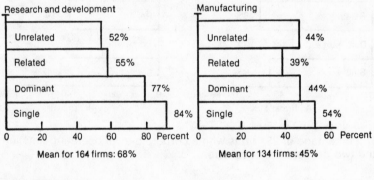

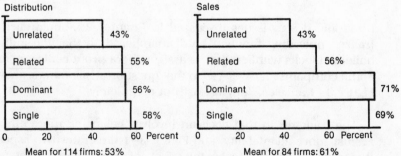

Note: The sample size differs for each function, and in all cases is less than the 291 firms in Figure 3-1.
Sources: Part Two, Exhibits C–12, C–13, C–14, C–15.

Mean percentage of each functional activity performed by a corporate-level operating unit, for firms having such units shown there are similar to those shown in Figure 3–1 because they are based on the same trade-off analysis. These data do provide evidence to suggest that corporate managers determine the functional authority of each profit center manager in a careful fashion, seeking the proper amount of disaggregation for each operating function that will achieve the best possible balance between efficiency and adaptability.

A fifth functional activity which we refer to collectively with the term "administrative services," is never completely decentralized—at least not by the firms in our sample. The reason why some administrative activities, particularly finance and accounting services and legal services, are almost always retained at the corporate level, at least to some extent, is to permit corporate managers to have direct functional authority for important corporate-wide activities which they do not wish to delegate to profit center managers. Nevertheless,

Figure 3–3
Diversification strategy and corporate-level administrative services

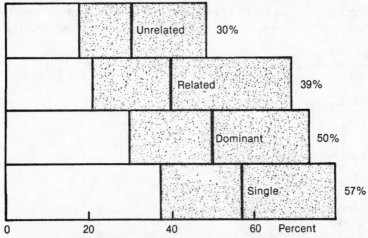

Note: Heavy line is the median percentage for companies in each category; shaded area is the interquartile range.
Source: Part Two, Exhibit D–6.

Percentage of the total cost of administrative services in each firm that are performed at the corporate level

as Figure 3–3 illustrates, most of our sample companies do assign some functional authority for administrative services to their profit centers, and the pattern that emerges reflects the same trade-off that we observed for the other four operating functions.

The third organizational design issue faced by corporate managers is: To which profit center should each functional pool of physical resources be assigned? We did not attempt to obtain detailed information about how our sample companies have answered that question because we could not think of a way to obtain—nor did we need—a quantified answer for each of the operating functions. Our intent in trying to obtain answers to all three of these organizational design issues was to permit us to construct a quantitative measure of the extent of functional authority for a "typical" profit center manager in each firm. Thus, we really did not need to know *which* profit center had functional authority for each specific pool of physical resources. Rather, our intent was to quantify the extent to which a typical profit center manager depended upon functional resources which were managed by other executives in the firm. We realized that those executives might be other profit center managers, but it was feasible to obtain data about interdependencies *among* profit center managers only for the manufacturing function. Interdependencies in the manufacturing function occur when a plant assigned to one profit center manager produces components or products that are then transferred to another profit center manager for further processing and sale. Such transfers of goods between profit centers are very common in decentralized firms, as the data in Figure 3—4 illustrate. The data

Figure 3– 4
Diversification strategy and transfers of good among profit centers

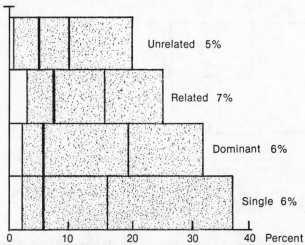

Note: Heavy line is the median percentage for companies in each category; three shaded blocks are the range for the following percentiles: 25–50 percent; 50–75 percent; and 75–90 percent.
Source: Part Two, exhibit B-4.

Percentage of total corporate cost of goods sold that is transferred among profit centers there are the cost of goods transferred as percentage of the cost of all goods manufactured in the firm. Only 15 percent of the companies in our sample reported that they did not have transfers of goods among their profit centers. More remarkably, the median percentage of such transfers is low, ranging from 5 percent to 7 percent without regard to the diversification strategy of the firm. The familiar pattern does emerge, however, when we look at the percentage of transfers for the firms in these categories that do the most such transferring. The data shown are for the respondent in each category which is at the 90th percentile, and we see that a Single Business firm has almost twice as many transfers as a firm with Unrelated Businesses.

Functional authority of profit center managers

Our next step, having obtained the data described above, was to find some way of combining the data for each of the five operating functions into a summary figure which would serve as an index of the total functional authority of a typical profit center manager in each firm. Constructing a separate index for each of the five operating functions was not particularly difficult, and our methodology is described and displayed in Sections C, D, and E of Part Two. The problem was that each such index was prepared on its own basis reflecting the nature of each functional activity. Thus, the index for functional authority over the sales activity is computed by calculating sales by the profit center manager's own sales force as a percentage of total profit center sales. A figure of less than 100 percent is a measure, in rough terms, of a profit center manager's partial functional authority for the selling activity. But for the manufacturing function, the percentage is calculated on the basis of the total cost of goods manufactured; for distribution it is based on the total value of the goods distributed; for administrative services it is based on the total cost of such services; and for research it is based simply on the "total research and development," without any further definition as to the cost or value of that functional activity. Designing our questionnaire in this fashion made it easier for our respondents to answer each of these questions, but it complicated our task of constructing a summary index.

One alternative that we considered was to calculate a weighted average of the five functional indices, using as weights the total cost of each functional activity as a percentage of the total cost for all five functions. There were two problems with this approach. First, we only had such data about the relative cost of each function for less than half the firms in our sample (see Exhibit 11 in Section A). But the second problem was more important; for the firms where we did have such data, the costs incurred in the manufacturing function were roughly ten times the costs incurred for sales and marketing, and we did not believe that a profit center manager's functional authority for manufacturing was ten times as important to him as his functional authority for sales. More likely, we thought, a "proper" weighting of the relative importance of each of the five functions would be different in each firm and should reflect the nature of the specific lines of business engaged in and the business strategy being pursued in each such line. We did not have, nor could we hope to get, such data. Thus, we decided to calculate the summary index as a simple average of the values of the five functional indices, and the results are displayed in Figure 3–5.

Figure 3–5
Diversification strategy and functional authority of profit center managers

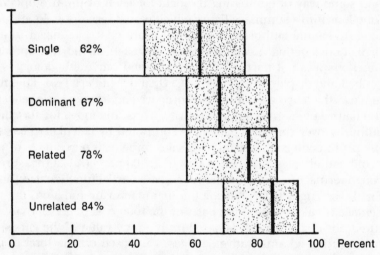

Notes: Heavy line is the median percentage for companies in each category; shaded area is the interquartile range.
   The data displayed here cannot be calculated directly from the earlier figures in this chapter. Please refer to Section E, Part Two, for an illustration of the calculation of this summary index.
   Source: Part Two, Exhibit E–5.

Simple average of the five functional authority indices in 234 firms

We readily admit that our index of the total functional authority of a typical profit center manager is crude at best, but it does seem to capture the essence of the underlying data. The first message in Figure 3–5 is simply that the diversification strategy of a firm does affect the functional authority of profit center managers. Because of the greater interdependencies among operating units in a Single Business firm, profit center managers have less functional authority than their counterparts in a firm that consists of a number of Unrelated Businesses. The second message in Figure 3–5 is that there is a wide variation in the amount of functional authority enjoyed by the typical profit center manager in our sample firms. The method used to classify each firm into one of four diversification strategy categories is somewhat arbitrary, but viewed as a spectrum there clearly are differences among our firms in terms of that strategy. At one end of that spectrum, a profit center manager at the 25th percentile of a Single Business firm has a functional authority index of 44 percent; at the other end of that spectrum, a profit center manager at the 75th percentile of an Unrelated Business firm has a functional authority index of 94 percent. Both executives are called profit center managers, but it is clear that that title covers a broad range of situations.

The main message in Figure 3–5, however, is that the vast majority of profit center managers in our sample do have physical custody of a substantial pool of functional resources. Are profit center managers independent or interdependent? Is a glass of water half full or half empty? For a median typical profit center manager, the glass is more than half full; he can feel a considerable degree of independence in managing his business because he has functional authority for roughly two thirds of the physical resources that are needed in his business. Let us turn now to see how that authority is translated into action.

PATTERNS OF PERCEIVED AUTONOMY

The ambiguous role of a profit center manager is rarely acknowledged as such in the parlance of business executives. A profit-seeking competitive corporation must be run crisply, with nice clean lines of responsibility and authority; there is nothing ambiguous about the chain of command displayed in a corporate organizational chart. Rather, the inherent ambiguity that comes with the territory of a profit center manager is encoded in the word *autonomy*. Managers, describing how their corporation is run, will commonly say, "We're organized into a set of autonomous profit centers," or "Our profit center managers have quite a lot of autonomy." We defined autonomy in the opening paragraph of this chapter as the "power to initiate change and the ability to influence events." Now we must elaborate on that set of words, trying to enrich our understanding of an elusive, multifaceted concept.

There are two pairs of operative words in that definition: power and ability, and initiate and influence. Words such as "to decide" on what action should be taken or "to make" an event occur are intentionally omitted from our definition because those verbs are too active. To quote Sloan once again, "an organization does not make decisions; its function is to provide a framework, based upon established criteria, within which decisions can be made."[1] The tone of that statement, and the last four words in particular, is passive and impersonal, and intentionally so. When a profit center manager initiates action he does not necessarily decide what action should be taken; many times his role is to identify the need for an action to be taken and to initiate a decision-making process that results in a determination of what action to take. Usually he is a participant in that process and is more or less influential in determining the outcome.

In many cases a decision simply emerges from this process and it may be impossible to say who really "made" the decision. A profit center manager identifies a problem on which he believes action should be taken and decides, for reasons to be discussed below, to discuss it with his boss. Usually, in presenting the issue, he will identify two or more courses of action and indicate the one that he prefers along with his reasoning for it. In the ensuing discussion, which may be quite brief, a better alternative may be discovered which both men immediately agree upon. Attempting to determine who made that decision is an exercise in futility, nor is it necessary, because both men "own" the decision. Nor is this decision-making process unusual; our survey indicates that, in fact, it is one of the common ways in which decisions are made in decentralized firms. Given that fact, it is no wonder that it is difficult to talk in tangible terms about the autonomy of a profit center manager.

Autonomy: The corporate perspective

Before examining autonomy from the profit center manager's point of view, it will be useful to take a corporate perspective on the concept. A primary reason why corporate managers decide to decentralize is to multiply the number of centers of initiative within the firm. They accomplish this by establishing a number of business units, each with its own market focus, and each run by an innovative profit center manager. But decentralization requires more than the

---

[1] Alfred P. Sloan, Jr., *My Years with General Motors* (New York: Doubleday, 1964).

design of a complex new responsibility structure; the behavior of those profit center managers must now be shaped in a very complex fashion. Each profit center manager does have a new, broader set of responsibilities than before, and each such manager must develop an appropriate sense of his autonomy to take action in fulfilling those responsibilities. For corporate managers this means expressing their "intended autonomy" for each subordinate, and to do this they must deal with two new, more subtle issues of organizational design:

1. How much autonomy is appropriate for a profit center manager?
2. How can a sense of that propriety be developed within each profit center manager?

The scope of a profit center manager's business responsibility is defined in terms of a market or market segment. It is fairly easy for corporate managers to convey to each profit center manager both the breadth of his responsibility, and the limits on that breadth, because the definition is in external and competitive terms. The organizational design issues arise in executing those responsibilities. There will be some actions which a profit center manager ought to initiate and execute without checking first with any executive at the corporate level—such as changing the price of his product in response to a competitor's action. An example might be household toasters manufactured by General Electric, where the profit center manager's action there is unlikely to have any side effects on the products sold by other profit center managers. But there will also be some situations where the profit center manager should check with one or more executives outside his profit center before changing the price of his product. Here, the example might be the Oldsmobile Division of General Motors, where it is clear that the change in price might have important impacts on both the Buick and Pontiac product lines. The task for corporate managers is to develop and convey to each profit center manager a sense of the constraints that restrict his ability to take independent action.

Constraints, or the lack thereof, on the autonomy of profit center managers fall into two broad types. Constraints of the first type are economic, having to do with both the magnitude of the action to be taken and the implications of that action on the activities of other operating units in the corporation. The need for these constraints was partially illustrated by the examples in the preceding paragraph. If the price revision on toasters was relatively small and subject to modification as the competitive environment evolves, it might be appropriate for the profit center manager to act independently. But General Electric also makes nuclear power plants for electric utilities and a price revision there might have a major impact on corporate performance over a span of several years. The manager of that profit center might find it appropriate to seek the advice of his direct superior and perhaps others in the management hierarchy before announcing a price change. At General Motors the desirability of seeking such advice about a change in the price of Oldsmobiles is due, in part, to the effect of that action on other product lines, but it is also true that corporate managers in that company know a great deal about pricing and competition in automobile markets. They have a knowledge of the business that enables them to give substantive advice on that issue.

Economic constraints on the autonomy of a profit center manager are relatively easy to specify in the form of written statements of policies and procedures. The economic appropriateness of these constraints on his autonomy are also easy for a profit center manager to understand and accept. Because these constraints are economic it is not even necessary to have an elaborate book of rules and regulations; a profit center manager is expected to possess both the perspective and judgment which will permit him to recognize the broader ramifications of any proposed action.

The second broad type of constraints on the autonomy of a profit center manager is social and psychological. These constraints are at least as important as the economic ones, but are much more subtle, both to define and to communicate. Taking independent action to deal with a difficult business problem is risky for a profit center manager. It is much easier simply to identify the need to take action and then carry the problem upstairs. That is appropriate in some cases, of course, but in other cases corporate managers would prefer for the profit center manager to act independently. From a corporate perspective, the problem is one of developing a *willingness* to act alone on the part of profit center managers under the appropriate circumstances; achieving this requires conscious management of the constraints caused by self-confidence, trust, and organizational climate. An occasional profit center manager may be viewed as "unwilling to accept responsibility," but more frequently he or she has quite a different perception of the situation.

The self-confidence of a profit center manager reflects the extent of his belief that he knows the right action to take in a given situation. Even if he is convinced, his willingness to take independent action is significantly colored by his relationship with his boss. He is more likely to act if he and his superior have worked together for a sufficient length of time to develop a mutual self-respect and a trust in each other's capabilities. Self-confidence and trust cannot be mandated in an organization, but corporate managers can seek to create a climate which encourages risk-taking and is tolerant of the inevitable mistakes that will occur. The organizational philosophy of decentralization has a major impact on the profit center manager's sense of his autonomy.

And what is the net result? If corporate managers are successful in conveying an understanding of these constraints, each profit center manager will have a sense of his autonomy which will be appropriate for the moment and will evolve over time as his own capabilities develop. The objective that corporate managers seek is a profit center manager who has the confidence to act alone on some occasions, the wisdom to seek counsel on other occasions, and the common sense to distinguish one occasion from another. Profit center managers do make such distinctions as we shall see in turning now to an examination of their autonomy as they perceive it.

Perceived autonomy of profit center managers

In order to learn more about the decision-making process in decentralized firms we designed a brief questionnaire to be completed by profit center managers in our sample companies. The questionnaire listed 20 "actions which could have an impact on your profit center." We defined five types of decision-making processes and, for each action, asked the respondent to indicate the type, "which most closely describes the way that the decision is 'typically' determined." For four of the five types, the process began with "*my initiative*. I identify an issue on which action appears necessary, and proceed as follows:". Within the "my initiative" processes, the short titles of the four choices were "my decision," "two-person decision," "multiperson decision," and "corporate decision." We explained that we were "interested in the extent of your influence in determining what action is taken . . . we are not asking whether you have the authority to decide, but whether you usually do make the decision without first discussing it with the others outside your profit center." The fifth type of decision-making process was defined as, "the need for an action of this sort is usually initiated by a higher level administrative department. . . ." The questionnaire is reproduced in Section H.

We distributed the questionnaire through the financial executive who had responded to our structural questionnaire, asking him to forward one copy to each of "three operating profit center managers who manage profit centers typical of the ones you had in mind in completing the first questionnaire." We also requested that the distribution be restricted to profit center managers who had been in their positions for two years or more, because we wanted a set of respondents who were familiar with their jobs and had had an opportunity to develop self-confidence in their abilities to handle their responsibilities. We were unable to discover or invent a concise way to measure the self-confidence of a profit center manager, so we substituted an arbitrary experience factor in the hope that this would screen out some of the dispersion caused by this constraint on the autonomy of profit center managers.

We also asked the profit center managers, "How many months have you reported to your present superior?" The responses ranged from 1 month to 25 years, with a median of about 36 months. The intent of this question was not to verify that the questionnaire had been sent to experienced profit center managers; rather, we wanted to identify those situations where the profit center manager's boss had recently been replaced by a new individual. Our hypothesis was that trust between a profit center manager and his superior can be an important potential constraint on the former's autonomy, and that trust can be developed only by working together over a period of time. This hypothesis has recently been elaborated significantly by Professor Gabarro.[2] We found that 26 of our 317 respondents had reported to their current superior for less than 12 months and that, in those cases, their perception of their autonomy was somewhat lower than the autonomy perceived by their counterparts with more mature relationships. The difference was small, but statistically significant, so we eliminated those respondents from any analyses in which we were trying to relate the perceived autonomy of the profit center manager to any of the structural or demographic characteristics of their firms.

The result of this screening was a sample of 104 corporations for which we had two or three respondents to the autonomy questionnaire who were experienced and trusted profit center managers. For each of these respondents we constructed an index of perceived autonomy based on his or her description of the decision-making process used for the 20 actions; the decision processes were scored from one to five with "initiated by others" scored as a 1 (lowest autonomy)

---

[2] John J. Gabarro, "Stages in the Development of Working Relationships," unpublished working paper, Harvard Business School, 1976. Our findings reported here are also consistent with those reported by F. A. Heller in *Managerial Decision Making* (London: Tavistock, 1971), although his research was conducted at a slightly lower organizational level.

and "my decision" scored as a 5 (highest autonomy). The score for each of the two or three respondents in each corporation was then averaged and rescaled on a range from zero to one in order to determine an index that was "typical" for profit center managers in that corporation.

The 20 actions listed in the questionnaire were grouped into four broad categories of decisions, and the results shown in Figure 3–6 are

Figure 3–6
Diversification strategy and perceived autonomy of profit center managers by type of decision

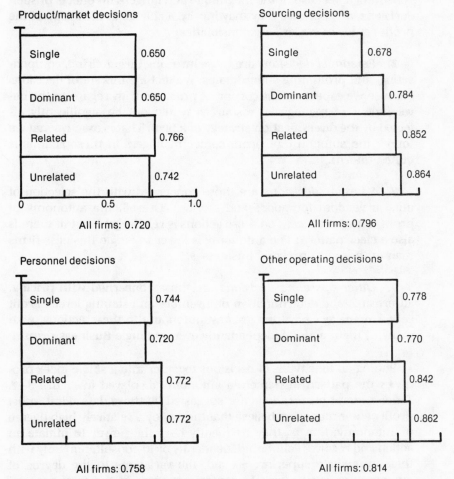

Product/market decisions

Single	0.650
Dominant	0.650
Related	0.766
Unrelated	0.742

0   0.5   1.0

All firms: 0.720

Sourcing decisions

Single	0.678
Dominant	0.784
Related	0.852
Unrelated	0.864

All firms: 0.796

Personnel decisions

Single	0.744
Dominant	0.720
Related	0.772
Unrelated	0.772

All firms: 0.758

Other operating decisions

Single	0.778
Dominant	0.770
Related	0.842
Unrelated	0.862

All firms: 0.814

Source: Part Two, Exhibit F–9. (Terms from this exhibit were divided by five to yield the numbers in the figure.)

Median score on perceived autonomy index (rescaled from zero to one)

presented at that level of summarization. An index value of 1.0 represents "my decision," 0.80 represents a "two-person decision," and 0.60 represents a "multiperson decision." The pattern of autonomy is somewhat different for each type of decision, and each deserves a brief comment.

1. *Product/market decisions* are those involving discontinuing or redesigning existing product lines, developing a new product line, expanding into new territories, etc. Profit center managers have the least autonomy for decisions of this sort, particularly in the less diversified firms where interdependencies among profit centers are greater. Even in the more diverse firms, however, autonomy is constrained because of the magnitude and longer-run effects of such decisions, and because they may involve a change in the scope of the profit center manager's responsibilities.

2. *Personnel decisions* are those involving hiring, firing, compensating, and promoting subordinates. We include this set of decisions because we expected that corporate practices with regard to the development of managerial resources would not be significantly affected by the diversification strategy of a firm. That is exactly what we found; the autonomy of profit center managers in these actions is quite uniform.

3. *Sourcing decisions* are those concerned with the selection of outside vendors for goods and services. Overall, the autonomy of profit center managers on these actions is relatively high, but there is also a clear pattern: The autonomy is lower in Single Business firms than in those in Unrelated Businesses.

4. *Other operating decisions* are those concerned with pricing, advertising, and determination of inventory and staffing levels. Profit center managers have the greatest autonomy in these actions, with many of them acting independently even in Single Business firms.

Putting all four types of decisions together into a single index produces the pattern of perceived autonomy displayed in Figure 3–7. Three general observations are suggested by those data. First, most profit center managers believe that they enjoy a relatively high degree of autonomy; that is, they frequently have the power to initiate an action and resolve it either independently or in consultation only with their immediate superior. Second, the variations in the degree of autonomy enjoyed by profit center managers in the four types of firms are significant in a statistical sense, but they are not dramatic;

Figure 3–7
Diversification strategy and perceived autonomy

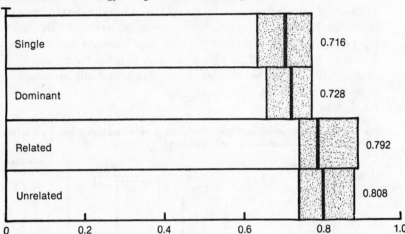

Note: Heavy line is the median score on the Perceived Autonomy Index (rescaled from zero to one); shaded area is the interquartile range.

Source: Part Two, Exhibit F–9. (Terms from this exhibit were divided by five to yield the numbers in the figure.)

the autonomy index for a profit center manager in a Single Business firm at the 25th percentile is 0.62 compared to an index value of 0.84 for a profit center manager at the 75th percentile in a firm consisting of Unrelated Businesses. Finally, our data do show that there are differences in the perceived autonomy of profit center managers that can be explained, in part, by the diversification strategy of their firms. This pattern is similar to the pattern observed earlier for the functional authority of profit center managers, and we will now turn to an examination of the relationship between these two patterns.

THE AUTHORITY/AUTONOMY RELATIONSHIP

Thus far we have described and displayed two indices that tell us something about the nature of the profit center manager's job and how he performs it. He is responsible for managing a profitable business, and the functional authority index is a measure of the extent to which he has physical custody of the corporate resources necessary to fulfill his responsibilities. The perceived autonomy index is a measure of his ability and willingness to take action more or less independently in meeting those responsibilities. The data for these two indices were provided by different people in each firm; a corporate financial executive supplied information about the functional au-

thority of a "typical" profit center manager in the firm, while two or
three experienced, trusted profit center managers responded to the
autonomy questionnaire. The metric used for the two indices is quite
different, but when they are both arrayed on a scale from zero to one
we can examine the relative relationship between authority and autonomy, as displayed in Figure 3– 8. A careful examination of that
relationship yields some useful insights about the management of
decentralized firms.

Figure 3– 8
Diversification strategy and the relationship between autonomy and authority
(medians for companies in each category)

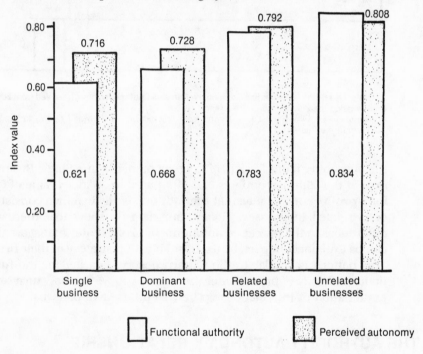

The first observation drawn from Figure 3– 8 is not an insight but a
documentation of the expected: A profit center manager who has
substantial functional authority also believes that his autonomy to
take independent action is relatively high. This relationship is not
surprising, of course, because both indices are measures of the independence of a profit center manager; one measure is physical and the
other is perceptual. The strength of the relationship, given the crude
nature of our authority index in particular, *is* surprising. For the
sample as a whole, the variation in the functional authority index

accounts for about one quarter of the variation in the perceived autonomy index.

The more revealing aspect of the relationship shown in Figure 3–8 lies in the variations in the autonomy index which are not explained by functional authority. Let us look first at the Single Business firms where the divergence is the greatest. A typical profit center manager in such a firm believes that he has more autonomy than he "has a right to believe" based on the physical resources at his disposal. The explanation for that phenomenon, we believe, reflects the success of corporate managers in developing a sense of autonomy in their profit center managers despite the fact that the economic constraints of interdependence do not permit them to endow their profit center managers with equivalent functional authority. Corporate managers do want each profit center manager to feel responsible for the success of his line of business so that he will be motivated to initiate change and influence events. In Single Business firms, enhancing a profit center manager's perception of his autonomy is good—but only up to a point. He is, after all, not completely independent, and his sense of autonomy must be managed so that it is less than, say, the autonomy perceived by a profit center manager in a more diversified firm.

Looking at the other end of the diversification spectrum, we see that profit center managers in firms with Unrelated Businesses perceive their autonomy to be somewhat less than might be expected based on their functional authority. Again, we see the hand of corporate managers at work, this time constraining the independent action of their profit center managers, particularly with regard to product/market decisions.

The primary message from the data that we have presented in this chapter is that the physical decentralization of corporate resources has a major impact on the decision-making behavior of profit center managers. These managers are the agents of change in decentralized firms; they are supposed to identify opportunities that might improve the performance of their businesses and then initiate the actions that will convert their ideas into realities. In order to achieve the desired result, a profit center manager must first identify the physical resources to be utilized and assess the effects of revising the current utilization of those resources. In order to cause a revision to occur, he then selects a decision-making process ranging across a spectrum from ordering the revision (based solely on his authority to do so) to discussing the proposed revision with one or more of his superiors and peers. Physical decentralization is important because a profit center manager is more likely to act autonomously when he or she has custody of the resources that are affected by the change.

Developing the "proper" sense of autonomy in each profit center manager is a delicate task for corporate managers. Fulfilling the objective may now be perceived as the result of the interplay of three important elements in the management of a decentralized firm. First, the philosophy of corporate managers about decentralization, and the way they act out that philosophy in dealing with their profit center managers, must surely be a major influence even though we cannot measure it. Second, the design of the responsibility structure of the firm—the distribution pattern of functional authority—plays a demonstrably important role. Finally, corporate managers also design a set of management systems that are intended to influence the behavior of profit center managers. The role of these systems, particularly the systems used to measure and reward the performance of profit center managers, also have an important effect on the perceived autonomy of profit center managers.

Chapter 4

Management systems: Measurements and rewards

PROFESSIONAL MANAGERS are systematizers. Collectively, they must make and execute a myriad of decisions—figuring out what to do and then getting it done. They strive to make good decisions, and one way to achieve that is to use good decision-making processes. An important part of a manager's task is to design a system of management and to develop a management process that will involve other members of the organization in figuring out what should be done and in getting someone to do it. In organizations as complex as a decentralized business firm, managers devote explicit effort to the design, development, and continued evolution of an elaborate set of management systems and processes.

The most important management system is the responsibility structure described in the two preceding chapters. It is important because it serves to identify the managers who will be involved in the primary management processes: strategic planning, budgeting, and monitoring performance. But the structural and procedural apparatus designed to assist managers in a decentralized firm is vast. A partial catalog would include the location, size and layout of physical facilities (thus determining the elemental authority structure); the size and composition of management committees; the size and location of staff departments; procedures for the recruiting, selection and evaluation of personnel; programs for the career planning and development of managers; executive compensation and reward systems;

policies and procedures for the authorization of capital expenditures; and, not least, systems for measuring the performance of the organization as a whole and of segments within it.

Of all these, the performance measurement system ranks second only to the responsibility structure in importance as a tool for managers. The reasons, to be explored at some length in the second section of this chapter, are essentially twofold: (1) The measurement system provides a financial structure for the firm, paralleling the responsibility structure, which serves as a common language for managers as they work together in the planning, budgeting, and review processes, and (2) the measurement system provides a performance metric which may play an important role in determining the financial rewards that managers receive. Before examining the importance of measurement systems, we shall first discuss the role of management systems generally. Then, the concluding section of this chapter will focus on the reward systems found in decentralized firms.

DECENTRALIZATION AND MANAGEMENT SYSTEMS

There are two broad types of managerial work—deciding what to do and getting it done—and management systems are intended to aid managers in both tasks. These tasks are highly interrelated, because they are performed simultaneously in a dynamic environment, and in a decentralized firm they are extremely complex because they require the simultaneous involvement of managers at several levels in the responsibility structure. Figure 4–1 is a conceptual schematic showing how these tasks of strategy formulation and implementation are accomplished by the people in an organization. We will discuss that briefly before turning explicitly to the role of management systems.

Strategy formulation and implementation

The task of strategy formulation is difficult, even for a relatively simple business. In such a business, strategy is determined, implicitly or explicitly, by a handful of corporate managers. The task is both analytic and intensely personal, and has been described best by Kenneth R. Andrews in his book, *The Concept of Corporate Strategy.*[1] In Andrews' view, the strategists seek to reconcile conflicting forces.

---

[1] Dow Jones-Irwin, Inc., Homewood, Ill., 1971.

Figure 4–1
Strategy formulation and implementation

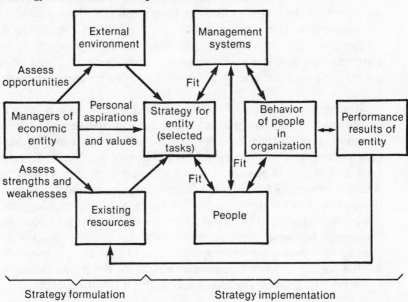

Strategy formulation   Strategy implementation

They must deal simultaneously with four questions: What *might* we do? What *can* we do? What do we *want* to do? and, What *should* we do?

Each of those questions requires careful thought, and none can be answered solely by rational analysis. Most corporations share a common external environment, and the identification and assessment of attractive opportunities rests heavily on the personal perceptiveness of the managers involved. Determining the capability of the organization to capitalize on opportunities also implies a rational assessment, but it is extremely difficult to be objective about one's own organization.[2] Finally, many corporations develop an explicit set of shared values, and those values plus a manager's personal aspirations and ethics are, appropriately, an explicit part of the task of strategy formulation. As Andrews says, in discussing the relevance of personal values in the determination of strategy, "somebody has to have his heart in it."[3]

For a simple economic entity, the result of this personal analysis by its managers is the definition of a "business strategy." Except in

[2] For additional insight here see, Howard H. Stevenson, "Defining Corporating Strengths and Weaknesses," *Sloan Management Review,* Spring 1976, pp. 51–68.

[3] Andrews, *Concept of Corporate Strategy,* p. 117.

the case of a total monopoly, each company in an industry seeks to find a place for itself among its competitors. In most industries, the major competitors are unlikely to change substantially over the next decade, and the thrust of technological and market development can be foreseen, however dimly. Defining a business strategy is an attempt to delineate the specific tasks that the business must perform particularly well if it is to be successful in a competitive environment.

Strategy formulation in a decentralized firm is an infinitely more complicated task.[4] The strategic issue for top managers in such corporations is the determination of a "diversification strategy," deciding how corporate resources shall be deployed, over time, among the various lines of business in the corporate portfolio. The strategic thought processes for such managers are, conceptually, the same as those shown in Figure 4–1, but the scope is much broader. Each of the individual lines of business in such a corporation, of course, still requires a business strategy of its own. To achieve this, corporate managers decentralize the responsibility, to a greater or lesser extent, for the formulation of business strategies to the profit center managers responsible for running each of the lines of business.

The General Electric Company in 1978 is a good example of the complexities of strategy formulation in an $18-billion decentralized firm. The responsibility structure specifies six levels of general managers (the approximate number of managers at each level is shown in parentheses): chairman/chief executive officer (1), vice chairman (2), sector executive (6), group executive (10), division general manager (50), and department general manager (150). For operating purposes, GE has more than 200 profit center managers. For strategic planning purposes, roughly 50 of these profit centers (or a set of related profit centers) have been identified as "strategic business units" (SBUs). The primary criterion for designation as an SBU is that the unit must sell mainly to external markets (not to other components of GE) against an identifiable set of competitors. Many divisions are SBUs, but some product departments qualify, as well as some groups.

The manager of an SBU at General Electric develops a proposed business strategy for submission to sector and corporate managers. In the review of these proposals, each SBU is classified into one of

---

[4] A more complete treatment of this task is presented in Richard F. Vancil, "Strategy Formulation in Complex Organizations," *Sloan Management Review*, Winter, 1976. That article is also reprinted in Peter Lorange and R. F. Vancil, *Strategic Planning Systems*, (Englewood Cliffs, N.J.: Prentice-Hall, 1977).

four corporate portfolio categories: invest to grow, selectivity/grow, selectivity/earnings, and harvest/divest. Not all lines of business, at GE or any other diverse corporation, have equal potential for growth, nor does any corporation have sufficient resources to fund all growth opportunities. Thus, GE's corporate managers must make some choices in allocating resources, and the proposals from the SBUs must be modified to accommodate to these difficult judgments. The result is a complex web of interrelated strategies, linking the corporation to each of its lines of business with an explicit statement of the business strategy that each profit center manager will attempt to implement.

The simultaneous implementation of a disparate set of business strategies in a decentralized corporation can best be achieved by assigning responsibility for each line of business or business segment to a profit center manager. There is little formal knowledge about the implementation process except that it involves people working together and people taking actions. The right-hand side of Figure 4 − 1 is an attempt to depict the process conceptually. Again, the chart applies to any defined economic entity: an entire diversified corporation, a product division within it, or a functional activity within a division.

One thing that can be said about implementation is that it is not a neatly scheduled execution of a preprogrammed set of actions. The term "selected tasks," in the center of Figure 4 − 1, is not a list of specific action steps; rather, it is a definition of the crucial activities which must be performed particularly well if the entity is to pursue its strategy successfully. The people in the organization must understand what those key activities are and why they are so important. Then, if they show a commitment to that strategy and if they are the right sort of people for the nature of the tasks to be performed, they will behave in a manner consistent with the organization's objectives and goals, and that behavior will lead to the desired performance results. An obvious point needs to be made explicit: the implementation of a strategy requires an organization composed of the right sort of people in terms of formal training, experience, and personality and psychological traits.

The other major box on the right half of Figure 4 − 1 shows the key role that management systems play in implementing strategy. The first thing to be said about management systems is, like the people in the organization, the systems must be appropriate for the organization's strategy. The key word in the chart is "fit."[5] The management systems for a steel mill would not work at all in a hotel chain. More subtly, the management systems for, say, the Hyatt Regency chain of hotels would be somewhat different from those employed by Holiday Inns. If properly designed, the management systems of an organization have an important influence on the behavior of people, increasing the likelihood that they will take actions that will contribute to the successful performance of the entity.

An important aspect of Figure 4−1 is that all the arrows on the right side of that chart are double-headed. The strategy for an organization is not determined independently of the type of people that are in it; those people may be the principal resource of the organization and the strategy may attempt to capitalize on the talents of those people. Success also begets success. If the performance results of the organization are good, morale goes up and the behavior of people in the organization improves. People acting collectively in an organization also develop norms which affect the type of people who feel comfortable in the organization; individuals either adapt to those norms or leave the organization. Management systems also change and evolve over time so that the people in the organization, individually and collectively, are comfortable with those systems. Finally, the management systems themselves may be a major resource of the organization—as those developed by, say, the McDonald's hamburger chain—and thus influence the strategy of the entity. We turn now to a closer look at those systems.

Purposes of management systems

Any economic entity of some size needs a set of formal management systems to facilitate the implementation of its strategy, and those systems must be tailored to fit both the strategy and the people

---

[5] This broad view of a set of management systems was first articulated and illustrated by Rensis Likert, who concluded: ". . . every component part of a particular management system fits well with each of the other parts and functions in harmony with them. Each system of management has a basic integrity of its own. . . . *The management system of an organization must have compatible component parts if it is to function effectively.*" (*The Human Organization,* New York: McGraw-Hill, 1967, p. 123; emphasis in the original.) Likert's definition of the components of a management system is presented there and in his earlier book, *New Patterns of Management* (New York: McGraw-Hill, 1961, pp. 223−33). The concept of "fit" was also discussed by Gene W. Dalton in *Motivation and Control in Organizations* (Homewood, Ill.: Richard D. Irwin, Inc., and the Dorsey Press, 1971); p. 20. A more elaborate conceptualization has recently been suggested by John P. Kotter in *Organizational Dynamics* (Reading, Mass.: Addison-Wesley, 1978).

in the organization. In the discussion that follows, we will now restrict our focus to the systems designed by corporate managers. A profit center manager will need to develop additional management systems which are appropriate for the nature of his business. He does so, however, within the framework of requirements imposed by his corporate superiors. We want to take a closer look at that framework.

In the second paragraph of this chapter we listed a number of specific management systems and procedures. That list was, at best, only partial, focusing on those systems that tend to be more formalized and more explicitly designed.[6] Our definition of management systems, however, is intended to be broad enough to include a variety of less formal practices and traditions which have an important effect on the organizational climate and culture. Within this entire set of management systems, the idea of "fit" is applicable again. All of these systems are operating simultaneously within a given organization, and the systems must be mutually supportive if the organization is to function effectively. Thus, the existence of a set of informal practices and traditions that cannot be explicitly changed in a preemptory fashion serves to restrict the freedom of managers when they want to change the more formal systems. As a result, although management systems do change in an organization, they tend to evolve rather slowly over time.

The best way to discuss the design of management systems, and the interrelationships between such systems, is in terms of the results they seek to achieve. While each system usually has one or more specific purposes of its own, in a broader sense we may synthesize three major purposes of management systems.

Human resource development. One major purpose of management systems is to ensure the continuing enrichment and renewal of the organization's human resources. Corporate-wide systems designed for this purpose vary greatly in their discipline and comprehensiveness. Some decentralized firms define a pool of executive manpower that reaches two or three levels down into their divisions. Most corporations of any size, to a greater or lesser extent, design

---

[6] For a comprehensive discussion of the full array of management systems and practices, see Jay W. Lorsch and Stephen A. Allen III, *Managing Diversity and Interdependence* (Boston: Division of Research, Harvard Business School, 1973), particularly chaps. 3 and 4. Their study focuses on corporate-divisional relations, but devotes relatively little attention to the structural design of measurement and reward systems. Their study and this one are both compatible and complementary.

formal systems to identify these managers, track their performance, ensure equitable compensation, and place them in competition for promotions across the entire corporation so that they may develop a coherent career path toward broader responsibilities. Executive development is essentially self-development, and many management systems facilitate that process. Management-by-objectives systems, and budgeting and reporting systems, enable a manager to set goals for his own performance and take pride in his accomplishments when his goals are achieved. Other forms of recognizing a manager's potential contributions also serve to motivate executives to increase their capabilities: attending a formal executive education program, or being appointed a member of a prestigious committee within the corporation, are only two examples.

Resource management. A second major purpose of management systems is to ensure the rational utilization of corporate resources. In addition to the management of human resources, other corporate resources—financial, physical, and technological—also require wise and conscious allocation. Long-range planning systems, and budgeting systems for both capital expenditures and continuing operations, play an important role here. At least as important, however, is the management process by which such resource allocation decisions are made. Important dimensions of this process include the size and role of corporate staff in reviewing divisional proposals and the extent to which committees are used to thrash out controversial decisions.

Shared purpose. Finally, a more subtle but perhaps most important purpose of management systems is to develop a sense of cohesiveness and shared purpose among corporate managers and their subordinates. If a corporation is to pursue multiple business strategies simultaneously, it is highly desirable to achieve some sort of consensus among corporate and divisional executives on what they are trying to do and why they are trying to do it. A profit center manager who "buys into" the corporate objectives and goals, and understands the rationale for corporate resource allocation decisions, also accepts a personal commitment to perform as promised within his or her sphere of responsibility. Planning and budgeting systems provide formal mechanisms for the process of developing shared purpose, but informal practices are also important. Many companies use executive conferences for this purpose, frequently holding them at convention centers that facilitate social interaction. Shared values, a qualitative step beyond the acceptance of mutual performance goals, are harder to build, particularly in highly diverse organizations.

But many less diverse corporations, with more homogeneous managers, do have a sense of tradition and heritage about the shared values that imbue an organization with its distinctive culture.

Management systems, designed and evolved by managers, are intended to institutionalize the way that each manager thinks about his role in the organization. He may be responsible for a profit center, but he knows it is not "his," and he must manage it in the context of the larger organization. Management systems, subtly and intricately interrelated, perform two functions simultaneously: (1) enhancing each manager's "sense of autonomy" over his sphere of operations, and at the same time, (2) creating a "web of constraints" that limits his autonomy in a way that he can understand and accept.

Two brief examples should serve to illustrate this point. First, consider a profit center manager who has risen to his position through conscious corporate management of his career path. He is a beneficiary of the corporation's executive manpower development system. At the same time, that system constrains his authority over his direct subordinates; he may lose a capable subordinate because of promotion opportunities available in other divisions. Another aspect of the profit center manager's job is to identify strategic opportunities for his business and to request an allocation of corporate resources to pursue them. Yet, he knows that his requests will be put into competition with proposals from other profit centers, and that he will not always win.

In both of these instances, being a part of a larger corporation is both a blessing and a curse. Compared to the job of the president of an independent corporation of equivalent size, a profit center manager has the benefit of access to a greater pool of corporate resources, both human and financial, than his or her counterpart. But that access has its price; he is responsible for the performance of his profit center but he lacks the unilateral authority to command that corporate resources be committed to that end. Management systems in decentralized firms are designed to help a profit center manager cope with that ambiguity.

MEASUREMENT SYSTEMS

Performance reporting systems, which include measuring the financial performance of profit centers, now become the focal point for the remainder of our study. As Sloan describes in his book, measurement is the key:

. . . It was on the financial side that the last necessary key to decentralization with coordinated control was found. That key, in principle,
was the concept that, if we had the means to review and judge the
effectiveness of operations, we could safely leave the prosecution of
those operations to the men in charge of them. The means as it turned
out was a method of financial control which converted the broad principle of return on investment into one of the important working instruments for measuring the operations of the divisions. . . .[7]

Measurement systems are critical to the effective management of a
decentralized firm, and this section presents a brief general discussion of why such systems are so powerful. Our focus here is restricted to financial measurements, but we are quick to acknowledge
that nonfinancial measures of performance are also extremely important. Nonfinancial measures, often stated in physical or statistical
terms, can provide data in natural functional categories that are focused on a particular operating unit and can be made available
quickly. At lower operating levels, nonfinancial data may be used almost exclusively, but such measurements do not have the characteristics nor the purposes of financial measurement systems, as discussed below.

Characteristics of financial measurement systems

One reason why financial measurement systems are so powerful is
simply the natural attributes of such systems. Four characteristics
that contribute to the power of financial measurement systems are
discussed below.

Disciplined by accounting. Financial measurement systems
have an inherent integrity that is unquestioned by operating managers. They may joke that accountants "cook the books," but they
know that the debits must equal the credits.

The real discipline of the accounting equation rests, ultimately, on
cash. All cash must be accounted for as to where it came from and
where it went. In order to handle a massive volume of such transactions, accountants develop a detailed set of rules that are almost inflexible in order to ensure that similar transactions are recorded in a
consistent manner.

---

[7] Alfred P. Sloan, Jr., *My Years with General Motors* (Garden City, N.Y.: Doubleday,
1964) p. 140. © 1963 by Alfred P. Sloan, Jr. Reprinted by the permission of the Harold
Matson Company, Inc.

The importance of this, in a managerial context, is sometimes overlooked. The accounting system provides the *only* detailed and inflexible set of rules that an organization imposes upon itself. Other rules in the organization, such as standard operating procedures, may also be quite detailed, but they are much more flexible. Written policies and procedures are instructive, but they may also conflict with one another. One personnel policy may specify certain minimum qualifications for a particular job; another may specify that a certain number of positions be filled by minority and female personnel. Most policies can be followed most of the time, but policies are also made to be challenged and changed—or sometimes, wisely, ignored. But no manager, unless he is party to fraud, would instruct his accountant to fail to record a transaction that would involve the receipt or disbursement of cash.

Comprehensive and pervasive. It is the need for cash, of course, that is pervasive in business organizations. The expenses of every last tiny operating unit must be paid. It is this fact which gives a financial measurement system its total scope, blanketing the entire organization and reaching into every nook and cranny. Every activity of any significance to the corporation will ultimately trigger a cash transaction and, thus, the accounting system gathers some data about all such activities. For a relatively brief period, in a particular subunit, events may occur that the accounting system does not capture. Machinery may break down and remain unrepaired, for example, but cash to repair it will be required if the unit is to continue operating. In the not-too-long run, there is no place to hide.

The pervasiveness of an accounting system does not automatically result in a financial measurement system that is valuable for managerial use. It does create the opportunity for such a system, however, as Sloan noted:

> . . . The reports, for example, were not usable for evaluation and comparison until they were set up on a uniform and consistent basis. Uniformity is essential to financial control, since without it comparisons are difficult if not impossible.[8]

Properly designed, a financial measurement system has the capability of aggregating the entire set of activities of an organization, expressed in financial terms. The other, important, capability is that such data can also be decomposed to whatever level of detail a manager may desire.

---

[8] Ibid., p. 143.

Mandatory and mature. A third characteristic of financial measurement systems is that every business organization must have one,
if only to file an income tax return. Corporations vary greatly in the
formality of their management systems; some do not prepare operating budgets, much less long-range plans. A few very large corporations refuse to draw formal organization charts, preferring to operate
in a relatively unstructured style. Some management systems are
nothing more than fads, here today and gone within a year or two, but
financial measurements are a mandated reality—and they have been
around for a long time.

The managerial implications of this are simply that it is hard to
ignore the data that the measurement system provides. The chief
executive, at least, cannot resist peeking at the data, seeking to answer
the question: "How well did we do?" But that question inevitably leads
to, "Why was our performance better or worse than I expected?" and
"Who is responsible for the performance variations?" With a relatively modest expenditure of effort, the base of raw data can be converted into an important managerial tool.

Adaptable to context. Finally, although a disciplined and comprehensive set of financial data must exist, those data may be manipu-
lated in a flexible and creative way, thus permitting managers to enhance their understanding of the economics of their business. Sloan,
again, said it well:

> . . . Each of these two elements—profit margin and rate of turnover of
> capital—Mr. Brown broke into its detailed components, a case, you
> might say, of aggregating and deaggregating figures to bring about a
> recognition of the structure of profit and loss in operations. Essentially
> it was a matter of making things visible. The unique thing was that it
> made possible the creation, based on experience, of detailed standards
> or yardsticks for working capital and fixed-capital requirements and for
> the various elements of cost. . . .[9]

The managerial payoff inherent in the flexibility of a financial measurement system is the primary reason why extremely complex
internal measurement systems have been developed by business corporations. It is possible for a manager, manipulating the economic
parameters of his business, to come to a more sophisticated understanding of the critical variables affecting profitability—he develops a better economic model of the business. This model can then
be codified and institutionalized through the design of the financial

---

[9] Ibid., p. 142.

measurement system, just as Donaldson Brown did for General Motors. The subsequent generations of managers are thus able to learn the essence of the business more quickly and, if they develop an even more sophisticated model of the business, the measurement system can be modified to reflect that.

There is one important limitation on this attribute of a financial measurement system that should be noted. Accounting, based on financial transactions and governed by the objectivity requirements of generally accepted accounting principles, does not always mirror the economic realities of a business. Successful research and development, for example, is not an expense but an investment that may have a handsome payoff. Nearly all the companies in our sample (see Section G for details) use the same accounting policies in designing their internal measurement systems that they use for external reporting. But despite the crude and sometimes arbitrary accounting methods that are externally imposed, most manufacturing corporations are able to design their financial measurement system so that it is of substantial help in improving their own understanding of the nature of their business and in communicating that understanding to others in the organization.

These characteristics of a financial measurement system give it great potential for assisting managers in running their organization more effectively. We turn now to how that potential is realized, looking at the purposes that a financial measurement system is designed to achieve.

Purposes of financial measurement systems

Another reason why financial measurement systems are so powerful is that, properly designed, they may contribute to satisfying several important managerial needs. Four major purposes of financial measurement systems are discussed briefly below.

Coordination. A key task for corporate managers in a decentralized firm is the development of a management process that will enable them to fulfill their responsibilities for corporate performance. Having decentralized authority and responsibility to their profit center managers, corporate managers play an integrative role, coordinating the activities of the various components to achieve the desired overall result. The most important elements of that process involve planning for and budgeting the allocation of corporate resources.

Financial measurement systems provide formal structure for the management process. Budgeting is a detailed, time-consuming task, reflecting a myriad of coordinated decisions about near-term operations. But budgeting is not an end in itself; budgets may need to be changed for a variety of reasons, so performance must be tracked against budgets in order to raise signals that changes may be needed. The routine historical financial reporting system measures performance results, and that highly structured system also provides the framework for planning and budgeting. The primary framework for the management process, of course, is the responsibility structure of the firm. In another sense, then, the financial measurement system is a quantitative overlay on the responsibility structure, assigning every element of revenue and expense to a particular individual position in the organization. Each manager can then present his plans and budgets and, because they are expressed in financial terms, they can be easily aggregated for higher level review and coordination.

Motivation. Another important task of corporate managers is to release the creative energies of each profit center manager so that as he pursues the parochial objectives of his own business he is also contributing to the achievement of a coordinated set of corporate objectives. Many management systems reinforce this, and the financial measurement system plays an important role. Each profit center manager has a defined sphere of business responsibility, and the common practice in decentralized corporations is to request each such manager to define his or her personal performance goals in financial terms for corporate review and approval. When that goal-setting process works effectively, the profit center managers then become committed to achieving their goals, thus helping to ensure that corporate performance goals will also be met.

In Sloan's view, the financial measurement system had exactly this desired result:

> . . . It increases the morale of the organization by placing each operation on its own foundation, making it feel that it is part of the Corporation, assuming its own responsibility and contributing its share to the final result. . . .[10]

In our view, motivating the desired performance by profit center managers is one of the most important purposes of financial measurement systems. All too often this point is stated, perversely we believe, as a need to evaluate the performance of profit center man-

---

[10] Ibíd., p. 50.

agers. Financial measurement systems, however, provide only a fraction of the relevant data that are appropriately used to evaluate the performance of a manager. And besides, history is dead, and there is little to be gained in crying over spilled milk. Instead, the financial measurement system is designed in an attempt to influence the behavior of the manager in the future, challenging him to look ahead—not over his shoulder—in order to meet and exceed the goals he has set for himself.

Operational guidance. Decentralization requires an explicit understanding between corporate managers and each profit center manager about the extent of his or her responsibility. Again, many management systems contribute to this definition, but the financial measurement system plays a unique role because it is so detailed. Each profit center manager knows specifically which elements of revenue and expense are within his sphere of responsibility and, implicitly, therefore, is told that these are the items to worry about to the exclusion of certain other items which are someone else's responsibility. Cordiner noted that measurement systems have "important values to decentralized management," and concluded by commenting:

> . . . all these points are directed at helping each decentralized manager and individual contributor measure and guide his own work, through self-discipline; they are not designed as a way for others to "second-guess" the manager of a component or the workers in his component. . . .[11]

In order to achieve this sort of detailed operational guidance for each profit center manager in a decentralized firm, the financial measurement system must not only be designed well, it must be used well. It is one thing for a corporate manager to pay philosophical lip service to the idea that decentralization means that he must allow his subordinates to make some mistakes if they are to learn. It is another thing for him to bite his lip when an unfavorable performance report hits his desk. A good performance measurement system can help a profit center manager to identify his own mistakes and to change his behavior in a way that will prevent recurrence of those mistakes. But the measurement system alone cannot achieve that result; both superiors and subordinates must work toward a relationship which will allow that learning to occur.

---

[11] Ralph J. Cordiner, *New Frontiers for Professional Managers* (New York: McGraw-Hill, 1956), p. 98. © 1956 by McGraw-Hill Book Company.

Monitor organizational effectiveness. Finally, financial measurement systems play a primary role in assisting corporate managers in their task of keeping informed about the operating effectiveness of their organization. Financial measurements are quite efficient for this purpose, permitting "management by exception" that quickly tells a corporate manager when and where to worry. Sloan, as usual, put the point well:

> . . . The figures did not give automatic answers to problems. They simply exposed the facts with which to judge whether the divisions were operating in line with expectations as reflected in prior performance or in their budgets.[12]

Wise managers, like Sloan, know that even the best financial measures contain inherent imperfections. It is not enough to look simply at the bottom-line performance of a profit center manager; the profit calculation contains too many variables, some of which reflect short-term performance while the impact of others may not be visible for months or years. Nevertheless, financial measurements are important because they are available frequently and are prepared on a consistent basis. Their purpose, in this regard, is to provide a starting point for further investigation.

Limitations of profit measurement systems

Financial measurement systems possess several important characteristics which permit them to aid corporate managers in fulfilling several important tasks. In decentralized firms, such systems are designed to measure the profit earned by each business segment for which a profit center manager is responsible. The design of an internal profit center measurement system is a complex and detailed task—directly analogous to the design of the responsibility structure for the firm—because design decisions are required for each and every element of corporate revenue and expense. We will examine those design issues and how they have been resolved by our sample companies in the next chapter. For the moment, however, it is sufficient to note that there are ample opportunities to make errors in the design of such systems. By errors we do not mean technical mistakes; the debits still equal the credits even in a system that is conceptually flawed. A conceptually perfect system is easy to define: it "fits," that is to say, it is tailored in such a way that it is consistent with the other management systems in the firm, most particularly the responsibility

---

[12] Sloan, *My Years with General Motors,* p. 142.

structure and the processes by which corporate managers convey the degree of intended autonomy for each profit center manager.

In our structural questionnaire, we asked corporate financial executives to describe in detail the design of their profit center measurement systems. In order to appraise that design, we asked the profit center managers in a subset of those firms for their opinions about the system. The phrasing of the question is shown below, and the responses are displayed in Figure 4—2.

Do you believe that profit, as it is routinely calculated for your profit center, fairly reflects the effectiveness of your performance as a manager, to the extent that such performance can be measured in financial terms?

Figure 4— 2
Fairness of the profit center measurement system as perceived by profit center managers

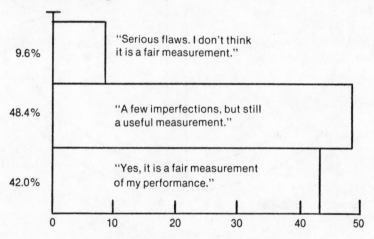

Percentage of 312 profit center managers

Source: Part Two, Exhibit F–28.

Less than 10 percent of our respondents thought that the profit center measurement system in their firm was seriously flawed, but nearly 50 percent believed that it had some imperfections. We asked both of those groups of respondents to comment on "the most important imperfections or flaws." More than 80 percent of them did comment, and in our analysis of those comments, we were finally able to assign most of them to one of four categories as shown in Figure 4—3.

Figure 4– 3
Comments on flaws and imperfections of profit center measurement systems
(percentages of 166 comments)

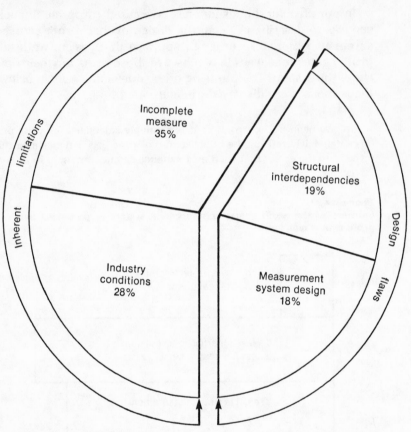

Source: Part Two, Exhibit F–28.

Two of the four types of comments were concerned with the inherent limitations of any system that attempts to measure the profit of an economic entity during a short period of time. One such limitation, referred to earlier, is caused by the inability of conventional accounting procedures to measure the economic consequences of current activities. Our respondents mentioned not only "investments" in research and development, but also expenditures to gain market share, improve their plant layout, and develop the managerial resources in their profit centers. Others, somewhat more cryptically, simply stated that, "short-term profits don't necessarily measure the long-term health or profit potential of my profit center." Comments of this sort were more common than for any of the other three categories; they made up more than a third of the comments that we classified.

A second inherent limitation is more specifically directed to the profit center measurement systems used by decentralized firms. The profit calculation may tell what the financial performance of the profit center was, but it does not tell how good that performance was. More than a quarter of the comments we analyzed said something like, "My profit performance last year may not have looked good compared to my budget or even to prior years, but in the light of the chaotic conditions that existed in our industry, I think my performance was outstanding." Corporate managers, responsible for the entire firm, may sometimes have similar feelings, but frequently they are able to compare the performance of their firm to other similar publicly held firms. The answer to the question "How well did we do?" must surely be "Compared to what?" For profit centers within a decentralized firm, obtaining timely and relevant comparative data that will permit the assessment of the performance of a profit center relative to its external environment may be difficult.

We were aware, of course, of both of these inherent limitations in profit center measurement systems. We attempted to forestall such comments by inserting a clause in the question, pointing out that we wanted the respondent to appraise the fairness of profit as a measure of his performance "to the extent that such performance can be measured in financial terms." One respondent underlined that clause, commented on the inherent limitations of profit measurement, and then said that except for those problems he thought their profit center measurement system was fair.

One interpretation of the fact that so many respondents said the measurement system was imperfect or flawed, and then commented on the inherent limitations of such systems, is that they simply did not read the question carefully enough (or that it was poorly worded). Another interpretation is that they did understand the question, and that their comments may really be taken as a commentary on the way that the profit center measurement system is used within their firms. Periodic profit can never be a perfect measure of a manager's current performance, and unless corporate managers use such data with sensitivity, they may exacerbate the frustrations that are expressed in the comments that we received.

Our real intent in asking profit center managers to appraise the measurement system in their firm was to identify those situations where the design of the system was flawed. We wanted to understand the nature of such flaws and, if possible, discover whether and how such flaws might be cured. Nearly 40 percent of the comments we received related to design flaws and could be classified into the two categories shown in Figure 4−3.

One type of design flaw is apparently caused by the complexities of the responsibility structure in a decentralized firm. The profit center manager's job is intentionally ambiguous—his business responsibility does exceed his functional authority—and for some of our respondents that gap was either so wide or so painful that they said, in effect, "Ouch!" A typical comment went something like, "It's not fair to hold me responsible for profit when I have no control over the sales force." A broader sampling of these comments is presented in Section F.

Comments on the other type of design flaw were more specifically aimed at the design of the profit center measurement system. The most frequent comments in this category were those pointing out the arbitrariness of allocations of corporate overhead and the sometimes shattering effect that a corporate change in accounting policy could have on the profit reported by a profit center. Sometimes we found it difficult to classify comments into one category or another. For example, "It's not fair that I have to absorb the manufacturing variances on the components that I buy from other profit centers," reflects both the interdependence of that profit center manager on others and a measurement system that assigns manufacturing variances to the receiving unit rather than the producing unit. Again, a representative sample of comments like these are presented in Section F.

Our detailed analysis of the comments on both types of design flaws produced some useful insights. Profit center managers who complained about structural interdependencies were more likely to be in firms where the typical profit center manager scored relatively low on the functional authority index. Put another way, these comments were substantive; they were made by profit center managers who were more highly interdependent on other units than the managers who did not make such comments. More importantly, managers who commented on either type of design flaw were more likely to have relatively low scores on the perceived autonomy index than managers who did not make such comments. Our conclusion from these data is that the design of a profit center measurement system is inextricably interrelated with the design of the responsibility structure of the firm and the degree of intended autonomy for its profit center managers. Comments about design flaws are really telling us that the "fit" among these three elements is poor, at least as perceived by the profit center manager.

Profit center measurement systems do have inherent limitations, and the design of such systems is intricate because they must be consistent with the responsibility, authority, and autonomy of the profit center manager. We shall explore the intricacies of that design in more detail in Chapter 5. For the moment, however, one closing comment is in order. Profit center measurement systems have the potential to be a powerful tool for corporate managers, and that potential is more likely to be realized if the measurement system is perceived as fair by the profit center managers. Only 42 percent of our respondents gave an unqualified opinion to that effect. But, if we take account of the fact that many of the comments we received were related to the inherent limitations, it appears that roughly two thirds of our profit center managers believe that the calculation of profit for their profit center is a fair measure of their performance stated in financial terms.

REWARD SYSTEMS

The rewards of being a profit center manager are multiple. First, there is the fun of it—the responsibility for managing a business that, for a while at least, he can think of as his own. Second, there is the power and status of the position—power that is overt and tangible in the form of physical resources remanded to his custody. Finally, there is the feedback, and that, too, comes in multiple forms: his performance is measured by the most important business yardstick, profit; if he can build a good record of performance, not necessarily measured solely financially, he may be promoted to a higher position; and, along the way, there is feedback in the form of financial compensation, a good salary and the prospect of a significant bonus. Decentralized firms use rewards of all these sorts to "turn on" their profit center managers, motivating them to initiate the actions that will result in high performance both for their profit centers and for the firm as a whole.

Before proceeding, an implicit assumption in the paragraph above needs to be made explicit: the personal psychological characteristics of an individual are a major determinant of whether he finds the job to be fun—or pure frustration. A profit center manager must have a high tolerance for the ambiguity that is inherent in his job, and that quality is relatively rare. In this study, by restricting our survey to profit center managers who have been in their jobs for two years or more, we hope that our respondents represent the type of individuals who do relish the rewards enumerated above.

Rewards and measurement

The profit center measurement system plays a central role in providing rewards to profit center managers. The very act of measuring the profit earned by the business poses a challenge to his or her professional capabilities. Profit center managers, by the time they arrive at that position, are already "successful," at least their potential for a general management position in their firm has already been recognized. Tangible rewards, power and money, come with the position and are more than trivially important. But most profit center managers realize that the more important rewards in the future are psychic rewards; the personal satisfactions that come from demonstrating to others that he does, indeed, have the capabilities to manage his business with sufficient skill to produce an increasing stream of future profits.[13]

Corporate managers, too, realize the paramount importance of psychic rewards in motivating the kind of initiative and action that they want from their profit center managers. Corporate managers seek, in a variety of ways, to make these psychic rewards more explicit, but the most important ways involve their personal interactions with individual profit center managers. Consider a profit center manager two or three levels down in the corporate hierarchy but with a firm grasp on the bottom rung of the general management ladder. One day he finds himself going down in the elevator with the corporate president who remarks, casually, "Jim, you're really doing a great job in the toy and game division, and we're all very proud of your performance." That dual recognition, both by name and by knowing about his performance, is probably worth more to that profit center manager than a minor, impersonal increase in his bonus.

But corporate managers, at least in our sample of firms, also put the corporation's money where their mouth is. Recognition, followed

---

[13] Monetary rewards, of course, may be important as a way of calibrating psychic rewards. For a fascinating article on managerial ambiguity in general, see Richard T. Pascale, "Zen and the Art of Management," *Harvard Business Review,* March–April 1978. He cites an American Management Association survey in which "49 percent of the respondents indicated that recognition for what they did was their most important reward."

by a smaller bonus at the end of the year, is faint praise indeed. Instead, both to guard against that event and to reinforce the importance of the psychic reward of good performance with a tangible one, most decentralized firms employ a more or less explicit link between the financial performance of a profit center and the size of the annual bonus received by its manager.

We asked the profit center managers in a subset of our sample firms to tell us about their incentive compensation: whether they received a bonus, how much it amounted to as a percentage of salary, and how the size of their bonus was determined. Annual bonuses are common in decentralized firms; 90 percent of our profit center managers said that they received one. Bonuses are also an important component of a profit center manager's annual cash income; the median bonus amounts to 25 percent of salary, and this median is fairly constant regardless of the diversification strategy of the firm. The most interesting finding, displayed in Figure 4−4, is the significant role played by current financial performance in the determination of a profit center manager's annual bonus.

For nearly two thirds of our profit center managers, the size of their annual bonus is determined by a defined formula rather than by reliance on a potentially subjective judgment by their superior. More surprisingly, for nearly half of those managers, their bonus was determined *solely* by the financial performance of their profit center. Even for those managers where a formula was not applied, their perception was that their annual bonus was affected, at least to some extent, by their financial performance. Only four percent of this sample said that financial performance was not an important factor in determining their annual bonus.

Bonuses and autonomy

We wanted to use these data to determine whether there was any relationship between the bonus system employed by a decentralized firm and the perceived autonomy of the profit center managers in that firm. To do so, we constructed a bonus index for each profit center manager who received a bonus. As described in detail in Section F, the index combined the size of a manager's bonus with the importance of financial performance in determining the size of the bonus. The five categories shown in Figure 4−4 were assigned values from 1 to 5. A profit center manager who received a bonus equal to

Figure 4– 4
**Importance of current financial performance in determining annual bonus
(percentage of 282 profit center managers)**

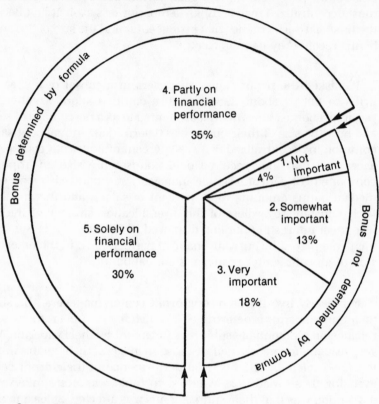

Source: Part Two, Exhibit F–4.

100 percent of his salary and determined by a formula based solely on financial performance would have a bonus index score of 500; another manager with a 10 percent bonus in which financial performance was not an important determinant would have an index score of 10. For the sample as a whole, scores on the bonus index ranged from 7 to 495.

This index, admittedly crude, did permit us to observe that there appears to be a significant relationship between the size and method of bonus determination on the one hand and the perceived autonomy of a profit center manager on the other. We divided the profit center managers into three equal-sized groups based on their score on the perceived autonomy index, and then calculated the median value of the bonus index for each group. The results, displayed in Figure 4–5,

Figure 4–5
Relationship between perceived autonomy and bonus index

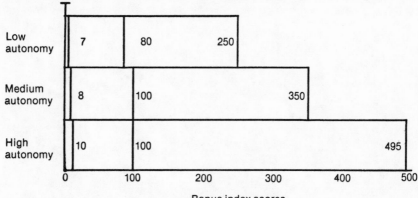

Bonus index scores

Note: Scores on the bonus index for 258 profit center managers, divided into three equal-sized groups in terms of their scores on the perceived autonomy index. Bonus index scores are the minimum, median, and maximum for managers in each group.
Source: Part Two, Exhibit F–7A.

indicate that there does appear to be a relationship between autonomy and the bonus system.

It is interesting to speculate about the nature of this relationship, and tempting to try to determine cause and effect. Is the bonus system performance-oriented because a profit center manager has relatively high autonomy? Or, does a profit center manager believe that his or her autonomy is relatively high because of the performance-oriented nature of the bonus system? The answer, we believe, is both. The most delicate task for corporate managers is to help each profit center manager develop an appropriate sense of his autonomy. Some profit center managers, more interdependent than others, should recognize that their autonomy is constrained. In that circumstance, a bonus system that placed a high value on the current financial performance of such a profit center would send a misleading signal to that profit center manager. Instead, a smaller bonus determined more subjectively can be used to recognize his performance as that of a team player. What Figure 4−5 shows, we believe, is an example of a good fit between one of the management systems in a decentralized firm reinforcing the intended perception of his autonomy by a profit center manager.

Chapter 5

The interdependence of profit center managers: Responsibility and control

DESIGNING a conceptually perfect profit center measurement system is a detailed and demanding task. Detailed because, if the system is to be comprehensive, it must encompass every element of revenue received and expense incurred by the corporation. Demanding because, if the system is to be conceptually perfect, it must fit with the other management systems that are used within the firm. The critical task in designing such a system is to ensure that it is consistent with the degree of perceived autonomy which corporate managers seek to develop in their profit center managers.

The reason a profit center measurement system needs to be designed at all is that profit center managers are *not* independent. A functionally organized firm needs a performance measurement system, but the design of that system is simple, or at least straightforward. The system in such a firm is frequently called a cost accounting system because it focuses on the efficient use of resources, matching the cost of inputs consumed against the production of goods and services. Each manager in such a firm is responsible for the operating costs incurred by one or more pools of functional resources, and the quality of his or her performance is measured by comparing those costs to an engineered standard cost, an expense budget, or less formal rules of thumb. Cost accounting systems may be elaborately detailed, and the performance variances measured by such systems may be disputed because the performance standards may be inappropriate, but there is rarely any dispute about the fact that the costs actually incurred in his unit are the costs for which the manager is responsible. Functionally organized firms have a single profit center—the corporate entity—and its profit is measured in accordance with generally accepted accounting principles.

Decentralized firms have far more complex performance measurement systems for two reasons. First, for purposes of measuring the profit of business units within the firm, conformance with externally imposed accounting procedures is not required; the designer of a profit center measurement system has great flexibility to mold it as a managerially useful tool. Second, and more important, a profit center measurement system must take cognizance of the fact that the utilization of some pools of corporate resources is shared among two or more profit centers. The existence of shared resources creates two important issues which must be resolved by the designer of a profit center measurement system:

1. Should the operating costs and capital investments for shared resources be assigned to the profit center managers who use those resources?
2. If so, what method should be used to assign the costs and investments to each profit center?

Answering the first question determines the "financial responsibility" of a profit center manager, and answering the second question affects his perception of his ability to "control" the utilization of shared resources. In this chapter, we will deal with each of those topics in turn.

FINANCIAL RESPONSIBILITY OF PROFIT CENTER MANAGERS

Many decentralized firms, as a part of their strategic planning process, review the "business charter" or mission of each of their profit centers every year or so. A definition of the business responsibility of a profit center manager, in terms of the specific product/ market segments that he is to pursue, can be expressed in a few dozen words. A definition of the financial responsibility of that profit center manager, in terms of the costs, revenues, and assets for which he is accountable, both reinforces the definition of his businesses and provides detailed elaboration about the scope of his specific responsibilities for each aspect of that business. A profit center manager who has no product development facilities within his own unit, and who is not charged for any of the costs of the corporate research and development activity, is told—explicitly or inferentially—that he is not responsible for the design of new products for his market. Such a situation is rare (only 15 of the 291 companies in our sample), but when that is the intent of corporate managers they can express it to a profit center manager both in the verbal definition of his business responsibility and the quantitative definition of his financial responsibility.

The intent of assigning business responsibility to a profit center manager is to create a center of initiative that would not otherwise exist. Corporate managers hope that he or she will develop a willingness to take actions that might otherwise not be taken. The intent of assigning financial responsibility to a profit center manager is to motivate the development of that willingness. He is told that his performance will be measured by the difference between a defined set of revenues and costs. If he takes no initiatives, the sheer momentum of his business will carry it for awhile, but a bottom line will periodically be struck—be it red or black—that tells something about how well he is doing. The inevitability of that periodic profit calculation serves to energize a profit center manager, challenging him—one might say obliging him—to cause actions to occur that will improve the profits earned by his business. Even if he lacks the functional authority to act independently, he is still responsible for attempting to initiate proposals for action that will affect either the magnitude of the costs incurred for his business, or the benefits from those expenditures, in a manner that will be favorable to the performance of his profit center.

Patterns of cost responsibility

The revenues earned by a profit center are easily measured; they result from the sale of goods or services for a defined set of products or markets. When we talk about the cost responsibilities of a profit center manager, we are concerned with two broad categories of costs: local costs and assigned costs. "Local costs" are the operating costs incurred by the physical resources for which a profit center manager has functional authority. Just as in a functionally organized firm, the measurement of those costs for each operating unit is easy, and a profit center manager is clearly responsible for the costs incurred in his operating units. "Assigned costs" are those costs which are charged to a profit center manager because he has shared in the utilization of resources that are under the functional authority of other managers in the firm. All decentralized firms have pools of resources that are shared among their profit centers to a greater or lesser extent. For the moment, we are concerned with the question of whether or not the cost of shared resources is assigned to profit center managers, deferring the question of how such assignments are made until the next section in this chapter.

We wanted to construct an index that would measure the cost responsibility of a typical profit center manager in each of our sample firms. To measure local costs, we simply took the functional authority index described in Chapter 3 and used it as a rough measure of the costs incurred in the operating units for which the profit center manager had physical custody. To measure assigned costs, we had to examine individually each of the five functional activities plus two costs incurred at the corporate level for interest expense and income taxes.

For the three primary operating functions (manufacturing, distribution, and sales), we discovered in the pilot testing of our structural questionnaire that any such costs that were not incurred within the profit center appeared to be universally assigned to the profit centers. For each of these functions, therefore, the assigned cost index was calculated as 1.0 minus the value of the functional authority index for that function. For example, if a profit center manager's own sales force produced 85 percent of his or her sales volume, the functional authority index for sales is .85. The remainder of the sales, produced by a corporate sales force for which the profit center manager is assigned part of the cost, yields an assigned cost index for sales of .15. For the other four items (research and development, administrative services, interest, and taxes), our pilot tests showed that there were variations among firms as to whether or not these costs were assigned to profit centers. The structural questionnaire included a question on each of these items, and the responses are displayed in Figure 5–1.

The patterns shown in Figure 5–1 indicate that there is a range of practice among our sample firms on the cost assignment issue, and that the range is only partially explained by the diversification strategy of a firm. For both research and administrative services, the decision to assign the cost of shared resources is apparently determined by the business strategy being pursued by a firm in its lines of business

Figure 5–1
Diversification strategy and assignment of corporate-level costs to profit centers

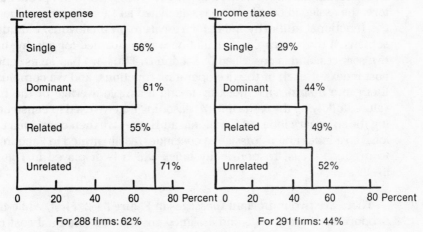

Research and development

Single	71%
Dominant	74%
Related	76%
Unrelated	69%

0   20   40   60   80 Percent

For 153 firms: 72%

Finance and accounting

Single	74%
Dominant	71%
Related	74%
Unrelated	73%

0   20   40   60   80 Percent

For 282 firms: 73%

Interest expense

Single	56%
Dominant	61%
Related	55%
Unrelated	71%

0   20   40   60   80 Percent

For 288 firms: 62%

Income taxes

Single	29%
Dominant	44%
Related	49%
Unrelated	52%

0   20   40   60   80 Percent

For 291 firms: 44%

Sources: Part Two, Exhibits C–9, D–10, D–27.

Firms which assign costs as a percentage of all firms that incur such costs at the corporate level.

rather than the diversity of those businesses. Assigning corporate expenses for interest and income taxes is more likely in the more diverse firms. Our analyses of these latter two items are presented in Section D but, except for diversification strategy, we were unable to discover any relationship between the decision to assign these costs to profit centers and any other characteristics of the firms in our sample.

For our purposes, however, the cost assignment decisions for interest and taxes can be ignored. The focus of our study is on how a profit center manager develops a perception of his autonomy for taking action that affects the operating results of his profit center. Operating activities do affect the capital requirements of the firm and the income taxes that it pays, and what we discovered is that some firms do include those costs in the calculation of profit at the profit center level, presumably to encourage their profit center managers to incorporate those expenses into their decision-making calculus. But our concern was not with that calculus but with the effect of operating interdependencies among profit centers on the autonomy of a profit center manager. Therefore, we decided that the cost responsibility index for a profit center manager should encompass only the five operating functions: research, manufacturing, distribution, sales, and administrative services.

We used the data in Figure 5−1 to calculate an assigned cost index for research and for administrative services. For research, if the cost of the corporate-level research activity was assigned to the profit centers, the assigned cost index was calculated as 1.0 minus the value of the functional authority index for research. An analogous, although somewhat more complex, calculation was performed for administrative services, and is described in Section D. Thus, we had an assigned cost index for each of the five operating functions, and we combined them into a summary index by taking a simple average of the five values, following the same line of reasoning that we used in constructing the summary index of functional authority. We then combined the local cost index and the assigned cost index, as illustrated in Section E, to produce a cost responsibility index which is displayed in Figure 5−2.

There are two important messages in Figure 5−2. First, while the proportion of local costs and assigned costs varies, the total cost responsibility of a typical profit center manager in our sample firms is not significantly affected by the diversification strategy of the firm. Nearly all of the profit center managers are responsible for nearly all of the operating costs of the five functional activities. A partial explanation of this phenomenon may be due simply to the fact that the profit figure calculated for each profit center is used by corporate managers for two purposes. One purpose, of course, is to influence the behavior of profit center managers by holding them responsible for operating results. But corporate managers also use the profit calculation in their strategic evaluation of the attractiveness of the

Figure 5–2
Diversification strategy and cost responsibility of profit center managers

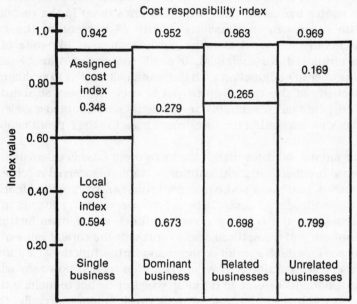

Note: Values shown for each index are the means for companies in each category.
Sources: Part Two, Exhibits E–5, E–8.

market segment represented by each profit center, and those assessments affect the allocation of corporate resources among the profit centers. For that purpose, apparently, corporate managers in our sample firms want to base their assessment on the total costs of being in a market segment, including the costs of shared resources.

The other message in Figure 5–2 comes as no surprise, but it is interesting to see it quantified: the cost responsibilities of a profit center manager always exceed the local costs of his functional resources to a greater or lesser extent. Corporate managers do use the calculation of profit to influence the behavior of each profit center manager, and the message they are sending to him in deciding to assign the costs of shared resources is that the scope of his initiative should not be restricted solely to the resources for which he has functional authority. A profit center manager shares in resources that are also utilized by others, and his responsibility in cludes trying to influence the management of those shared resources.

Patterns of asset responsibility

The second important aspect of the financial responsibilities of a profit center manager is the corporate investment in the resources that he utilizes in his business. Nearly 85 percent of the companies in our sample calculate the "investment base" (the value of the assets employed) for each of their profit centers, presumably using that number in conjunction with the profit calculation to evaluate the productivity of the capital employed in each business segment. As with the profit calculation, our respondents have adopted a variety of practices in calculating the investment base for their profit centers.

Our survey indicates that, if the investment base is calculated, the universal practice is to include the asset values of external receivables, inventories, and plant and equipment that can be directly identified with a specific profit center. These core assets are analogous to the local costs for the primary operating functions of manufacturing, distribution, and sales; these assets represent the capital value of the resources for which a profit center manager has functional authority. There are several other types of corporate assets, however, where our respondents diverge in deciding whether or not to include these items in the investment base of their profit centers. Broadly, these assets fall into two categories: (1) shared resources (cash, intracompany receivables, shared plant and equipment, and headquarters facilities), and (2) nonoperating assets (other investments and goodwill). The decision by corporate managers to assign none, some, or all of these assets to a profit center manager has the effect of defining for him the extent of his financial responsibilities for managing the assets utilized in his business.

In order to observe the pattern of asset responsibilities across our sample firms, we calculated an asset responsibility index for each respondent. The value of that index ranges from zero (for those firms that do not calculate an investment base for their profit centers) to 1.0 (for those firms that assign all assets to their profit centers); it is a rough measure of the comprehensiveness of the asset responsibilities of the profit center managers in our sample. This index is analogous to the cost responsibility index described above in that it is not based on the dollar magnitude of the costs or assets involved in an activity but only depicts the scope of the activities for which a manager is financially responsible. The calculation of the asset responsibility index is illustrated in Section G, and the summary results are shown in Figure 5−3.

Figure 5-3
Diversification strategy and asset responsibility of profit center managers (distribution of assets responsibility index)

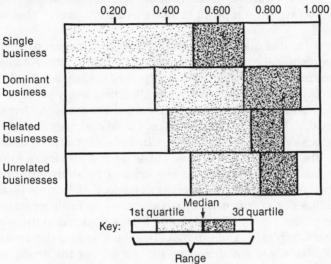

Source: Part Two, Exhibit G-11.

The pattern shown in Figure 5-3 reinforces the findings reported previously, in that there is a relationship between the interdependencies of a profit center manager and the extent of his or her financial responsibility for corporate assets. In contrast to the cost responsibility index, however, the comprehensiveness of asset responsibility is much more sensitive to these interdependencies. Single Business firms again present the most interesting case: it is fairly common in such firms to assign a share of the operating costs of shared resources to profit centers, but much less common to assign a share of the investment in those resources.

Responsibility and autonomy

As might be expected, because it is certainly intended, financial responsibility for costs and assets affects a profit center manager's perception of his autonomy. From a profit center manager's point of view, financial responsibility for shared resources constitutes the "right to worry" about the utilization of those resources; an obligation, if you will, to be concerned about the benefit/cost effect that those resources have on the profit performance of his or her business. The designer of a profit center measurement system has to decide whether the costs and investments for each pool of shared resources should be assigned to the profit center managers, but the criterion for that design decision is better framed as a different question: What do we want a profit center manager to worry about?

The "we" in that question are the corporate managers of the firm, not some technical expert on the design of profit center measurement systems. It is the corporate managers, of course, who design the responsibility structure of the firm, deciding how many profit centers to have in order to implement their corporate strategy. Corporate managers also design the pattern of functional authority for the firm, difficult decisions that must be made by balancing off the desire to maximize the benefits of economies of scale and the desire to minimize the interdependencies that are created by shared resources. Corporate managers, then, use the opportunity to define the financial responsibilities of a profit center manager as a way to elaborate on the overly simplified organizational design that is depicted in the organization chart. Typically, the interdependencies among the operating units in the firm are not shown on that chart, but the profit center measurement system can be used to capture those interdependencies. Corporate managers must decide which of these interdependencies they wish to bring to the explicit attention of a profit center manager, and they implement that decision by assigning the costs of shared resources to him.

Assigning the costs of shared resources to a profit center manager does affect his perception of his autonomy. Figure 5−4 shows the relationship between the cost responsibility index and the perceived autonomy index for typical profit center managers in our sample firms. As was true in our discussion in Chapter 3 about authority and autonomy, the situation in Single Business firms is the most interesting. A profit center manager in such a firm is highly interdependent on other operating units, compared to his counterparts in more diversified firms. He senses, appropriately, that his autonomy is less than it would be if he had more functional authority. Nevertheless, because he is accountable for a substantial amount of costs assigned from other operating units, he feels that he has responsibility for the utilization of shared resources, and he is willing to initiate proposals that will permit him to influence the way that those resources are managed.

The result is that financial responsibility for assigned costs mitigates, in part, the diminished sense of autonomy that might be perceived by a profit center manager who is highly interdependent on

Figure 5–4
Diversification strategy and the relationship between responsibility and autonomy

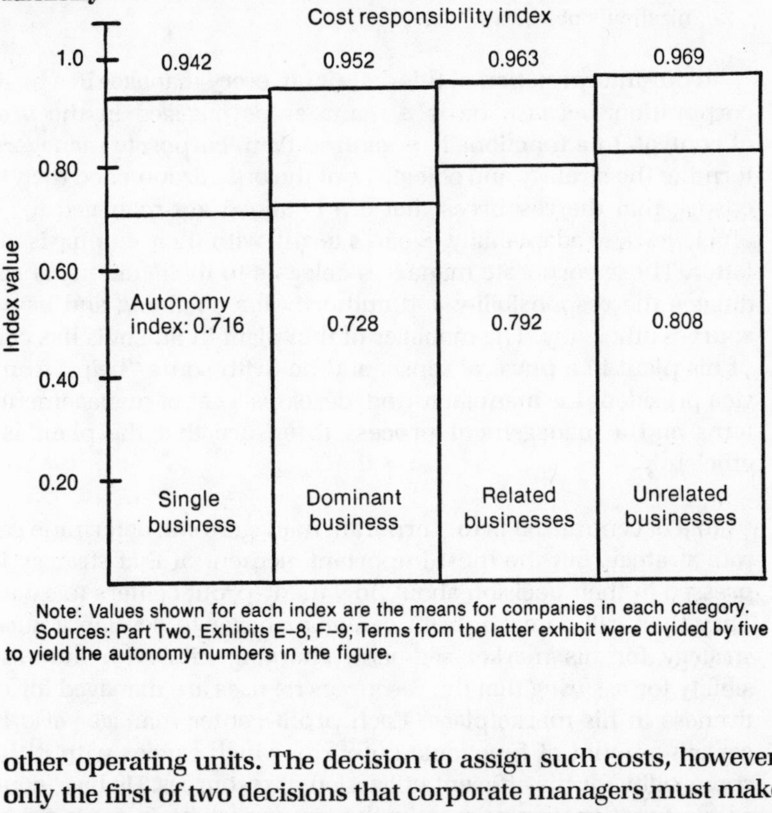

Cost responsibility index

	Single business	Dominant business	Related businesses	Unrelated businesses
Cost responsibility index	0.942	0.952	0.963	0.969
Autonomy index	0.716	0.728	0.792	0.808

Index value (1.0, 0.80, 0.60, 0.40, 0.20)

Note: Values shown for each index are the means for companies in each category.
Sources: Part Two, Exhibits E–8, F–9; Terms from the latter exhibit were divided by five to yield the autonomy numbers in the figure.

other operating units. The decision to assign such costs, however, is only the first of two decisions that corporate managers must make in designing a profit center measurement system. We turn now to the second decision which involves a further fine-tuning of a profit center manager's perceived autonomy: his ability to control the utilization of shared resources.

CONTROL OF SHARED RESOURCES

Control is a common everyday word with a variety of meanings in practical use. Thus far in this book, we have avoided using the word, although it has appeared in our quotes from Sloan when he talked about "coordinated financial control." The word will now appear frequently in the remaining pages.

Anthony developed the best formal definition of what Sloan was talking about. He defines "management control" as

. . . the process by which managers assure that resources are obtained
and used effectively and efficiently in the accomplishment of the organization's objectives.[1]

In our interpretation of this definition, every manager in a business
corporation, *because* he is a manager, is engaged in the *process*
of control. In a functionally organized firm, corporate managers determine the strategy and objectives of the organization and then try to
ensure that the resources that are obtained are managed for both
efficiency and adaptability (Sloan's term), with their emphasis on the
latter. Those corporate managers delegate to their functional subordinates the responsibility and authority for obtaining and using resources efficiently. The manager of that plant in St. Louis has control
of his plant in a physical sense, and he (with some "help" from the
vice president for manufacturing) develops a set of management systems and a management process to ensure that the plant is run
efficiently.

In a decentralized firm, corporate managers still determine corporate strategy, but the most important element of that strategy is expressed in their decision about how many profit centers to establish.
They then call on each profit center manager to develop a business
strategy for his market segment, charging him with the responsibility for assuring that the resources he uses are managed for effectiveness in his marketplace. Each profit center manager also has a
certain amount of functional authority which carries with it the responsibility for the efficient utilization of resources. He has "control"
of his functional resources in the sense that he is responsible for
both the efficient *and* effective utilization of those resources. There
may be some difficult decisions to be made in balancing those twin
objectives, but the philosophy of decentralization is that the profit
center manager can make those decisions as well and probably better
than corporate managers can.

The delicate problem of management control in a decentralized
firm is the management of shared resources. By what process can
corporate managers assure that each pool of shared resources is
managed for both efficiency and effectiveness? In a few instances,
such as those 15 companies where all the research and development
is done in a corporate lab and none of the costs are assigned to profit
centers, corporate managers answer that question by holding the

---

[1] Robert N. Anthony, *Planning and Control Systems: A Framework for Analysis* (Boston: Division of Research, Harvard Business School, 1965), p. 17.

functional manager responsible for both tasks; by absolving their profit center managers of financial responsibility for those costs, they are, in effect, telling them not to worry about how effectively the corporate research function is performed. But the far more common answer to that question, as demonstrated by the data in the previous section, is to assign the cost of shared resources to each profit center manager who uses those resources. When this is done, we have a situation in which a functional manager is responsible for the efficient utilization of a pool of shared resources and a profit center manager is responsible for the effective utilization of those resources. The issue still remains: what decision-making process shall be employed to achieve a satisfactory balance between those twin objectives?

Cost assignment practices

In broad terms, the resolution of that issue lies in the actions that corporate managers take to affect each profit center manager's perception of his autonomy for actions involving shared resources. Multiple signals will be sent, but one signal that can be examined in some detail is that transmitted by the profit center measurement system. The design of such a system must include an answer to the question: How shall we measure the costs of shared resources that are assigned to profit centers? In answering that question, corporate managers help each profit center manager to enhance his understanding of the extent of his autonomy regarding shared resources.

Corporate managers in our sample firms have found an almost bewildering array of answers to that question. Our structural questionnaire asked a corporate financial executive in each firm to describe the accounting procedure that was used in assigning the costs of each operating function to profit centers. A full display of their responses is presented in Sections B, C, and D; a summarization of those responses for four of the operating functions is shown in Figure 5—5.

For analytical purposes, we found it useful to group the detailed descriptions of cost assignment practices into three categories. One common category is to take the costs incurred at the corporate level and to assign those costs to profit centers by prorating the corporate cost on the basis of profit center sales, profits, or assets. A second common method, called "negotiate" in Figure 5—5, does not involve a

Figure 5– 5
Cost assignment methods for corporate-level operating functions

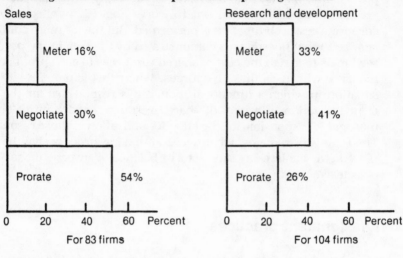

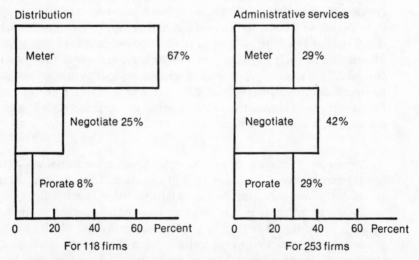

Note: Values shown are the percentages of firms using each method, for firms having a corporate-level activity.
Sources: Part Two, Exhibits C–30, C–32, C–33, C–34, D–16.

mathematical calculation; the cost assigned may be based on an estimate of the usage of the shared resource by each profit center, or may
simply be negotiated between the profit center manager and the
manager in charge of the corporate functional activity. The third
method, somewhat less common, is to assign the cost based on the

actual usage of the shared resource by each profit center. This is called the "meter" method in Figure 5−5, although that does not necessarily imply the existence of a digital read-out device.

The main message in Figure 5−5 is that there is no common pattern of cost assignment practices for these four functions employed by our sample firms. For some functions, however, it is possible to understand the logic behind the most common practice. Assigning the cost of a corporate sales force based on the volume of sales that it produces for each profit center is probably viewed as "fair" by a profit center manager even though that cost figure is not as informative as one which reflects the efforts of that sales force to sell the products in his or her line. For a company with a centralized distribution network, computer-based information systems make data on the volume of goods moved for each product line readily available; assigning the costs of physical distribution based on actual usage is fair and is also a rough measure of the effort expended for each profit center. For corporate-level administrative services, a proration method of one sort or another is the most common practice; metering a particular profit center's "usage" of, say, the corporate public relations department may rarely be feasible. We find that all three cost assignment methods are commonly used to assign the costs of corporate research and development, and perhaps the most interesting finding is that each of the three methods is used by some firms for each of these four functional activities.

For the manufacturing function, costs may be assigned to profit centers from either a corporate-level manufacturing activity and/or from other profit centers. These cost assignment methods are commonly called transfer prices because the amount of cost assigned to a profit center is determined by attaching a value to each unit of a product that it receives from other plants within the firm. The full array of transfer pricing pratices is displayed in Sections B and C, and summarized in Figure 5−6. In that figure, "cost" may be either variable manufacturing costs or those costs plus a share of manufacturing overhead, measured at either standard cost or actual cost. A "cost plus" price is determined by a formula which provides a defined profit for the plant that manufactured the product. In some firms the price may be arrived at by "negotiation" between the manager with functional authority for the plant and the profit center manager who is receiving the product. "Market" may be based on either external pricing information or on the list price at which the product is sold by the manufacturing plant to external customers.

Figure 5– 6
**Transfer pricing methods for intracompany shipments
of goods**

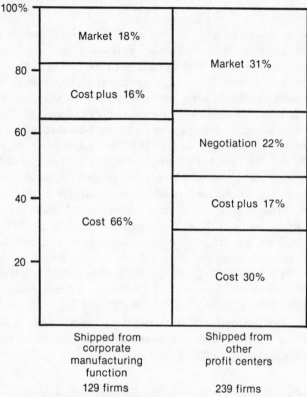

Shipped from   Shipped from
corporate   other
manufacturing   profit centers
function
129 firms   239 firms

Note: Values shown are the percentages of firms using each method,
for firms having such shipments.
Sources: Part Two, Exhibits B–10, C–31.

Figure 5–6 tells us that transfer prices are set differently depending upon who the internal supplier is. A corporate-level manufacturing activity, intended to serve two or more profit centers, is not itself a
profit center, and so it commonly transfers its products at cost. When
the internal supplier is another profit center, however, the transfer
price is usually higher than the cost of manufacture, thus permitting
a selling profit center to earn some or all of its normal profit margin
on the internal sale. But again, the more interesting finding is that
each of the four methods of setting transfer prices for either type of
internal supplier is used by some of the firms in our sample.

Control and autonomy

While the preceding paragraphs offer a possible explanation for the most common cost assignment practice in our sample firms, our real interest is in trying to understand the reasons for variations in practice. The selection of a cost assignment method affects a profit center manager's control of shared resources. He is not responsible for the efficient management of shared resources, a functional manager is; but a profit center manager does have more or less responsibility for the effective utilization of shared resources, and the cost assignment method tells him something about the extent of this responsibility and about the degree of his autonomy to affect the way that shared resources are utilized.

The three cost assignment methods shown in Figure 5 — 5 illustrate this point. One third of the companies in our sample apparently view their corporate research activity as a contract laboratory; a profit center manager is charged for the cost of the work done on behalf of his product line and, presumably, he can "buy" more or less research, depending upon his judgment about the effectiveness of such expenditures. On the other hand, one quarter of the firms assign the cost of corporate research as a simple proration across all profit centers. Here, the message to the profit center manager is equally clear: his allocation of research costs does not permit him to evaluate the effectiveness of the corporate research expenditures on behalf of his product line. Presumably, the nature of research in such corporations is such that a single project may benefit several profit centers; if so, the cost assigned to any single profit center may be less than the value of the research performed. The very act of assigning research costs to a profit center manager tells him that he should worry about that benefit/cost relationship, and thus he will behave somewhat differently than the profit center managers in the 15 firms referred to earlier where research costs are not assigned. But the proration method of cost assignment also tell the profit center manager that his influence over the nature of research to be performed is indirect at best. His control over the quantity of research resources that is obtained by the corporation, and the way those resources are used, is clearly less than that of a profit center manager who is charged for research on a metered basis.

We made a major effort, described in Sections E and G, to use the data on cost and asset assignment methods to construct management control indices that would serve as summary measures of a profit center manager's control over the utilization of shared resources. We hoped that a cost control index would demonstrate the effect of cost assignment methods on the perceived autonomy of a profit center manager. At the summary level, embracing all five operating functions, we were unable to construct an index which would demonstrate that relationship; the myriad of cost assignment methods used across the five functions is apparently too diverse to be compressed into a single index. Our effort to construct an asset control index was also fruitless. Nevertheless, we continue to believe that control and autonomy are related, and this belief was buttressed to some extent when we examined a profit center manager's control of costs for each of the operating functions individually.

For the manufacturing and distribution functions, a profit center manager's control of shared resources is not significantly affected by the method used to assign the cost of those resources to him. The assigned costs are those incurred in producing and shipping physical products, and it is the profit center manager who determines the number of units to be produced. In effect, these costs are assigned on a metered basis; the unit of measure is the unit of product. The cost per unit of product manufactured is determined by the method of transfer pricing used in the firm, and these methods do vary as we saw in Figure 5 – 6. But the major factor determining transfer prices within a firm is the business strategy that it is pursuing, as we saw in the example of the appliance manufacturer in Chapter 2. From the point of view of a profit center manager, he negotiates for the best price that he can obtain no matter whether the supplier is an internal or external plant, but he can still control his total costs because he decides how many units to buy.

For the selling function, we did discover a relationship between the interdependence among profit centers sharing a corporate sales force and the method used to assign the cost of that sales force to the profit centers. In those firms where a corporate sales force is responsible for most or all of the selling function, the most common method of cost assignment is a proration based on the sales made for each profit center. In those firms where the corporate sales force is relatively unimportant, its costs are more likely to be assigned based on the actual effort expended on behalf of each profit center. As with the research function discussed above, we believe this is another example of how the selection of a cost assignment method can influence a profit center manager's concern for the effective utilization of shared resources. We believe that corporate managers decide to retain a centralized sales force in those situations where they expect to reap substantial economies of scale. In those circumstances, corporate managers also retain the primary responsibility, along with the functional manager of the sales force, for assessing the benefit/cost relationship and for determining how large the sales force should be and how it should be utilized. Profit center managers in such firms can each attempt to influence the utilization of the sales force in behalf of their profit center but, because of the way that the cost is assigned to them, they realize that they have relatively little control over that function.

Finally, in the administrative services function we did discover one statistically significant relationship that lends credence to our theory that the method used to assign costs to a profit center affects the profit center manager's perception of his or her autonomy. In one of the questions in the autonomy questionnaire, profit center managers were asked to describe the decision-making process they used when the action under consideration was "hiring a consultant for assistance in developing or modifying operating systems (such as production scheduling or accounting)." In firms that have a centralized electronic data processing (EDP) facility, work of this sort might be done for a profit center by personnel at the corporate level. When the costs of the corporate EDP facility are assigned to profit centers based on metered usage, we found that profit center managers felt they had more autonomy for deciding to hire a computer consultant than their counterparts in firms where the corporate EDP costs were assigned by some method of proration. The reason here seems obvious: When a profit center manager is charged for his utilization of the corporate EDP facility on a metered basis, he knows that he is responsible for assessing the benefit/cost ratio of using the shared resource. It may be a shared resource, but from his perspective he is able to make a relatively independent decision about whether to utilize the resource or not; his independence of action is roughly equivalent to that involved in hiring an outside consultant.

On the other hand, however, when the effective utilization of corporate EDP resources is retained at the corporate level (as implied by a proration method of cost assignment), a profit center manager is less likely to hire an outside computer consultant without first discussing the proposed action with others because he knows that his action might not be in the best interests of the corporation as a whole. If he believes that one of his computer-based systems needs modification, he can initiate action either in the form of a request for assistance from the corporate EDP facility or, perhaps, in the form of a proposal to hire an outside consultant to do the job. Either way, his influence on the decision of whether, when, and how the job is to be done is likely to be less than that of a profit center manager whose EDP costs are assigned on a metered basis.

The design of a profit center measurement system requires decisions about whether the cost of shared resources should be assigned to each profit center manager and, if so, how the cost assignment calculation should be performed. The answers to both questions are intended to influence the degree of a profit center manager's concern for the effective utilization of shared resources and his perception of his autonomy involving those resources. Assigning, or failing to assign, cost responsibility for shared resources tells a profit center manager what to worry about; the method of cost assignment, in effect, tells him how much to worry.

Our data suggest that when the interdependence among profit center managers on a pool of shared resources is relatively low, each such manager will believe that his control of assigned costs is relatively high because costs are more likely to be assigned on a metered basis. This enhanced control over assigned costs affects a profit center manager's perception of his autonomy, and he is more likely to take independent action. When the interdependence among profit centers is relatively high, the decision to assign cost responsibility for shared resources is a signal to a profit center manager that he should be involved in the decision-making process about the utilization of those resources, but, because the method of cost assignment tends to be a proration, he realizes that his control over those resources is relatively limited and is less likely to take independent action.

We have suggested elsewhere that a principal criterion for the design of a profit center measurement system is "goal congruence,"[2] the system should measure performance in such a way that a profit center manager is encouraged to make decisions that are in the best interests of the corporation taken as a whole. To the extent that higher corporate profits are in the best interests of the corporation, then a profit center manager who attempts to increase the profits of his profit center is acting in the corporate interest *if* the profit center measurement system does not mislead him about what the corporate interests really are. But both corporate managers and profit center managers know that a periodic profit calculation is in-

---

[2] Richard F. Vancil, "What Kind of Management Control Do You Need?" *Harvard Business Review*, March–April 1973.

herently imperfect, and the limited utility of that number is further compounded by the existence of shared resources within the firm. Taken all by itself, the profit center measurement system is too cryptic and impersonal to serve as the only guidance for the actions of profit center managers.

In decentralized firms, the congruence that is needed is a congruence of understanding between corporate managers and each profit center manager about the extent of his autonomy. It is his perception of his autonomy that leads each profit center manager to select the appropriate decision-making process for each action that he wishes to initiate, and it is that process that assures that the decision which is finally made is taken in the best interests of the corporation as a whole. Corporate managers have many ways of influencing a profit center manager's perception of his autonomy, as we will review in the next chapter. The profit center measurement system is an important tool for corporate managers in this regard, and they mold its design so that it reinforces the other signals they are sending to a profit center manager about the extent of his autonomy. The design of a profit center measurement system may be said to be conceptually perfect when the signals that are received by a profit center manager influence his perception of his autonomy in the manner intended by corporate managers.

Chapter 6

A theory of decentralized
management

IN THE PRECEDING FOUR CHAPTERS we have dwelt at length with three familiar management concepts: authority, responsibility, and autonomy. Our purpose in that discussion was to make operational the meaning of those terms in decentralized firms by attaching descriptive modifiers to each. "Functional authority" thus becomes a physically tangible fact for each manager; we use that term to refer to the corporate resources that have been placed under his custody. "Financial responsibility" thus becomes an explicitly defined set of quantified measurements for each manager; we use that term to refer to the set of corporate activities for which he is accountable. "Perceived autonomy" thus becomes a descriptor of the decision-making processes in decentralized firms; we use that term to refer to the willingness of a profit center manager to take more or less independent action as he seeks to improve the performance of his business.

In this chapter we now attempt to interrelate these three primary concepts not only to each other but also to other concepts which, while less well defined, are clearly important: corporate strategy, managerial philosophy, management processes, and rewards. The intent here is not to summarize what has been said earlier so much as to synthesize this set of concepts into a practical framework, a theory about how decentralized firms are managed. That conceptual scheme is displayed in Figure 6–3, but before discussing that it will be useful to focus briefly on the primary actors in such firms: the profit center manager and the corporate managers who seek to define his job and to influence his behavior.

THE PROFIT CENTER MANAGER

The focus of our theory of decentralized management is on the profit center manager because his is the new role that is created by the decision to decentralize the firm. The new role is different from that of key second-level managers in a functionally organized firm, and we have attempted to identify some of the important dimensions of that difference in Figure 6-1. The first thing that must be said is that a discussion in terms of stereotypical roles and dimensional dichotomies is doubly dangerous; the differences may be overdrawn and are inevitably simplistic. Nevertheless, there are important differences, and comparing the two roles helps us to appreciate the task of a profit center manager.

Figure 6-1
Profit center managers and functional managers: Dimensions of the task

Dimensions	Profit center manager	Functional manager
Strategic		
Orientation	Entrepreneurial	Professional
Relevant environment	External	Internal
Objective of task	Adaptability	Efficiency
Ambiguity of task	High	Low
Operational		
Responsibility	Broad, cross-functional	Specialized, single function
Authority	Less than responsibility	Equal to responsibility
Interdependence on others	May be high	Usually low
Performance evaluation		
Measurements	Profit, growth, return on investment	Costs, compared to standards or budgets
Quality of feedback	Slow, garbled	Rapid, accurate
Risks and rewards		
Risk of failure	Higher	Lower
Compensation potential	Higher	Lower

As individuals, there are important similarities among high-level managers in any successful business organization. They tend to be intelligent, energetic and ambitious, and they value the psychic rewards that come from their work regardless of whether they are functional managers or profit center managers. For a functional manager, however, psychic rewards are related to the recognition of his professional competence in his area of specialization. He is responsible for a fairly homogeneous set of activities, and the ambiguity of his task is relatively low because he has physical custody (authority) of the resources he is responsible for and is relatively independent of the activities in other functions. He focuses his energies on those resources, trying to manage them efficiently as measured by reasonably precise performance standards.

In contrast, the task of a profit center manager is much more like that of a corporate president or an independent entrepreneur. He is responsible for a business, defined in terms of an external, competitive market, and his task is to be proactive in that market, mounting initiatives that will continually adapt his products to the changing needs of his customers. One reason that his job is ambiguous is that even a "successful" initiative may not affect his measured profitability for months or years, and in the interim a changing environment may befog or confound the reasons for his success. Another source of ambiguity, in contrast to the president's job, arises because a profit center manager shares in the utilization of corporate resources that are under the functional authority of other managers: he is responsible for the financial results of his business even though he lacks direct control over all the resources that his business requires.

This distinction—the bottom line, if you will—between the tasks of profit center managers and functional managers is extremely important for the successful management of a decentralized firm. Managers are individuals, and individuals are sufficiently different that it is possible to find the competent people that are needed to fill both types of jobs. Some part of the individual differences that allow a manager to be happy in one role whereas he would be miserable in the other may be explained by differing preferences for the risks and rewards of successful performance: a profit center manager accepts a higher risk of failure and may be more highly paid if he succeeds. But there are also many other reasons why individuals prefer different tasks. One of the most important tasks of corporate managers is selecting the right individuals to serve as profit center managers. Or, one might almost say, to facilitate the process of self-selection by potential profit center managers. However selected, when the choice is right the result is a profit center manager who accepts and relishes the ambiguity of his job, and is eager to work jointly with corporate managers to forge an effective system of decentralized management.

CORPORATE MANAGERS:
ORGANIZATIONAL CLIMATE

The key to decentralization lies in helping each profit center manager to develop a proper sense of what his role entails. Corporate managers accomplish this in a variety of ways, as we will see in a moment, but the primary way that they influence his behavior is by their own behavior which, in turn, reflects their philosophy of management and style of leadership. Corporate managers are individuals too, and while their tasks may be similar in most decentralized firms, their approach to those tasks may be quite different. Lorsch and Allen documented these differences in a small sample of firms and found that some part of the difference is explained by "management assumptions about organization." Excerpts from statements by two of the presidents in that study are reproduced in Figure 6–2.

Demographically, Firms 2 and 4 are quite similar in terms of size, number of profit centers, and the degree of diversity among their lines of business. Philosophically, however, it is clear that each of these two presidents has a quite different opinion about how his

Figure 6–2

Management Assumptions about Organization

Statements by Two Corporate Presidents

Firm 2

In this company we lean toward complete decentralization. Every division has responsibility for its own growth and profitability. We want these divisions to think of themselves as separate companies. Within the constraints posed by our financial resources, we let the divisions move in the directions they want as long as they can produce a reasonable level of earnings. Of course, we want them to dream and move into exciting new areas; but the onus is on them and we're not going to force them.

When you're as diversified as we are, you must have substantial decentralization. With our dissimilar product lines, trying to quarterback decisions at the corporate level would be extremely hazardous. Not long ago, some people recommended that we establish staff functions at the corporate level in areas such as engineering, purchasing and manufacturing. I think this misses a lot of things. First, our divisions are so diverse that I fail to see how these centralized functions could play a constructive role. Second, and perhaps more important, as you begin

---

Figure 6– 2 (continued)

building a large corporate staff, you suddenly find that the division manager is no longer the sole determinant of his own profitability. So, then, how can you judge his performance? . . .

All this talk about decentralization comes down to getting competent top-level division managers and giving them plenty of room to maneuver. If they get into trouble, you try to go along with them for a while and help where you can. If you find it increasingly difficult to believe that they will produce what they promise, then perhaps it's time to get a new manager. If this doesn't work, then we'd consider disposing of the division."

Firm 4

The biggest issue of all is to decide whether you are going to be an operating or a holding company. Are you going to be decentralized or centralized? If you have too much centralization, you destroy the profit center manager's creativity. But if you have too much decentralization, you're in trouble before you know it. I feel that we have struck a definite balance between these two extremes.

Our control system is the guts of our approach—i.e., flexible budgeting. We know every element of cost by divisions and by groups. It is the corporate staff's responsibility to get in and ask what we need to know, e.g., fixed costs in relation to margin, variable costs, profit mix, plans about pricing. The division manager, in turn, is evaluated against these elements. This leads to questions about his authority, and these limits are worked out as a result of the control system. . . .

I insist that we are an operating company and that we must know as much as we can humanly know about division operations. To accomplish this end we also have operating management committees for each group, which consists of corporate and group officers and which meet every two months. In these meetings group and division people present their plans and results. They have to explain every single discrepancy on the cost control charts. Plus they must give "make good" reports on capital programs. If they don't make good, we respond by putting more and more controls on their capital decisions."

Source: Excerpted from Jay W. Lorsch and Stephen A. Allen III, *Managing Diversity and Interdependence* (Boston: Division of Research, Harvard Business School, 1973), pp. 55–58. Used by permission of Harvard University Press.

"decentralized" firm will be managed. It is tempting to characterize the difference as a dichotomy—an operating company versus a holding company—but the president of Firm 4 makes it clear that he is really talking about a "balance point" somewhere along an undefined conceptual spectrum where the two ends are labeled "centralization" and "decentralization."

The excerpts illustrate that it is possible for two presidents to select different points on that spectrum, and that choice leads to the creation of an organizational climate that would clearly produce different behavior on the part of profit center managers in the two firms. "Climate" is a rich, all-encompassing organizational concept, produced by the dynamic and simultaneous interaction of a great many variables. Three types of climatic variables that have important effects on the perceived autonomy of a profit center manager are discussed briefly below: structural constraints, formal processes, and personal interactions.

Structural constraints that affect the ability or willingness of a profit center manager to act independently occur in a variety of guises. The most overt forms are written policy statements and standard operating procedures which either prescribe the action to be taken under specified circumstances or spell out the decision-making process that is to be followed for certain kinds of actions. The latter type of situation is the more important because it typically focuses on large resource commitments or on the utilization of shared resources. The most common structural mechanisms that are established to constrain independent action on these decisions are corporate staff offices and management committees.

Decentralized firms vary greatly in terms of both the size and power of corporate staff and the role of committees, but it is not uncommon for a profit center manager to need the concurrence of a staff officer and/or the approval of a committee before he or she can take a specified action. Perhaps, more importantly, in many situations the actions that require concurrence or approval are not completely delineated; it is simply the existence of the staffs or committees that add to the ambiguity of a profit center manager's job as he decides whether or not to seek counsel before acting. How that choice is made, of course, is influenced by other aspects of the managerial climate in the firm.

Formal processes for the routine managerial tasks of planning, budgeting, and monitoring the performance of each profit center also serve to create an organizational climate that is consistent with the philosophy and style of the corporate managers. All decentralized firms have a more-or-less formal set of processes for these purposes, formal processes in the sense that the schedule of meetings may be prepared for as much as a year in advance and each meeting has a specified topical agenda and a specified set of participants. The important variations among decentralized firms in this regard are not the fact that such meetings occur but the frequency and length of the meetings, the degree of detail in which topics are discussed, and the breadth of participation by other managers. A profit center manager who must participate in frequent, long, and detailed discussions of his business in meetings attended by corporate staff as well as line officers will have a quite different perception of his autonomy than one who has a brief, quarterly, one-on-one meeting with his direct superior.

Finally, organizational climate is fundamentally determined by personal interactions among managers—by how managers behave in those meetings and in the myriad of unscheduled informal contacts that they have with each other. The reason managers travel great distances to have face-to-face contact is that written or spoken words cannot convey the entire message—body language and other forms of nonverbal behavior still play a critical role in building and maintaining effective interpersonal relationships: "When I told the boss what I'd done, all he said was 'that's OK,' but he frowned a little and squirmed around in his chair." A profit center manager who might make the foregoing statement is also saying that, next time, he might check his proposed action with his boss before proceeding to implement it.

Corporate managers, using these practices and others, more or less explicitly, inevitably create a managerial climate for their organization. In our view, that climate is the single most important determinant of a profit center manager's perception of his autonomy. While that assertion is not documented by this study, we doubt that many managers in decentralized firms would question its validity. Corporate managers in such firms encourage a profit center manager to be innovative and entrepreneurial while at the same time constraining his freedom of action. The climate that corporate managers create does provide signals that affect a profit center manager's behavior, but so too do the other signals they send, such as their definition of his authority and responsibility. We turn now to a discussion of the interrelationships among these concepts and how these multiple signals affect the management of decentralized firms.

AUTONOMY AND DECISION-MAKING PROCESSES

Finally, daily, somebody has to decide to take action. In a decentralized firm, the key managerial issue is not really "Who should decide?" but "When should a profit center manager decide independently rather than seek the counsel of one or more of his peers or superiors?'' It is the profit center manager who has the obligation to initiate adaptive change in his business segment, and it is he who must figure out how to translate his initiatives into successful realities. Corporate managers help him cope with this latter task by designing a web of management systems as shown in Figure 6−3. The focal point of that design is a profit center manager's perception of his autonomy—his *current* understanding of the appropriate decision-making process to be followed in order to cause an action to occur. Although this conceptual scheme is labeled ''A Theory of Decentralized Management,'' it might well be subtitled ''The Education of a Profit Center Manager'' because corporate managers design and use these systems to convey the intended autonomy that they want each profit center manager to have.

Autonomy, intended and perceived, is an ephemeral concept primarily because it is dynamic, it ebbs and flows over time. Figure 6−3 is a static depiction of the factors that affect a profit center manager's perception of his autonomy, and we will discuss those factors first in static terms before dealing with the dynamics of an ongoing firm.

Figure 6− 3
A theory of decentralized management

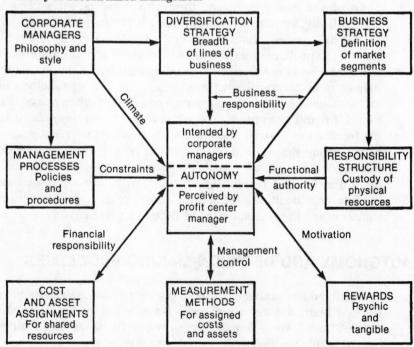

Corporate strategy, at a point in time, reflects the current intentions of corporate managers concerning the lines of business in which to engage (diversification strategy) and, within each line, the specific market segments to be pursued (business strategy). These critical choices, at least in most large U.S. manufacturing firms, lead to decentralization, creating a need for multiple market foci and leading to the establishment of a set of profit center managers, each responsible for the activities of the firm within a defined market segment. The definition of the business responsibility of a profit center manager, usually stated in terms of a competitive, external market, is his mandate to act as an agent of change. The scope of his charter defines the arena within which he is to act more or less autonomously in adapting his products to meet the current and future needs of his customers.

The responsibility structure that corporate managers then design is intended to make the autonomy of a profit center manager more explicit and tangible by giving him physical custody of some of the corporate resources that he needs to operate his business. The problem for corporate managers is that, depending on the heterogeneity of the business(es), there may be significant operating economies of scale to be gained if some functional activities are organized to serve the needs of two or more profit centers. The functional authority (physical custody) for these shared resources is assigned to a corporate-level functional manager rather than to one or more profit center managers. A major finding of this study is the documentation of the significant role that functional authority plays in affecting the perceived autonomy of a profit center manager. He has physical custody of a pool of functional resources of greater or lesser magnitude; the greater his functional authority is, the more likely he is to be able—and willing—to take independent action.

Finally, at a still important but clearly tertiary level, corporate managers use their design of the profit center measurement system to affect the behavior of each profit center manager concerning his utilization of the shared resources for which he lacks functional authority. The measurement system defines the financial responsibility of a profit center manager; it is consistent with, but more detailed and explicit than, the charter that describes his business responsibility. By deciding whether or not to assign a portion of the operating costs and asset values of shared resources to a profit center manager, corporate managers convey their intent about his or her need to be concerned with the effective utilization of those resources. By deciding how such cost and asset assignments are made, corporate managers dampen or enhance a profit center manager's sense of control over the efficient utilization of shared resources.

An important characteristic of these two sets of decisions concerning measurement system design is that they do not send a primary signal about the autonomy of a profit center manager. Corporate managers, by their definition of business segments and their distribution of functional authority, determine their intended autonomy for each profit center manager. The design of the measurement system helps to ensure that that message gets through, reminding the profit center manager periodically of whether and to what extent he should be concerned with the management of shared resources. The double-headed arrows in Figure 6—3 are intended to convey this symbiotic relationship between perceived autonomy and the design of the profit center measurement system. Similarly the system designed for determining the annual bonus award also affects perceived autonomy because it reflects the intended autonomy determined by corporate managers.

Dynamically, the life of a profit center manager in a decentralized firm is much more complex than the neat diagram in Figure 6—3 seems to imply. Everything changes over time, of course, but at least two separate tempos deserve comment. One tempo beats to the rhythm of the corporate evolution of leadership, strategy, and structure, and even that consists of a medley. Corporate managers change, either as they mature in their jobs or when a new president is appointed, and this affects the autonomy of a profit center manager. His autonomy may increase as trust develops during a lengthening relationship with his boss, and as his boss becomes increasingly confident of his knowledge of a disparate set of businesses. A profit center manager's autonomy is also likely to be affected by new faces in the corporate offices, bringing somewhat different managerial philosophies, new leadership styles, and an evolutionary change in organizational climate.

Corporate strategy and structure also evolves over time as environmental conditions, and corporate aspirations, change. One expression of strategic change is structural: an increase or decrease in the number of profit centers in the firm, bringing with it modifications in the charters of business responsibility and/or changes in functional authority.[1] Even without strategic changes, technological

---

[1] A recent study by Stephen A. Allen III, documents the fact that such changes are not infrequent. See "Organizational Choices and General Management Influence Networks in Divisionalized Companies," *Academy of Management Journal*, vol. 21, no. 3 (1978).

changes may increase or decrease the benefits from large-scale operations, thus causing or permitting more or less centralization of functional authority with a concomitant impact on the autonomy of a
profit center manager.

A second important dynamic affecting the ongoing management of
a decentralized firm is the current operating performance of each
profit center. From one year to the next, even if there is no change in
corporate leadership, strategy, or structure, a particular profit center
manager's autonomy may change significantly. The change is more
dramatic if the results from his profit center begin to fall seriously
short of expectations. Under those circumstances, as the president of
Firm 2 stated it, you "help where you can," and the profit center
manager's freedom to take action without corporate counsel may be
sharply curtailed.[2] In contrast, a profit center manager with a
lengthening record of more-than-satisfactory performance is likely to
find his autonomy increases as corporate managers spend their time
where it is needed most.

Speaking dynamically, then, it is the management process—the
way that corporate managers and profit center managers work
together—that provides the continuous fine-tuning of decision-
making processes in decentralized firms. The more formally structured elements in Figure 6–3, business responsibility, functional authority, financial responsibility, management control and motivation,
provide a framework for an unending managerial dialogue. But at any
point in time, the autonomy of a profit center manager is subject to a
failure of communication; his current perception may not jibe perfectly with his boss' intention. And so they continue to talk.

Autonomy is the word used by managers to permit them to talk
about the ambiguity of a profit center manager's role. Decentralization is an organizational philosophy that inevitably creates ambiguity
in that role, by holding a profit center manager responsible for the
financial performance of a business and, at the same time, withhold-
ing from him the functional authority to control shared resources.
The testimony to the success of decentralization in U.S. manufacturing firms is all around us. Decentralization works not only because it
is a powerful concept but also because corporate managers work at
making it work. Having designed an ambiguous role, they also design

----

[2] See Lorsch and Allen, *Managing Diversity and Interdependence.* Their study
documents that corporate managers do adapt the amount of time spent with each
profit center manager, devoting more attention to those with the poorest *relative* performance among the profit centers in the firm.

a management process and a set of management systems to help
themselves and their profit center managers cope with that ambiguity. The result is, indeed, the best of both worlds: multiple centers
of initiative, and a spectrum of decision-making processes that are
used selectively to ensure that the benefits from interdependency are
not lost.

PART TWO

DETAILED
FINDINGS AND
ANALYSES

Introduction to part two

THE DIVISION of this book into two parts is a reflection of the two broad purposes of this study. First, we hoped to make a contribution to the theory of management in a relatively underresearched field: the relationships between general managers at the corporate and divisional levels in decentralized manufacturing firms. The evolution of such a theory clearly benefited from having access to a large body of empirical data, but we hoped that the theory would be intuitively appealing on its own and it is presented in Part One as a cohesive whole, with only moderate references to the underlying data.

Second, we wanted to collect and disseminate that body of empirical data simply because (1) it appeared feasible to do so, (2) the task had not been done by others, and (3) the resulting data might spark provocative insights in the minds of other researchers. For this purpose, a quite different form of presentation is appropriate, and we hope that the format used in Part Two provides convenient access to the data.

This introduction to Part Two is not intended to serve a reader as an entry point to this book; we assume that the reader has read at least Chapter 1 for an overview of the scope and methodology and Chapter 6 for a summary of the major concepts. Additional methodological description is contained in each of the sections of Part Two, as outlined briefly below.

Part Two consists of eight sections, offered as more or less discrete sets of topical data. Section H presents the questionnaires that we used, and Section A describes the design of those questionnaires and the demographic characteristics of our sample. The largest unified mass of data we collected was focused on the operating structure of our respondents (called "functional authority" in Chapter 3) and their cost assignment practices (called "financial responsibility" in Chapter 5). These data are presented in Sections B, C, and D and then converted into summary indices in Section E. Another set of data, the "autonomy" data gathered from individual profit center managers, is presented and analyzed in Section F. The final set of data, on asset assignment practices used for the calculation of the investment base, is displayed in Section G.

The presentation in each section follows a relatively standard format: (1) the raw data from a segment of the questionnaires are displayed, (2) those data are cross-tabulated against the demographic variables described in Section A, and (3) the data are then cross-tabulated against each other and against the data found in the preceding sections. The analysis, thus, is progressive and serves to explain why the sections are arranged in the sequence described above.

Each section begins with its own summary of what it contains and, as will be noted, each is attributed to an individual researcher who took primary responsibility for executing the analysis within the guidelines laid down by the principal investigator. Those researchers, plus other colleagues mentioned in the Acknowledgements, comprise the "we" that speak in the first person throughout this book. For this introduction, however, it seems to me that the singular pronoun is more appropriate. As the principal investigator, I am responsible for the basic orientation of the project, for the statistical methodology employed, and for the resulting caveats that must be raised concerning the quality of the data presented here. Each of these topics is discussed briefly below, concluding with a section that shares some of the disappointments that I encountered along the way—unresolved problems which, I hope, will be viewed as opportunities by other researchers.

Orientation of the study

When told that the Financial Executives Research Foundation (FERF) was interested in sponsoring a study on decentralization and profit center measurement, my first question was whether they would consider a large-scale empirical survey. Subsequently, of course, they did commission such a survey, and the basic die was cast. There were three reasons why I wanted to take this approach. First, although the use of profit centers in decentralized firms was a mature and pervasive practive by the early 1970s, no prior survey of measurement practices had been done. I knew that most large firms had internal accounting policy manuals and that, with FERF sponsorship, we could ask chief financial officers to describe what those policies were. In short, some potentially interesting data were available, and collecting them seemed worth the effort.

More important, FERF did not restrict the project to measurement practices, and this meshed nicely with my broadening interest in management systems generally. Only a year or two earlier, the Doctoral Program at Harvard Business School had been restructured, and I had been one of the founders of a new Special Field called Administrative Systems. The creation of this field was intended to facilitate research that cut across our prior, parochial foci, embracing the mutual interests that several of us had in the interrelationships among organizational behavior, management control, and the implementation of corporate strategy. I knew that, with the willing cooperation that FERF could provide, I might also be able to gather strategic and behavioral data from the respondent firms. This led to the development of the "initial hypothesis" (Figure 1–1 in Chapter 1) which was the cornerstone of my proposal to FERF.

Finally, I wanted to attempt a major empirical survey because I believed that I personally was ready for such an approach. I am a true disciple of situational analysis as taught by the case method; a believer in the "contingency theory of management," to use the current label. I know that each business firm—and each profit center in such a firm—is unique and that, by definition, there are no pat, universal solutions to *important* management issues. If there were, we wouldn't need highly paid managers to deal with those issues. In order to learn that, I have paid my clinical dues. Although I have been a full-time academic for the last 20 years, my conservative estimate is that I have spent an average of 50 days per year on-site at more than 200 business organizations, engaged in casewriting, research, consulting, or some combination thereof.

The problem with clinical experience is that, while the clinician may learn a great deal, relatively little of that is easily communicable to others. I felt that I owed it to my students—and to myself—to try to pull together what I had learned, and that the process of doing that

might be facilitated by accepting the obligation to undertake the FERF
study and by amassing some empirical data to serve as a foil for my
clinical data base.

The result of adopting this approach can only be described as an
exploratory study. I did not delineate a set of hypotheses to be tested
by the data. Rather, I viewed my task as one of trying to invent new
instruments which might measure some of the important dimensions that account for some of the differences in the ways that decentralized firms are managed. Only after that effort was completed, in
late 1977, was I able to gain a better perspective on what I was doing.
Fritz Roethlisberger's magnificent autobiography was published at
that point, and he devoted three chapters to "Levels of the Knowledge
Enterprise."[1] In his terms, I was attempting to climb the knowledge
tree, starting from my clinical perch, by performing elementary measurements of elementary concepts that might subsequently lead to
"analytical knowledge" that had prescriptive power.

Viewed more pragmatically, I entered the project knowing that
decentralized firms used a wide variety of practices in measuring
"profit" internally. I was attempting to identify other attributes of
such firms that might have explanatory or predictive value for the
design of profit center measurement systems. Two of those attributes
turned out to be related to familiar concepts like "authority" and
"autonomy" and so I focused my efforts on relating those attributes
to the "responsibility" of a profit center manager, inferring the scope
of his responsibility from the design of the profit center measurement system.

Whatever I was doing, my colleagues called it "fishing in the data,"
and only the more civil among them legitimatized my activities with
the kinder label of exploratory research. With several dozen pieces of
raw data for each respondent, I was seeking to discover relationships
that I could rationalize and accept, and seeking to meld the set of such
relationships into a cohesive pattern. Data reduction was almost
mandatory, and I tried a variety of methods to create summary variables for the elementary concepts of authority, responsibility, and
autonomy. At one point, I kept an informal diary of these sequential
efforts, finally coming to refer to it as my "Catalog of Blasted Theo-
ries" —blasted because I rejected each attempt if the resulting sum-

---

[1] *The Elusive Phenomena* (Boston: Division of Research, Harvard Business School,
1977). The reference here is to part V, chaps. 20, 21, and 22, and, in particular, to his
summary diagram on p. 393.

mary variables had no explanatory power, and then I blasted that attempt because it had wasted my time.

The result, I think, is that I caught a small fish, but a "keeper." I make no pretense at having "proven" any aspect of the theory summarized in Chapter 6; the data cannot prove a theory that they helped me to invent. And the theory is in no sense a new paradigm for management scientists. All I can claim is that it is a more elaborate and more comfortable way of thinking about the problem than I would have been able to articulate if I had not mucked around in the data.

With that general warning about what has been done here, let me alert the reader to three specific caveats about some of the data and analyses that appear in Part Two.

Caveats for the reader

First, the whole idea of trying to calculate a summary measurement or index for a concept like "authority" is suspect. The very act of summarization entails not only a loss of data, it also belies the underlying uniqueness of each respondent. There are, for example, seven firms in the sample for which the summary Functional Authority Index is calculated as .85 (rounding to two decimals). All analyses using that index treat those firms as identical, even though they obviously are not. Further, the specific, simplistic linear transformation that was used to calculate that index from the raw data is hard to defend on the basis of either logic or fact; it was simply the best we could do with the data we had. Similar criticisms apply to the "autonomy" index, and these criticisms are compounded when we then find a strong correlation between the two indices and claim that it is the major finding from this study.

One thing that can be said in defense of such indices is that we also searched for specific authority-autonomy relationships at the micro level, using two bits of raw data as described in Section F. The correlations that are found there are less subject to the above criticism, and the summary indices, in some sense, simply capture the underlying reality. The major argument for our approach, however, is that the relationship ought to exist—I believe that it does—and the indices shown here may serve as an initial step toward a more sophisticated measurement of these concepts.

Next, the autonomy data have at least three inherent flaws that may limit their utility both in this study and as an instrument for further research. First, we have averaged the data again, combining the responses from two or three profit center managers in order to create a response that is more likely to be representative for the firm, but losing the uniqueness of each manager's situation. Second, the individual respondents were selected by someone in the corporate financial office. We asked him to pick "typical" profit center managers, but he may have tried to help us too much by picking the "best" ones. Third, the 14-month time delay between the structural questionnaire and the autonomy questionnaire caused a potential nonrespondent bias for which we made no attempt to correct, and in some cases there were surely structural changes in the interim which would make it inappropriate to match up the two types of data.

Finally, although we defined a "profit center" at the beginning of our structural questionnaire, we (intentionally) did not define a "typical" profit center. We did not do so because we couldn't figure out how to do it without getting into organizational levels and General Electric, for example, then had three levels of profit centers (now four) nested under the corporate office. The measurement data may not be damaged much by this omission; again, GE's internal profit measurement policies apply to profit centers at all levels. However, the data on the operating structure of functional activities is suspect. Those data reflect a corporate perspective, not necessarily that of a "typical" lowest-level profit center that may also share (unquantified) resources with other profit centers at that level. Most suspect are the two variables "Number of Profit Centers" and "Profit Center Sales" because they are both derived from a single question in the demographic questionnaire, and that question made no reference to the organizational level of a "typical profit center."

These are, in my opinion, the major caveats for the reader to be aware of as he approaches the data, but others of a more detailed nature are also flagged in the section to which they apply. Any designer of a survey instrument would almost surely do some things differently if he were starting from scratch again. So might I, but finally, what you see is what you get.

Opportunities for future research

I am, by nature, an optimist, and so I can't resist labeling the disappointments that I suffered in this study as opportunities for achievement in future research. I will briefly discuss three such "opportunities," and then close by mentioning some of the more conventional sort.

I had hoped that one result of this study would be the development of a taxonomy for labeling different types of profit centers. Such a classification scheme would be most useful—as demonstrated by the value to this study of Rumelt's taxonomy of diversification strategy. At the moment, the single term "profit center" is too broad, covering wide variations in the authority and autonomy of profit center managers. Our efforts to classify profit centers based on the manager's scope (and/or type) of functional authority, or on his or her perceived autonomy for various categories of decisions, were fruitless; we could not discern any natural break-points in the data.

The opportunity to develop such a scheme may lie down one of two paths. The "business strategy" of a firm has a direct impact on the number of profit centers it creates, and on their interdependence. Thus, one approach might be to develop a taxonomy for business strategies, and hope that it might map over into a taxonomy for profit centers. Another approach, suggested by the General Electric strategic planning system discussed in Chapter 4, would be to classify profit centers in terms of the relative importance of external (rather than captive) markets. Even if these probes do not work, the search should continue; our ability to understand decentralized firms would be greatly enhanced by a richer language.[2]

A second disappointment—although my expectations were not high—was the inability to demonstrate that decentralized firms that are "well managed" will have superior economic performance compared to those that are not. In the context of this study, "well managed" would mean firms where there is a good "fit" between intended and perceived autonomy and between that autonomy and the other management systems shown in Figure 6—3, Chapter 6. We did make one attempt to relate fit to economic performance, defining fit as the absolute value of the residuals from the regression equation for the authority-autonomy relationship, but to no avail.

I remain skeptical that it will ever be possible to demonstrate a relationship between performance variables, such as Earnings-per-

---

[2] As this book goes to press, I have learned of a new study which may contribute to the resolution of this important issue. See Derek F. Abell, *Defining the Business: The Starting Point of Strategic Planning* (Englewood Cliffs, N.J.: Prentice-Hall, in press).

Share Growth Rate or Return on Investment, and the quality of a set of managers or management systems. I do believe that such a relationship exists, but there is too much static in the performance variables, not to mention the measurement problems on the managerial variables. Still, efforts in this regard would carry a high payoff—at least in terms of recognition for the researcher—and there are a lot of optimists in the world.

My third disappointment in this study is that I have been unable to say anything definitive—or even mildly useful—on the subject of transfer prices. To my knowledge, our data are the only empirical data ever gathered on the topic, and we had plenty of other data to help explain the variations in practice that we found. But no pay dirt, only a dry hole. The issue remains as a perennial puzzle for academicians, while practitioners continue to cope. I wish the best of good fortune to the next researcher to tackle this problem.

Finally, despite all these caveats about the data and despite disappointments in some parts of the analysis, I hope this study will spark further research in the management of decentralized firms. One natural extension from this study might be to expand the effort to understand a profit center manager by using psychological and personality tests to measure his tolerance for ambiguity and other characteristics. Another potential contribution would attempt to develop refined or different instruments to measure the elementary concepts that have been the focus of this study. In particular, multivariate statistical analysis of the raw data may yield better summary variables and/or suggest insights toward the construction of better measurements.

In my view, however, new, broad-gauged clinical studies continue to rate first priority. The weakest links in the web of factors influencing autonomy in Figure 6–3 are those labeled "climate" and "constraints"—weakest in the sense of being the least documented and the least understood. We need to enhance our understanding of the roles of staff personnel and of management committees and, more generally, to become better sensitized to the nuances of the management processes by which general managers engage each other. Deep, intensive clinical studies are not only the best way to obtain such understanding, they are the only way. Breakthroughs along this dimension are likely to be less dramatic, or even recognizable, but my personal belief is that the next branch up in the knowledge tree of decentralized management is likely to be reached by a clinician who performs elementary measurements of elementary concepts such as style, culture, and climate.

Section A

Methodology; demographics of the sample*

Contents

Exhibits

* This Section was prepared by Lee E. Buddrus.

SUMMARY

This section describes the selection and composition of the 291 manufacturing firms that completed the questionnaire entitled "Profit Measurement and Decentralization." Seven demographic characteristics of these firms are defined and displayed: one portrays the "diversification strategy" of the firm, one measures size in sales revenues, three measure various aspects of financial performance, and two measure the number of internal profit centers and the sales revenue of a typical profit center in each firm. These seven characteristics are used repeatedly in subsequent sections in our efforts to analyze and explain the variations in management practices among these firms. The final topic in this section is the interrelationships among these seven characteristics.

SELECTION OF THE SAMPLE

Exhibit A—1 shows the response rate to our first questionnaire (the structural questionnaire). The 291 manufacturing companies listed under the column "Number of Usable Questionnaires" is the sample group used throughout this study.

The questionnaire was mailed to 1,010 members of the Financial Executives Institute (FEI) who were located at the headquarters office of their corporation. The selection was not random; we wanted a sufficient number of respondents from very large firms to assure an adequate representation from that group. In terms of the size of respondent firms, the results are shown in Exhibit A—2. We received relatively few responses from firms with sales under $100 million; most of our respondents might be considered large or very large.

Although the structural questionnaire was designed specifically for manufacturing firms, the mailing list included a variety of other types of firms. As shown in Exhibit A—1, the mailing list included 684 manufacturing firms and 326 nonmanufacturing firms. The data in Exhibit A—1 suggests something about the pervasiveness of profit centers within U.S. business corporations. Forty-six percent of the manufacturing firms returned the questionnaire whereas only 28 percent of the nonmanufacturing firms did so. Of the manufacturing respondents, 17 reported that their firm did not have two or more profit centers; of the remaining 296 responses 5 were not usable for other reasons. It would be an overstatement to conclude that 95 percent of U.S. manufacturing firms have profit centers; many people who received the questionnaire may have failed to return it *because* they had no profit centers. The formidable length of the questionnaire, however, was also a deterrent to responding. On balance, it seems safe to conclude that a substantial majority of large manufacturing firms have profit centers.

Of the nonmanufacturing firms, the lower response is due to both the factors mentioned above, plus two others. Some people who received the questionnaire may have had profit centers in their firms, but did not respond because the questionnaire was clearly designed for manufacturing businesses. But for the nonmanufacturing firms taken as a whole, the response rate in terms of usable questionnaires was less than half that for the manufacturing firms. We believe that, in part, this low response is due to the fact that profit centers are less common in nonmanufacturing firms.

DEVELOPMENT, TESTING, AND ADMINISTRATION OF THE QUESTIONNAIRE

In order to conduct our research, we needed five types of data—data on the functional operating structure in each corporation, data on profit measurement, data on the companies' diversification strategy, demographic data, and data on the perceived autonomy of profit center managers. The development, testing, and administration of the structural questionnaire which sought the first four sets of data is described in this section. The development, testing, and administration of the autonomy questionnaire is described in Section F, "Perceived Autonomy and Fairness."

Our research on the available survey instruments failed to locate a questionnaire that was comprehensive enough to gather the structural and measurement data we needed. We were able to select a few specific questions from previous surveys, but most of the questionnaire design was the result of the combined efforts of the research team. The final design is reproduced in Section H. The questions on structure and measurement fall into three broad categories, each described in more detail in subsequent sections.

1. Transfers between profit centers (Section B).
2. Corporate operating functions (Section C).
3. Corporate administrative services and other expenses (Section D).

We also sought information concerning assignment of assets to profit centers, and the relationship of corporate financial accounting to profit center accounting (Section G).

A major issue which had to be resolved in the initial phase of the study was the definition of a profit center. These exists in different companies, and in some cases even in the same company, a range of profit center levels; for example, profit centers at the product level, the division level, and the group level. After reviewing several academic definitions of the word "profit center," we arrived at the following definition:

> A profit center is defined as any fairly independent organizational unit, accountable separately for its performance, for which some measure of profit is determined periodically. (Examples include decentralized divisions or departments, and product groups.)

We knew that in calculating profit for profit centers, variations in the calculation might exist in the same company. We therefore asked the respondent to answer the questions with regard to how profit was *typically* calculated for profit centers.

The respondent was asked to answer the questions only for domestic profit centers which were not separate legal entities; our research task would have been unmanageable if we asked for data on the calculation of profit for foreign profit centers. And, we felt that profit center calculations for separate legal entities might be motivated strictly by legal rather than managerial considerations. Some respondents, however, were companies which were U.S. subsidiaries of foreign-owned companies.

The questions on structure, measurement, and diversity were reviewed both with academicians and with consultants from Management Analysis Center. The result was a questionnaire that required approximately 30 minutes to one hour to complete.

Our first questionnaire was designed to be completed by the chief financial officer. We felt that the chief financial officer had the most knowledge and access to persons and data regarding operating structure, the calculation of profit, and the diversity of the firm. He was also motivated to participate in the study because he was a member of the Financial Executives Institute.

The questionnaire was tested with four financial officers located in the Boston area. Their suggestions for modifications were recorded as they were actually completing the questionnaire. We then revised and modified the questionnaire, sent it to FEI's Committee on Corporate Reporting for another test, and revised the questionnaire again. With regard to certain specific questions, particularly the question on interest expense, we performed more tests with two of the Boston financial officers mentioned above.

A letter, shown in Section H, was sent from Mr. Ben Makela of FEI to our selected sample of respondents requesting their participation in the study. The letter also stated that, in addition to contributing to their profession, assisting us in the study would result in a computer-generated analysis being sent to them that would summarize their responses versus the responses of all participants in the study. We were careful to assure the respondents that under no circumstances would any individual company be identified as having given a particular response and only if they permitted it would we publish the company name as a participant in the research. One week later we sent the questionnaire to the sample group.

The response rate was fairly impressive. Most of the questionnaires were returned within a four- to six-week period. We had made contigency plans in the event that we received a low response rate. These plans were not used. Questionnaires continued to arrive for six months afterward. The final tally, as noted above, is given in Exhibit A−1. From our mailing list of 684 manufacturing firms 42 percent responded with usable questionnaires that we could enter into our data base. We felt that this high response rate for such a long and complicated questionnaire was somewhat remarkable in itself.

In addition to requesting the return of completed questionnaires, we also asked the respondent to supply us with a company organization chart with a typical profit center circled, and an annual report. Because some firms in our sample were private we did not always receive the annual report, but most companies did comply with our request.

We first reviewed the questionnaire answers to see if the questionnaire was usable. In cases where the respondent's answer was unclear, we either dropped the answer from the data base (treating it as a missing value) or telephoned the respondent and asked for a clarification. The organization charts and annual reports were checked to determine if we were receiving answers for "typical domestic" profit centers.

The questionnaires were then coded and entered into the data base. This sample was analyzed using both Analysis of Quantitative Data (AQD) and the Statistical Package for the Social Sciences (SPSS). Most of our analysis involved cross-tabulations.

DIVERSIFICATION STRATEGY

We decided to use a set of diversification categories designed by Richard P. Rumelt. Rumelt's categories are well documented in his book, *Strategy, Structure, and Economic Performance,*[1] and have the virtue of being fairly natural, strategic categories, rather than purely mechanical tabulations of SIC codes. The classifications can be merged into four broad categories of single business, dominant business, related businesses, and unrelated businesses. Rumelt's categories and the four groupings we selected for analysis are shown in Exhibit A–3 for our research sample.

A Single Business firm is defined as one which derives 95 percent or more of its revenues from a single product or service or a line of closely related products and services. A Dominant Business firm is one in which such a product line accounts for 70 to 95 percent of its revenues. A Related Businesses firm is one in which no single product line accounted for as much as 70 percent of total revenues, but more than 70 percent of the revenues come from a group of related product lines. An example of a related businesses firm would be a diversified firm that made cameras, photographic film, dyes, pigments, and textile chemicals. While textile chemicals are not obviously related to cameras, in this firm the link is clear between the product lines. An Unrelated Businesses firm is one which has less than 70 percent of its revenues coming from any single business and less than 70 percent of their revenues are related. Rumelt also defines vertically integrated businesses based on the sales revenue derived from a vertical chain of processes.

The problem with Rumelt's scheme is that one must still make a subjective judgment regarding the market boundaries of the largest single business unit, and one must also decide subjectively what constitutes a related business. Rumelt did this by personal examination of the annual reports and other public data for his sample companies in 1949, 1959, and 1969. We were interested in a much larger sample of companies in 1974, and because our sample consisted of FEI members it did not always correspond to Rumelt's sample. Therefore, we were faced with the choice of making our own subjective classification of the companies in our sample or of allowing the companies to classify themselves based on a set of questions which were derived from the Rumelt research. We decided on the latter approach and

---

[1] Boston: Division of Research, Harvard Business School, 1974.

developed the set of questions reproduced in Exhibit A−4. The exit point to Question 24 determines the classification of the company.

The advantage of allowing the respondents to answer these questions is that we easily obtained classifications as of 1974. A disadvantage of allowing the respondent to make the classifications is that we lost the opportunity to track the dynamics of diversification over time by the companies that were in both our sample and in Rumelt's. If one assumes that the hypothesis illustrated by Figure 1−1 of Chapter 1 is correct—that the profit center measurement system of a corporation is related to the diversity of its lines of business—then one might also suggest that a change in the profit center measurement system will follow chronologically a change in the degree of diversification. Thus, the profit center measurement system in place today may be related to yesterday's diversification. Because of the difficulty in obtaining prior year classifications of diversification, we settled for the diversification classification as of 1974.

As illustrated in Exhibit A−5 we did attempt to compare, for those companies which were both in Rumelt's sample and in our sample, the answers obtained by using Rumelt's approach versus the questionnaire approach. Out of 27 possible companies which we could compare, 40 percent of the questionnaire respondents classified themselves exactly in one of the same ten unconsolidated categories (shown in Exhibit A−3) as Rumelt classified them using public data for 1974. Thirty percent classified themselves in one of the ten categories adjacent to the category Rumelt would have used. Fifty-five percent classified themselves exactly in one of the same four broad categories (shown in Exhibit A−3) as Rumelt classified them. Thirty-five percent were in an adjacent category to one of the four broad categories. The classification of ten percent was completely different from Rumelt's classification.

These discrepancies arose because of the human judgment required of such a classification scheme. One could argue that the respondent is too biased to be objective. Or, to the contrary, one could argue that the respondent is in a better position to make the classification than Rumelt. This latter argument also hinges on how well one believes the questions are phrased to achieve objective answers. In the final analysis, both Rumelt's personal approach and the questionnaire approach depend on subjective judgments of business diversity and this is bound to lead to a discrepancy between classifications made using the two approaches.

OTHER DEMOGRAPHIC CHARACTERISTICS

We collected demographic data from the annual reports sent with the first questionnaire, from public sources, and from a short demographic questionnaire which accompanied our second-stage mailing (reproduced in Section H).

Exhibits A—2, 3, 6, 7, 8, 9, 10, and 11 display frequency distributions of the demographic data. The diversification strategy data contained in Exhibit A—3 show a relatively even distribution among the four broad categories. The largest single category in our sample is the Unrelated-passive type of business. Exhibit A—2 presents 1974 sales data for the sample and indicates that 27 percent of the companies are in the $1 billion or more category. Nevertheless, the distribution of respondents in terms of sales revenue covers a broad spectrum. The profit margin as a percent of sales data in Exhibit A—6 indicates that most respondents are in the 2.5 to 5.5 percent range. Exhibit A—7 gives return-on-investment data. Return on investment was defined as the ratio of profits after tax to total assets. Exhibit A—8 reports the compound rate of growth in earnings per share for the ten years, 1964—74.

The top half of Exhibit A—9 gives the size of a "typical" profit center as a percent of corporate revenues. This data was collected in 1975 using the short demographic questionnaire in Section H. We used this data to compute the average number of profit centers in a company. The result is shown in the bottom half of Exhibit A—9. Sixty percent of the 127 companies have between 6 and 20 profit centers. (The low number of companies included is due to the 44 percent response rate—127 out of 291—to our second mailing.) We also used the data in Exhibits A—2 and A—9 to construct Exhibit A—10 which gives the sales of a typical profit center. While these two profit center variables are appropriately construed as "structural" variables, we decided to include them with the demographic variables because we thought they might serve as a surrogate for a firm's "business strategy" as discussed in Chapter 2.

Exhibit A—11 presents an analysis of major income statement expense categories. We gathered these data for possible use as weighting factors in constructing the summary variables on authority, responsibility, and measurement (see Section E).

DEMOGRAPHIC INTERRELATIONSHIPS

Our study was not designed with the intent of identifying interrelationships between demographic variables. For example, we did not intend to explore in detail the relationship between the diversification strategy of a firm and the firm's financial performance. However, we did collect a great deal of demographic information on 291 manufacturing firms, and so we present here the results of a brief analysis we performed on the interrelationships between the demographic variables. This presentation will familiarize the reader with the type of analysis we performed in the subsequent sections.

The seven demographic variables are listed in Exhibit A—12 in the form of a correlation matrix. Of course, the matrix is symmetrical around the diagonal axis.

The first interesting observation of Exhibit A—12 is that diversification is not correlated with any of the financial performance measures—profit margins, EPS growth rate, or return on investment. As illustrated in Exhibit A—13, it does appear that dominant business firms have a slight edge in performance. Such firms tend to be found in the higher performance categories more often than they are found in the lower categories, while the other types of firms either tend to be low performers or equally spread among the categories.

Exhibit A—12 also reveals that for our sample there is no relationship between diversification strategy and sales revenue. Although our sample did not have many small firms in Unrelated or Related Businesses, it did have quite a few large Single Business firms, thus blurring any possible correlation between diversity and sales.

Surprisingly, Exhibit A—12 also shows that there is no correlation between diversification strategy and the number of profit centers. One could hypothesize that the more diverse a firm, the greater the need for profit centers. However, it appears that even Single Business firms are as likely to decentralize operations as more diverse firms. Exhibit A—12 does indicate a correlation between total sales revenue and the number of profit centers in a firm.

The remaining correlations indicated by Exhibit A—12 are not surprising. An example of one of these correlations is shown in Exhibit A—14 which crosstabs profit margins with the EPS growth rate. The exhibit simply states that high-growth companies also tend to be profitable companies. High-growth companies also have a high return on investment as illustrated in Exhibit A—15. Statistical measures shown at the bottom of Exhibits A—14 and A—15 attest to the strength of these relationships. Kendall's Tau C is the correlation coefficient between a pair of variables.[2] In both cases the probability that the relationship shown could be caused by mere chance is nil; the relationship is significant with only a .0000 chance of random error. R^2 is a measure of the amount of the total variance that is explained by the relationship between the two variables. In both cases the relationship accounts for about one quarter of the total variance.

Finally, one should note that there is no correlation between total sales revenue and any of the financial performance measures, nor is there any correlation between profit center sales revenue and any of the financial performance measurements.

As indicated in Exhibit A—11, we also collected data on major income statement expense categories. We therefore searched for relationships between these data and diversification strategy, sales revenue, and the number of profit centers. (We excluded the possibility of finding correlations between the financial performance variables and these expense categories because of the inherent negative bias of such a correlation. For the same reasons we did not search for correlations between expense categories.) Both diversification strategy and the number of profit centers were found to be unrelated to any of the expense categories. No correlations were found for sales revenue versus any of the expense categories except for sales revenue versus administrative expense. The correlation is displayed in Exhibit A—16 and simply states that large companies spend a smaller percentage of their sales dollars on administrative expenses than small companies. Some economists would predict that administrative expenses would decrease due to economies of scale while other economists would predict an increase due to the large bureaucracy. In either event, the R^2 statistic reports that the relationship accounts for only 10 percent of the total variance.

---

[2] See Hubert M. Blalock, *Social Statistics* (New York: McGraw-Hill, 1972).

Exhibit A–1
Respondents to the structural questionnaire

Type of industry	Total questionnaires mailed	Respondents		Usable questionnaires	
		Number	Percent of total	Number	Percent of total mailed
Manufacturing firms.............	684	313	46	291	42
Nonmanufacturing					
Utilities.......................	52	27	52	17	18
Retailers and wholesale trade ..	95	19	20	15	16
Services	30	10	33	9	30
Holding companies	57	9	16	4	7
Financial	20	8	40	8	40
Insurance.....................	22	8	36	6	27
Real estate	6	4	67	3	50
Transportation	30	3	10	1	3
Other.........................	8	3	38	3	38
Miscellaneous	6	—	—	—	—
Total Nonmanufacturing	326	91	28	66	20
Total all firms	1,010	404	40	357	35

Exhibit A–2
Sales revenue (1974 corporate sales revenue for 269 respondents)

Sales revenue (in $ millions)	Respondents		
	Number	Percent of total	Cumulative percent
0–24	3	1	1
25–49	4	1	2
50–99	23	9	11
100–199	48	18	29
200–299	34	13	42
300–399	19	7	49
400–599	33	12	61
600–999	33	12	73
1,000 or more...............	72	27	100
Total	269	100	

Exhibit A-3
Diversification strategy (291 respondents)

Strategic classifications	Number of respondents	Percent of total	Group label	As grouped Number of respondents	As grouped Percent of total
Single business	17	6	Single business	59	20
Single business—vertically integrated	42	14			
Dominant business—vertically integrated	40	14	Dominant business	80	28
Dominant business—constrained	19	7			
Dominant business—linked	14	5			
Dominant business—unrelated	7	2			
Related business—constrained	42	15	Related business	65	22
Related business—linked	23	8			
Unrelated—acquisitive	19	6	Unrelated business	87	30
Unrelated—passive	68	23			
Total	291	100		291	100

Exhibit A–4
Classification of diversification strategy

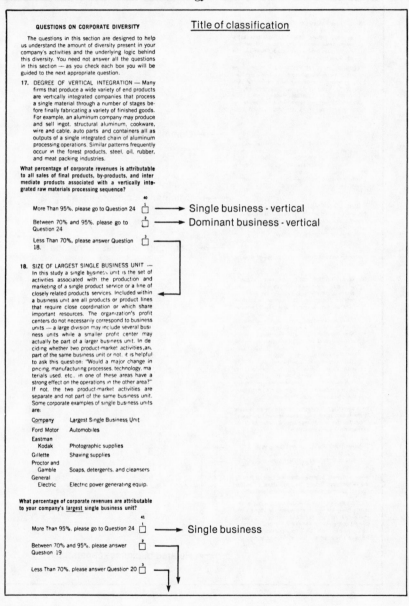

QUESTIONS ON CORPORATE DIVERSITY

The questions in this section are designed to help us understand the amount of diversity present in your company's activities and the underlying logic behind this diversity. You need not answer all the questions in this section — as you check each box you will be guided to the next appropriate question.

17. DEGREE OF VERTICAL INTEGRATION — Many firms that produce a wide variety of end products are vertically integrated companies that process a single material through a number of stages before finally fabricating a variety of finished goods. For example, an aluminum company may produce and sell ingot, structural aluminum, cookware, wire and cable, auto parts and containers all as outputs of a single integrated chain of aluminum processing operations. Similar patterns frequently occur in the forest products, steel, oil, rubber, and meat packing industries.

What percentage of corporate revenues is attributable to all sales of final products, by-products, and intermediate products associated with a vertically integrated raw materials processing sequence?

More Than 95%, please go to Question 24 ☐ → **Single business - vertical**

Between 70% and 95%, please go to Question 24 ☐ → **Dominant business - vertical**

Less Than 70%, please answer Question 18. ☐

18. SIZE OF LARGEST SINGLE BUSINESS UNIT — In this study a single business unit is the set of activities associated with the production and marketing of a single product service or a line of closely related products services. Included within a business unit are all products or product lines that require close coordination or which share important resources. The organization's profit centers do not necessarily correspond to business units — a large division may include several business units while a smaller profit center may actually be part of a larger business unit. In deciding whether two product-market activities are part of the same business unit, it is helpful to ask this question: "Would a major change in pricing, manufacturing processes, technology, materials used, etc., in one of these areas have a strong effect on the operations in the other area?" If not, the two product-market activities are separate and not part of the same business unit. Some corporate examples of single business units are:

Company	Largest Single Business Unit
Ford Motor	Automobiles
Eastman Kodak	Photographic supplies
Gillette	Shaving supplies
Proctor and Gamble	Soaps, detergents, and cleansers
General Electric	Electric power generating equip.

What percentage of corporate revenues are attributable to your company's largest single business unit?

More Than 95%, please go to Question 24 ☐ → **Single business**

Between 70% and 95%, please answer Question 19 ☐

Less Than 70%, please answer Question 20 ☐

Title of classification

Exhibit A– 4 (*continued*)

19. You have indicated that 70 to 95% of corporate revenues are derived from a single dominant business activity. Check the statement below which best describes the relationship between the company's minor business activities and this dominant business.

COMMON SKILL OR RESOURCE   most of the minor businesses are related to the firm's dominant business and to one another by some central skill, concept, or resource. Corporate examples are IBM (EDP technology) and Outboard Marine (in which chain saws, snowmobiles and lawnmowers are closely related to the engine used in its dominant outboard motor business).

☐ ➡ **Dominant business - constrained**

LINKED RELATEDNESS   not all of the minor businesses are closely related to the dominant business, but most have at least some relationship to other corporate activities. For example, a company's dominant farm equipment business might be related to a smaller fertilizer business which in turn related to a petrochemical plastics business.

☐ ➡ **Dominant business - linked**

UNRELATED   most of the minor business activities are unrelated to the company's dominant business. For example, Philip Morris' beer, hospital supplies, razor blade and gum businesses are unrelated to its dominant cigarette business.

☐ ➡ **Dominant business - unrelated**

After completing this question please go to Question 24.

20. RELATED BUSINESSES   A business is part of a group of "somehow related businesses" as long as it is tangibly related to at least one other business in the group. Thus photographic film cameras, dyes, pigments and textile chemicals form a group of related businesses. While textile chemicals is not obviously related to cameras, in this firm the links are clear: cameras   film   dyes   textile chemicals. Examples of firms whose preponderance of businesses are somehow related are 3M (tape, adhesives, coated paper, film, microfilm equipment, projectors etc.) and Miles Laboratories (pharmaceuticals, lab supplies, medical electronics). Examples of firms engaging in unrelated businesses are Ford (automobiles and trucks, electronics), Xerox (copiers, digital computers) and OLIN (aluminum, plastics, publishing, arms and ammunition).

What percentage of corporate revenues is attributable to the largest group of somehow related businesses? (Note: You may wish to read all of Question 20 before answering this specfic question.)

Less Than 70% please go to Question 21   ☐

70% or More please answer question below   ☐

Which statement best describes the logic underlying the relationships among the businesses within the "largest group of somehow related businesses?"

COMMON SKILL OR RESOURCE   the businesses in this group are mostly related through some common central skill or resource so that each is related to most of the others. For example industrial chemicals specialty chemicals fibers plastics and drugs are related by a common skill in chemical technology.

☐ ➡ **Related business - constrained**

Exhibit A–4 (*concluded*)

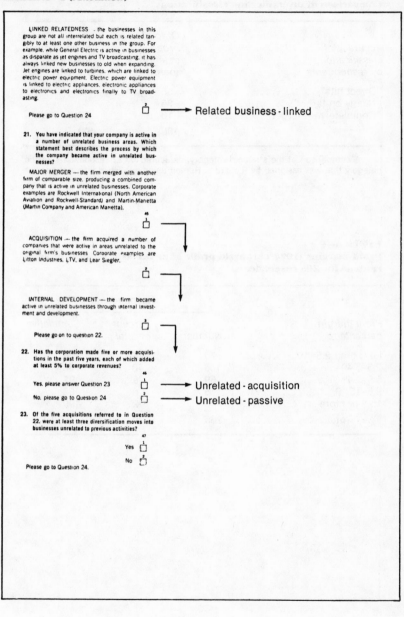

LINKED RELATEDNESS – the businesses in this group are not all interrelated but each is related tangibly to at least one other business in the group. For example, while General Electric is active in businesses as disparate as jet engines and TV broadcasting, it has always linked new businesses to old when expanding. Jet engines are linked to turbines, which are linked to electric power equipment. Electric power equipment is linked to electric appliances, electronic appliances to electronics and electronics finally to TV broadcasting.

Please go to Question 24 → **Related business - linked**

21. You have indicated that your company is active in a number of unrelated business areas. Which statement best describes the process by which the company became active in unrelated businesses?

MAJOR MERGER — the firm merged with another firm of comparable size, producing a combined company that is active in unrelated businesses. Corporate examples are Rockwell International (North American Aviation and Rockwell-Standard) and Martin-Marietta (Martin Company and American Marietta).

ACQUISITION — the firm acquired a number of companies that were active in areas unrelated to the original firm's businesses. Corporate examples are Litton Industries, LTV, and Lear Siegler.

INTERNAL DEVELOPMENT — the firm became active in unrelated businesses through internal investment and development.

Please go on to question 22.

22. Has the corporation made five or more acquisitions in the past five years, each of which added at least 5% to corporate revenues?

Yes, please answer Question 23 → **Unrelated - acquisition**

No, please go to Question 24 → **Unrelated - passive**

23. Of the five acquisitions referred to in Question 22, were at least three diversification moves into businesses unrelated to previous activities?

Yes

No

Please go to Question 24.

Exhibit A– 5
Comparison of diversification classifications*

Accuracy of classification by respondents	Of four broad categories (percent)	Of ten original categories (percent)
"Direct hits"	55	40
"Nearly on target"	35	30
"Completely off target"	10	30
	100	100

* A comparison of the strategic category, as scored by 27 respondents, to the category that was assigned by Richard P. Rumelt using published information.

Exhibit A– 6
Profit margins (1974 corporate profit after tax as a percent of sales revenue for 265 respondents)

Profit margin percentage	Respondents		
	Number	Percent of total	Cumulative percent
Less than 2.5	70	26	26
2.5–5.49	106	40	66
5.5–9.49	69	26	92
9.5–15.49	15	6	98
15.5 or more	5	2	100
Total	265	100	

Exhibit A– 7
Return on investment (1974 corporate profit after tax as a percent of total assets for 253 respondents)

Percent return on investment	Respondents		
	Number	Percent of total	Cumulative percent
−20	1	0.4	0.4
− 6	1	0.4	0.8
− 5	1	0.4	1.2
− 4	1	0.4	1.6
− 2	3	1.2	2.8
− 1	2	0.8	3.6
1	11	4.3	7.9
2	16	6.3	14.2
3	29	11.5	25.7
4	23	9.1	34.8
5	34	13.4	48.2
6	30	11.9	60.1
7	22	8.7	68.8
8	27	10.7	79.5
9	14	5.5	85.0
10	17	6.7	91.7
11	5	2.0	93.7
12	5	2.0	95.7
13	2	0.8	96.5
14	3	1.2	97.7
15	2	0.8	98.5
18	1	0.4	98.9
19	1	0.4	99.3
22	1	0.4	99.7
23	1	0.4	100.1
Total	253	100.0	

Exhibit A– 8
EPS growth rate (increase in earnings per share from 1964 to 1974, expressed as a ten-year compound growth rate for 245 respondents)

Percent growth rate	Respondents		
	Number	Percent of total	Cumulative percent
0–2	64	26	26
3–5	28	11	37
6–9	60	25	62
10–15	55	22	84
Over 15	38	16	100
Total	245	100	

Exhibit A– 9
Size of a typical profit center as a percent of corporate revenues
(127 respondents)

Size (percent)	Respondents		
	Number	Percent of total	Cumulative percent
0–5	22	17	17
5–10	35	28	45
10–20	41	32	77
20–30	19	15	92
30–40	5	4	96
40–50	5	4	100
Total	127	100	

Number of profit centers (127 respondents)

Number of profit centers	Respondents		
	Number	Percent of total	Cumulative percent
2–3	10	8	8
4–5	19	15	23
6–10	41	32	55
11–20	35	28	83
Over 20	22	17	100
Total	127	100	

Exhibit A– 10
Profit center sales (1974 sales for a typical profit center for 122 respondents)

Sales of typical profit center (in $ millions)	Respondents		
	Number	Percent of total	Cumulative percent
4	2	1.6	1.6
6	2	1.6	3.2
9	1	0.8	4.0
11	8	6.6	10.6
13	2	1.6	12.2
19	12	9.8	22.0
20	1	0.8	22.8
23	8	6.6	29.4
25	16	13.1	42.5
26	2	1.6	44.1
34	1	0.8	44.9
38	10	8.2	53.1
53	6	4.9	58.0
60	4	3.3	61.3
63	3	2.5	63.8
68	1	0.8	64.6
75	14	11.5	76.5
88	1	0.8	77.3
113	2	1.6	78.9
120	3	2.5	81.4
125	4	3.3	84.7
150	11	9.0	93.7
175	2	1.6	95.3
200	2	1.6	96.9
250	3	2.5	99.4
450	1	0.8	100.2
Total	122	100.0	

Exhibit A– 11
Expense analysis (expenses by major functional categories, stated as a percentage of 1975 sales revenue)

Category of expense	Percent of 1975 sales revenue				Number of valid respondents
	Mean	Median	First quartile	Third quartile	
Cost of goods sold	71.0	74.0	65.0	80.0	132
Research and development	1.7	1.3	0	2.0	130
Sales and marketing	8.0	6.0	3.0	11.0	113
Distribution	2.4	1.0	0	4.0	110
Administration	5.8	5.5	3.0	7.0	121
Interest	1.6	1.5	.5	2.0	133
Other income and expense	.3	0	−1.0	.5	132
Taxes	3.8	3.0	1.5	5.0	133

Exhibit A– 12
Correlation matrix for seven demographic variables

	Diversi-fication	Sales revenue	Profit margins	EPS growth rate	ROI	Profit center sales
Diversification	—					
Sales revenue	Pos., No	—				
Profit margins	Neg., No	Pos., No	—			
EPS growth rate	Neg., No	Pos., No	Pos., Yes*	—		
Return on investment	Neg., No	Pos., No	Pos., Yes	Pos., Yes*	—	
Profit center sales	Neg., No	▨	Pos., No	Pos., No	Pos., No	—
Number profit centers	Pos., No	Pos., Yes	Neg., No	Neg., No	Neg., No	▨

Notes: 1. "Yes" means the relationship is significant at the .01 level.
      2. The shaded boxes indicate a highly significant but artifactual correlation. Data for profit center sales were calculated by dividing sales revenue (corporate) by the approximate number of profit centers in the firm.
* Detailed support in Exhibits A–14 and A–15.

Exhibit A– 13
Diversity versus financial performance

	Profit margin category			
Diversity category	0–2.49%	2.5–5.49%	5.5% and over	Total
Single business	34%	32%	34%	100%
Dominant business	14	39	47	100
Related business	34	39	27	100
Unrelated business	28	46	26	100

	EPS growth rate category					
Diversity category	0–2%	3–5%	6–9%	10–15%	Over 15%	Total
Single business	36%	7%	18%	21%	18%	100%
Dominant business	18	9	22	26	24	100
Related business	30	12	29	21	7	100
Unrelated business	24	15	27	21	13	100

	Return on investment category			
Diversity category	4% or less	5–7%	7% and over	Total
Single business	30%	37%	33%	100%
Dominant business	29	30	41	100
Related business	44	29	27	100
Unrelated business	36	39	25	100

Exhibit A– 14
Profit margins versus EPS growth rate (number of firms)

Percent profit margins	EPS growth rate					
	0–2%	3–5%	6–9%	10–15%	Over 15%	Total firms
0–2.49	42	5	8	9	4	68
2.5–5.49	18	17	32	16	14	97
5.5–9.49	4	5	17	25	11	62
9.5–15.49	0	0	2	5	6	13
Over 15.5	0	1	1	0	3	5
	64	28	60	55	38	245

Kendall's Tau C = 0.39034   Significance 0.0000
R^2 = 0.23189 →

Exhibit A–15
Return on investment versus EPS growth rate (number of firms)

Percent return on investment	EPS growth rate					
	0–2%	3–5%	6–9%	10–15%	Over 15%	Total firms
−20–2	24	2	4	2	1	33
3–4	20	10	6	8	4	48
5	1	6	16	4	5	32
6–7	6	5	19	14	5	49
8–9	3	0	11	14	8	36
10–22	0	5	3	13	14	35
	54	28	59	55	37	233

Kendall's Tau C = 0.47685   Significance 0.0000
R^2 = 0.28658 →

Exhibit A– 16
Sales revenue versus administrative expense (number of firms; administrative expense is a percent of sales revenue)

Administrative expense	Sales revenue			Total firms
	$50–199 million	$200–599 million	$600 million or more	
0–4%	7	16	19	42
5–7	11	19	13	43
8–19	12	7	8	27
Total	30	42	40	112

Kendall's Tau C = 0.24795   Significance 0.0003
R^2 = 0.10896 →

Transfers between profit centers*

Contents

Exhibits

---

* This section was prepared by Srinivasan Umapathy.

SUMMARY

Sections B, C, and D present the results of the parts of our survey that explored the interdependencies between profit centers and corporate headquarters. The raw data used came from responses to questions in the structural questionnaire dealing with the transfers from one profit center to another, the shared use of corporate level operating functions, and the administrative support provided at the corporate level for the profit centers. The sections divide the presentation into three logical parts: Section B focuses on the transfers between profit centers, Section C discusses corporate operating functions, and Section D analyzes corporate-level administrative services and other expenses. Each of the sections begins by examining the extent of the interdependencies and then turns to the methods used to account for them.

There are three types of transfers that take place between the profit centers of a company:

a.   Transfer of goods from one profit center to another.
b.   Joint use of common facilities (usually one of the profit centers is responsible for maintaining the common facility and its costs are assigned to users).
c.   Transfer of services between profit centers.

This section examines the characteristics of these three types of transfers. It is based on the responses to the following questions in the structural questionnaire (Section H).

		Questionnaire
Question number(s) and title		page number
5, 6	Transfer of goods between domestic profit centers	6
9	Allocation of common facilities costs	9
10	Transfer of services between profit centers	9

First, this section displays information on the extent of the three types of transfers between profit centers. Then, focusing on the most important of these three—the transfers of goods—the text examines its relationships with the seven demographic variables (described in Section A).

Second, this section displays the various methods used for assigning the costs associated with the three types of transfers. Methods for pricing the goods transferred, for assigning costs of common facilities, and for charging for services rendered are presented and are subsequently correlated with the seven demographic variables. The correlation analysis identifies the demographic factors that might explain the methods used for transfer pricing.

EXTENT OF TRANSFERS BETWEEN PROFIT CENTERS

People often claim that profit centers in their pure form are in principle substantially independent of other operating units within the same firm. Such profit centers operate as self-contained entities with their own capability for sales, distribution, administration, and R&D. A collection of such profit centers within a single firm generates no transfer pricing problems, and performance evaluation is a straightforward process that is free of conflict.

Even if profit centers like this could exist, however, they would forfeit many of the contributions that a profit center structure can bring to a firm. When profit centers depend on each other to help carry out their operating plans, there is potential for valuable synergies. "The fact that a divisionalized company is more than a sum of its parts is evidenced through the intricate pattern of interdivisional relationships which can establish itself within a large divisionalized company."[1]

Our study shows that most large decentralized U.S. manufacturing firms demonstrate some degree of interdependence between profit centers. About 85 percent of the profit centers transfer goods, and transfers of services and joint use of common facilities exist in 55 percent and 71 percent of the companies, respectively. Thus, the notion of truly independent profit centers is rare if not absent in U.S. manufacturing firms. The companies in our sample split up their operations into interdependent profit centers, even though this policy introduces problem areas such as transfer pricing administration and profit center performance evaluation.

The extent of transfers of goods between profit centers was estimated by the respondents in one of two ways. Either (1) they gave the percentage of intracompany cost of sales elimination to total external cost of sales (if transfers of goods are treated as a purchase and sale

---

[1] David Solomons, *Divisional Performance: Measurement and Control* (New York: Financial Executives Research Foundation, 1965), p. 160.

transaction with a profit built into the transfer price), or (2) they estimated the value of goods transferred between profit centers as a percent of the corporate total value of goods manufactured (if transfers are based on costs). The choice of basis for estimating percentages enabled companies to report extent of transfers using measures commonly employed in their operations.

Of the 291 companies in the sample, 249 (85 percent) report that they transfer goods among profit centers, and 237 of them report the extent of such transfers. A frequency distribution of those responses is given in Exhibit B−1. The mean extent of transferred goods for those that do transfer goods is 12.7 percent of total corporate cost of sales. Less than 23 percent of the 279 respondents report transfers in excess of 15 percent, and the largest transfer is 65 percent.

The sharing of common facilities and the transferring of services occur in most firms, also, as shown in Exhibit B−2. Of 288 companies, 204 (71 percent) report that they have common facilities which are used jointly by two or more profit centers and 159 (55 percent) have transfers of services between profit centers.

DEMOGRAPHIC ANALYSIS OF TRANSFERS BETWEEN PROFIT CENTERS

The extent of transfers of goods between profit centers varies from 0 percent to 65 percent. Transfers of services and facilities also vary from company to company. In order to identify the causal factors for such wide variations, we explored the relationships between the extent of transfers between profit centers and the seven demographic variables (defined in Section A). Only transfers of goods are discussed here, and Exhibit B−3 summarizes the results. No significant relationship exists for either EPS growth rate or number of profit centers, but Exhibits B−4 through B−8 display the relationships for the other five demographic variables.

Diversification strategy bears a negative relationship with the extent of transfers of goods. Exhibit B−4 indicates that companies with lower levels of diversification (Single Business and Dominant Business) are more involved in inter-profit center transfers of goods than companies with higher levels of diversification (Related and Unrelated Business categories). This point is not surprising since a set of profit centers representing Unrelated Businesses are more likely to be independent and so fewer transfers of goods between profit centers are required. The accompanying table highlights this fact still further:

Percentage transfers of goods	Diversification strategy	
	Unrelated businesses	Others
Less than 10%	72 (85%)	119 (62%)
10% or more	13 (15%)	75 (38%)
Total	85 (100%)	194 (100%)

Among highly diversified firms, it is unusual to find transfers of goods between profit centers accounting for more than 10 percent of the cost or value of a profit center's finished goods, yet among other firms it is common.

At the bottom of Exhibit B−4, we show characteristics of the distribution of the measure of transfer of goods for each of the diversification categories. The information there demonstrates the above point even more clearly. For Single Business respondents, on average 13 percent of goods are transferred in from other profit centers; among respondents for Unrelated Businesses, however, 7 percent of goods are transferred.

Sales revenue is highly positively correlated with the percent transfer of goods. Typical profit centers in large companies tend to produce finished goods that include large amounts of goods and materials obtained from other profit centers. In smaller companies, goods from other profit centers are less important. Exhibit B−5 presents the cross-tabulation results. The reasons behind this relationship are not entirely clear. One suspects an intervening variable is involved, and diversification strategy is a likely candidate. The positive relation goes a long way, though, to support Solomons' comment quoted above about the importance of inter-profit center exchanges in large, dynamic firms.

Not surprisingly, then, both profit margins and return on investment—two key measures of financial success—are positively related to the extent of transfers of goods. Exhibits B−6 and B−7 show these relationships. Though we again suspect that some intervening variable or variables may be involved, these results demonstrate quite clearly that higher profit center interdependencies seem to occur in the more successful firms.

Finally, Exhibit B—8 details the positive correlation between profit center sales and transfers of goods. Since profit center sales figures were obtained for each company by asking what percent of total company sales a "typical" profit center generated, the results here for profit center sales do not add much to the insights offered by Exhibit B—5 (transfers of goods versus sales revenue). The positive relation is preserved; companies whose profit centers each do a high dollar volume of business demonstrate a high degree of profit center exchange.

TRANSFER PRICING POLICIES

As seen earlier, a majority of the companies do not have truly independent profit centers. Consequently, they must face the problem of pricing transfers of goods and services, and assigning costs of common facilities. The policies a company selects is a key issue because transfer prices have a direct bearing on the profits for which profit center managers are held responsible. An inappropriate transfer price might cause not only a misleading signal about profit center profits, but even worse might motivate the profit center manager to initiate actions that are incorrect from the total company point of view. Hence, companies invest considerable amounts of executive time on transfer pricing problems in an effort to ensure that profit center managers are motivated to behave in a manner that is in the best interests of the company. Let us now examine the various methods used for pricing transfers between profit centers.

Transfer pricing policies for goods

As indicated above, the extent of transfers of goods between profit centers was estimated in one of two ways, reflecting the basis on which transfers are valued. Companies either handle transfers as purchase and sales transactions or as exchanges valued at cost, and our survey revealed that of the 237 companies who report the extent of their transfers of goods, 162 companies (68 percent) handle transfers of goods as a purchase and sale transaction including a profit in the transfer price, while 75 companies (32 percent) transfer goods at cost. That is, over twice as many companies treat transfers as purchases and sales as treat transfers on the basis of cost.

The methods used by these companies for pricing goods transferred between profit centers are summarized in Exhibit B—9. There are as many as 11 methods used for pricing transfers of goods. Of the companies which treat transfers of goods as a purchase and sale, nearly a third use negotiations to arrive at transfer prices, and about 40 percent of them make use of either list prices or competitor's prices. Full manufacturing costs (standard or actual) are used by over 70 percent of the companies which specify transfer prices on a "cost basis."

An interesting question before us is whether we can identify the causal factors that are associated with transfer pricing policies. Before attempting such an analysis, we grouped the transfer pricing methods into five broad categories—variable cost, full cost, cost plus, negotiation, and market price. These five categories fall along a continuum of transfer pricing methods ranging from the use of cost-based prices to the use of market-price-based prices. This spectrum reflects the varying degrees to which a profit-center-to-profit-center transaction resembles a marketplace exchange. Applying these categories to our data we obtain the grouped transfer pricing policies for goods displayed in Exhibit B—10.

It is interesting to note that variable costs are used for establishing transfer prices in only about 5 percent of the companies. From a business perspective, this is not surprising because the profit center managers of supplying divisions would have little incentive to produce if their output were to be transferred on the basis of variable costs. Full costs are used by nearly a quarter of the companies. Thus, about 70 percent of the companies specify transfer prices on the basis of cost plus, negotiation, and market price. These methods obviously require more time and effort than methods equating transfer prices to variable or full costs. The fact that over two thirds of the companies use the more cumbersome methods of transfer pricing perhaps indicates the care with which such prices are arrived at and their importance in motivating profit center managers.

Methods used for assigning costs of common facilities

Common facilities are used jointly by two or more profit centers in 204 companies. The methods they use for assigning costs for common facilities are summarized in Exhibit B—11. Nearly 70 percent of the respondents use square feet as the basis for assigning costs for common facilities and this choice perhaps reflects the fact that the main type of facility used jointly by profit centers is shop floor or office space.

The methods used for assigning costs have been classified into three broad categories—prorated; estimated use, negotiation, etc.; and actual use. These three categories are arranged in an order reflecting the increasing degree of control over assigned costs which the method provides to a profit center manager. Of these categories, the actual use methods permit a profit center manager to reduce costs by using less space in his joint facility, and these methods are used by nearly 75 percent of the companies. The prorated methods of assigning the costs imply the profit center manager has no such cost control and these methods are used by less than 10 percent of the companies. Thus, nearly three quarters of the firms in our sample are interested in ensuring that the profit center managers are concerned about the extent of their actual utilization of joint facilities.

Methods used for assigning costs of services transferred

Of the 159 respondents who transfer services between profit centers, 156 specified their transfer pricing policies. Exhibit B—12 gives the frequency distribution of methods they use for assigning costs of services transferred. More than half the companies base their assignment of costs of services on actual usage and nearly a quarter of the companies use the method of negotiation between profit center managers. Only 2.6 percent of the respondents do not assign costs of services to the profit centers using the services. The methods used have been grouped in the exhibit into four broad categories: No charge; prorated; estimated use, negotiation, etc.; and direct usage. Once again, the three groups are arranged to reflect the increasing potential for management control.

We find a good correlation between the pattern observed in the methods used for assigning costs of common facilities and those used for assigning costs for services transferred. In both cases, nearly all the firms choose to make the profit center manager aware of the costs by assigning him a share of the costs in one way or another. A majority of firms encourage the profit center manager to control these costs through the use of cost assignment methods that allow him to affect the costs through his own actions. These methods help ensure that profit center managers make judicious use of common facilities and service departments.

DEMOGRAPHIC ANALYSIS OF TRANSFER PRICING POLICIES

After this review of the various methods used for transfer pricing, we now explore how demographic characteristics of companies correlate with the choice of transfer pricing or cost assignment methods. The analysis, we hoped, would partially explain why each company chooses the methods it uses, and then would suggest guidelines for deciding among the alternative transfer pricing policies. The results do not provide any clear answers, but they are quite interesting. The correlation matrix for the seven demographic variables (introduced in Section A) and the three transfer policy variables (goods, facilities, and services) is displayed in Exhibit B−13.

No significant correlations exist between the demographic variables and either (a) the assignment of costs of services transferred or (b) the assignment of costs for joint use of common facilities. Thus, the demographic variables do not explain the methods used for pricing such transfers.

A statistically significant correlation is observed, however, involving transfer pricing policies for goods. The methods used for assigning costs of goods transferred is associated with sales revenue, revealing that there is some truth to the notion that larger companies tend to use different transfer pricing methods than smaller companies. The cross-tabulation for this pair of variables is displayed in Exhibit B−14. The observed positive correlation means that in larger companies the transfer price is close to the market price end of the pricing spectrum (which, as discussed above, stretches from cost-based transfer prices to market-based ones). From Exhibit B−14, we can see that essentially all companies with sales over $400 million avoid using variable costs for valuing transferred goods. Smaller firms, however, are more likely to use cost-based valuation methods. Note also that smaller companies show more variety in their transfer pricing methods.

Returning to Exhibit B−13, we see that all the demographic variables are positively related to transfer pricing policies for goods. Though most of the relationships are not highly significant, for the companies in our sample, there is a clear trend: the more financially successful companies are more inclined to use market-based prices. From this we might infer that companies which try to maintain the independence of the profit centers by using market-based prices tend to be more successful.

From the above discussion, it is clear that though transfer prices are very important, we have not been successful in our attempt to explain why a particular manufacturing firm makes use of a particular method for transfer pricing. An answer to this question would be quite useful to practitioners involved in transfer pricing issues, and hence this topic offers much potential for further research.

Exhibit B–1
Transfers of goods between profit centers

Percent transfers of goods	Number of respondents	Percent of all respondents	Percent of respondents with transfers
0	42	15.1	—
1–3	55	19.7	23.2
4–7	60	21.5	25.3
8–15	58	20.8	24.5
Over 15	64	22.9	27.0
Total	279	100.0	100.0
Minimum		0.0	1.0
Median		5.0	8.0
Mean		10.8	12.7
Maximum		65.0	65.0
Standard deviation		12.8	13.0

Exhibit B–2
Transfers of services and joint use of common facilities

A. Common facilities
Responses to the question: "Do you have any common facilities (plants, offices, etc.) which are used jointly by two or more profit centers?"

	Number	Percentage
Yes	204	70.8
No	84	29.2
Total	288	100.0

B. Services
Responses to the question: "Do you have transfers of services between profit centers?"

	Number	Percentage
Yes	159	55.2
No	129	44.8
Total	288	100.0

Exhibit B– 3
Correlation matrix of the seven demographic variables and transfers of goods

Demographic variable	Sign of Kendall's Tau	Significance at 1% level	Detailed exhibit
Diversification strategy	Negative	Yes	B–4
Sales revenue	Positive	Yes	B–5
Profit margins	Positive	Yes	B–6
EPS growth rate	Positive	No	
Return on investment	Positive	Yes	B–7
Profit center sales	Positive	Yes	B–8
Number of profit centers	Positive	No	

Exhibit B– 4
Transfers of goods versus diversification strategy (number of respondents)

Percent transfers of goods	Diversification strategy				
	Single business	Dominant business	Related businesses	Unrelated businesses	Total
0......................	12	12	7	11	42
1–3	3	11	12	29	55
4–7	15	16	12	17	60
8–15	11	13	17	17	58
Over 15	16	23	14	11	64
Total	57	75	62	85	279

Kendall's Tau $C = -0.12110$ Significance = 0.0091

$R^2 = 0.038*$

Distribution of transfers of goods					
First quartile	2%	2%	3%	1%	2%
Median	6	6	7	5	5
Mean	13	13	11	7	11
Third quartile	16	19	15	10	15
Ninety percentile	37	33	25	20	30

* Computed without cut points for "percent transfers of goods."

Exhibit B–5
Transfers of goods versus sales revenue (number of respondents)

Percent transfers of goods	Sales revenue				
	$0 to 199 million	$200–399 million	$400–999 million	$1 billion or more	Total
0	17	6	6	5	34
1–3	15	8	16	13	52
4–7	23	12	11	8	54
8–15	9	12	14	20	55
Over 15	9	13	18	22	62
Total	73	51	65	68	257

Kendall's Tau C = 0.17063   Significance = 0.0001
R^2 = 0.047*

* Computed without cut points for "percent transfers of goods."

Exhibit B–6
Transfers of goods versus profit margins (number of respondents)

Percent transfers of goods	Profit margins (as a percent of sales)*			
	0 to 2.49%	2.50 to 5.49%	5.50% or more	Total
0	13	9	12	34
1–3	12	28	11	51
4–7	19	19	13	53
8–15	11	25	19	55
Over 15	14	18	28	60
Total	69	99	85	253

Kendall's Tau C = 0.11166   Significance = 0.0123
R^2 = 0.022†

* The categories for profit margins are condensed here to simplify the display.
† Computed without cut points for "percent transfers of goods."

Exhibit B-7
Transfers of goods versus return on investment (number of respondents)

Percent transfers of goods	Return on investment				
	Less than 4%	4 to 6%	6 to 9%	9% and over	Total
0	7	6	10	6	29
1–3	14	12	15	9	50
4–7	17	9	12	11	49
8–15	7	16	16	12	51
Over 15	9	11	19	19	58
Total	54	54	72	57	237

Kendall's Tau C = 0.10095   Significance = 0.0124
R^2 = 0.047*

* Computed without cut points for "percent transfers of goods."

Exhibit B-8
Transfers of goods versus profit center sales (number of respondents)

Percent transfers of goods	Profit center sales*				
	Less than $20 million	$20–34 million	$35–75 million	Over $75 million	Total
0	6	1	4	4	15
1–3	6	3	1	8	18
4–7	8	6	4	8	26
8–15	5	7	11	2	25
Over 15	3	8	17	7	35
Total	28	25	37	29	119

Kendall's Tau C = 0.18874   Significance = 0.0015
R^2 = 0.076†

* The categories for profit center sales are condensed here to simplify the display.
† Computed without cut points for "percent transfers of goods."

Exhibit B– 9
Transfer pricing policies for goods

| Method used* | Number of companies which treat transfers of goods | | | | | |
| | As a purchase and sale | | On cost basis | | Total | |
	Number	Percent	Number	Percent	Number	Percent
Variable standard	4	2.6	2	2.7	6	2.6
Variable actual	0	—	4	5.4	4	1.8
Full standard	2	1.3	27	36.5	29	12.8
Full actual	5	3.3	26	35.1	31	13.7
Profit on sales	6	3.9	0	—	6	2.6
Profit on investment	6	3.9	1	1.4	7	3.1
Negotiation	48	31.4	4	5.4	52	22.9
Full cost + mark up	18	11.8	6	8.1	24	10.6
Competitor's price	24	15.7	3	4.1	27	11.9
Market price—list	38	24.8	0	—	38	16.7
Market price—bid	2	1.3	1	1.3	3	1.3
Total	153	100.0	74	100.0	227†	100.0

* See question 5 in the questionnaire in Section H for the phrasing used to describe each method.
† Of the 249 companies which reported that they transfer goods between profit centers, 227 specified whether they treated transfers of goods as a purchase and sale or on cost basis, as well as the method used for transfer pricing.

Exhibit B– 10
Transfer pricing policies for goods—grouped

| Method used | | Respondents specifying method used | | | |
		Number		Percent	
Variable standard ⎤ Variable actual ⎦	Variable cost	7 ⎤ 4 ⎦ 11		2.9 ⎤ 1.7 ⎦ 4.6	
Full standard ⎤ Full actual ⎦	Full cost	30 ⎤ 31 ⎦ 61		12.5 ⎤ 13.0 ⎦ 25.5	
Profit on sales ⎤ Profit on investment ⎥ Full cost + Mark up ⎦	Cost plus	7 ⎤ 7 ⎥ 40 26 ⎦		2.9 ⎤ 2.9 ⎥ 16.7 10.9 ⎦	
Negotiation ⎦		53		22.2	
Competitor's price ⎤ Market price—list ⎥ Market price—bid ⎦	Market price	28 ⎤ 41 ⎥ 74 5 ⎦		11.7 ⎤ 17.2 ⎥ 31.0 2.1 ⎦	
Total		239*		100.0	

* Of the 249 companies which reported that they transfer goods between profit centers, 239 specified the transfer pricing policies.

Exhibit B– 11
Methods used for assigning costs of common facilities

Method used		Respondents specifying method used			
		Number		Percent	
Prorated on assets	⎤	3 ⎤		1.5 ⎤	
Prorated on sales	Prorated	5 ⎬ 19		2.5 ⎬ 9.4	
Prorated on operating costs	⎦	11 ⎦		5.4 ⎦	
Combination	⎤	15 ⎤		7.4 ⎤	
Other	Estimated use, nego-	2 ⎬ 35		1.0 ⎬ 17.3	
Negotiation	tiation, etc.	17		8.4	
Square feet and negotiation	⎦	1 ⎦		0.5 ⎦	
Square feet	⎤	140 ⎤		69.3 ⎤	
Personnel	Actual use	5 ⎬ 148		2.5 ⎬ 74.3	
Square feet and personnel	⎦	3 ⎦		1.5 ⎦	
Total		202		100.0	

Exhibit B– 12
Methods used for assigning costs of services transferred

Method used		Respondents specifying method used			
		Number		Percent	
No charge	⎤		4		2.6
Prorated on sales	⎤ Prorated	6 ⎤ 22		3.8 ⎤ 14.1	
Prorated on operating costs	⎦	16 ⎦		10.3 ⎦	
Negotiation	⎤ Estimated use, nego-	35 ⎤		22.4 ⎤	
Combination	tiation, etc.	9 ⎬ 45		5.8 ⎬ 28.8	
Budgeted usage	⎦	1 ⎦		0.6 ⎦	
Direct usage	⎤		85		54.5
Total		156		100.0	

Exhibit B–13
Correlation matrix of the seven demographic variables and transfer pricing methods

	Methods used for assigning costs						
	Transfer of goods			Common use of facilities		Transfer of services	
Demographic variable	Sign of Kendall's Tau	Significance at 1% level	Detailed exhibit	Sign of Kendall's Tau	Significance at 1% level	Sign of Kendall's Tau	Significance at 1% level
Diversification strategy	Pos.	No		Pos.	No	Neg.	No
Sales revenue	Pos.	Yes	B–14	Neg.	No	Pos.	No
Profit margins	Pos.	No		Neg.	No	Pos.	No
EPS growth rate	Pos.	No		Pos.	No	Pos.	No
Return on investment	Pos.	No		Neg.	No	Pos.	No
Profit center sales	Pos.	No		Neg.	No	Neg.	No
Number of profit centers	Pos.	No		Neg.	No	Pos.	No

Exhibit B– 14
Transfer pricing policies for goods versus sales revenue (number of respondents)

	Sales revenue*				
	$0–199 million	$200–399 million	$400–999 million	$1 billion or more	Total
Variable cost	6	1	1	2	10
Full cost	19	10	15	13	57
Cost plus	14	7	9	9	39
Negotiated	6	14	16	14	50
Market price	14	14	17	26	71
Total	59	46	58	64	227

Kendall's Tau C = 0.15210   Significance = 0.0020

* The categories for sales revenue are condensed here to simplify the display.

Section C

Corporate operating functions*

Contents

Exhibits

---

* This Section was prepared by Richard G. Linowes.

SUMMARY

This section presents the survey results for four operating functions performed at the corporate level for the benefit of the profit centers. The functions reported here are manufacturing, distribution, sales, and research and development (R&D). The data come from the respondent answers to the following questions in the structural questionnaire (Section H):

Question number and title	Questionnaire page number
1 Manufacturing costs	3
2 Research and development	4
3 Selling costs	5
4 Distribution costs	6

First, this section displays information on the existence of corporate-level operating functions, and summarizes the extent to which the four shared corporate functions perform the operations required by the profit centers. The measures of extent are then compared with the demographic variables (Section A) and with each other.

Second, it describes measures of profit center authority over the four operating functions, and compares them with measures of profit center financial responsibility for the operating functions. The first set of measures, on functional authority, looks at the percent of a profit center's needs that are met by the profit center itself. The second set of measures, on financial responsibility, describes the degree to which the profit center must bear the costs for all operating functions performed on its behalf.

Finally, this section examines the various cost assignment methods that are used by each of the four corporate operating functions to assign costs to the profit centers. It introduces a new set of variables that reflect the "management control" of the profit center manager—his ability, based on the method of cost assignment, to affect the amount of corporate functional costs that are assigned to his profit center. Using these recoded variables, the narrative explores the relationships that the management control indices have with each other, with the demographic variables, and with the measures of extent of corporate operating functions.

EXTENT OF CORPORATE OPERATING FUNCTIONS

Operations often are performed at the corporate level in decentralized firms. For some companies, centralized operations play a significant role. In the first part of this section, we explore the existence of centralized operations and analyze the extent to which they provide the goods and services needed by the profit centers.

In Exhibit C−1 we find the percent of companies in our sample that have some centralized operations for R&D, manufacturing, distribution, and selling. We see that well over half of the companies have some form of centralized R&D, whereas less than a third employed centralized selling. The prevalence of corporate manufacturing and distribution falls somewhere between these two. Notice that the most customer-oriented functions, selling and distribution, are least likely to have any centralized operations.

Knowing that a centralized operation exists does not tell us how important a role it plays for the company as a whole, and for each profit center in particular. To measure the extent of the operations performed at the corporate level, we constructed the following scale for each operating function:

Range of extent of corporate-level operation	Assigned value
None	0%
1–30%	15
30–70	50
70–99	85
All	100

The structural questionnaire asked respondents to indicate the extent of corporate-level operations, using the ranges on the left. For analytical purposes, we assigned the single values on the right—roughly the midpoints of the intervals—to the responses in order to calculate averages. We shall see how these were used shortly.

While the survey asked respondents to use the above scale for the four operating functions, the questions were phrased somewhat differently for each function. For manufacturing, it asked what percentage of the *profit center's* needs are met by corporate-level manufacturing. For distribution and selling, it asked what percentage of *total company* needs are met by the corresponding corporate operation.

And for research and development, it addressed *total company* needs, but it permitted responses either for all research together or for basic and applied research separately.

These apparent differences in format of the questions do not distort the substance of the results. The questionnaire was designed in part to investigate the degree of dependence of the "typical" profit center on corporate operating functions. One way to obtain such information is to ask what percentage of a *profit center's* needs are met by centralized operations. Another way to obtain this information is to ask what percentage of *total company* needs are met by centralized operations, and then to assume that centralized operations are as important for the "typical" profit center as they are for the company as a whole. Both of these approaches were used in the questionnaire.

For research and development, there was no simple way to make sense of the results for the respondents who considered separately basic and applied research. To handle this problem, the data on basic R&D was ignored for these 24 respondents and only their applied R&D activities were included in the analysis below.

In Exhibit C−2 we summarize the responses to the four questions on the extent of corporate operating functions. These counts are analyzed further by function in the next four exhibits: Exhibits C−3 through C−6. If we examine manufacturing, for example, we note that the counts in the second line of Exhibit C−2 also appear in the first column of Exhibit C−4. The latter exhibit tells us that 54 percent of the respondents have no corporate-level manufacturing; this figure is consistent with the second row of Exhibit C−1 because the other 46 percent (100 percent − 54 percent) of respondents must have some centralized manufacturing. (This cross-checking does not work exactly for the other functions since the number of respondents varied slightly from question to question.) Exhibit C−4 also tells us that only 5 percent of all respondents perform all their manufacturing at the corporate level.

How much of each operating function is performed at the corporate level on average for these decentralized companies? Using the scale introduced above, we calculated two averages for each function. For manufacturing, for example, the last line of Exhibit C−4 tells us that (1) roughly 21 percent of all manufacturing is performed at the corporate level, and (2) of those companies with some centralized manufacturing, roughly 45 percent of all manufacturing is performed centrally. We calculated these averages by first assigning the midpoint of each interval to all responses in that interval, then by summing the assigned values and by dividing by the number of responses.

It is interesting to note the high degree of importance of centralized operations for the companies that have centralized operations. This fact occurs most noticeably with centralized selling (Exhibit C—6). Whereas on average only 18 percent of a company's selling function is performed at the corporate level, if one looks only at companies that have some centralized selling one finds on average 61 percent of selling performed at the corporate level. These numbers suggest that if operating functions can be performed effectively centrally, then centralized operations tend to predominate.

The extent variables for the four corporate operating functions appear together as cumulative frequency distributions in Exhibit C—7. The graphs show the cumulative percent of respondents versus the extent that operating functions are performed at the corporate level. That is, given the extent that a "typical" profit center depends on centralized operations in one company, the graphs show the percent of responding companies whose profit centers are less dependent on centralized operations.

The survey studied two other issues surrounding the research and development function. First, corporate R&D itself sometimes is treated as a profit center. The survey revealed that 14 percent of the companies studied handled their research and development efforts in this manner, but only about half of these made corporate R&D a profit center for all projects. These results appear in Exhibit C—8.

Second, the costs for R&D performed at the corporate level sometimes are not assigned to the profit centers—in contrast to the treatment of the costs of the other operating functions. Exhibit C—9 shows that this nonassignment of costs is surprisingly common. Forty-two firms, roughly 27 percent of the respondents, indicated that they do not charge the profit centers for centralized R&D work. Part of the explanation for this apparently reflects the nature of the R&D activity. Though not shown in the exhibit, the survey revealed that in 27 of those 42 firms, part of the R&D activity is performed within the profit centers. This part is, most likely, the "applied" R&D, while "basic" R&D is centralized and the cost of it not assigned. Only 15 firms in the sample performed all R&D at the corporate level and assigned no costs to profit centers.

The results reviewed thus far show that the more customer-oriented an operating function is, the lower the chances that it will have a centralized component. When there is a centralized component, however, it very likely plays an important role in the company—handling usually over 50 percent of the load. Our pilot testing of the structural questionnaire led us to adopt the assumption that corporate-level costs are always assigned for centralized manufacturing, distribution, and selling to the profit centers, but we make no such assumption for corporate R&D since it does not assign its costs in over a quarter of the companies studied. R&D sometimes functions as a separate profit center, but only in approximately one case out of seven.

DEMOGRAPHIC ANALYSIS OF CORPORATE OPERATING FUNCTIONS

We turn now to an examination of the relationships between the extent of corporate operating functions and the demographic variables introduced in Section A. These variables included measures of each company's diversification strategy, size, and financial performance. This study is exploratory in nature, so we present here only those associations that we find to be significant.

First, we note that the existence of corporate-level operating functions varies with diversification strategy. Exhibit C–10 shows the number of respondents in each diversification category whose companies have centralized operations for the four operating functions. For example, 40 Single Business companies have some corporate-level R&D, whereas only 25 Single Business companies have some corporate-level selling. These figures become more meaningful when we compare them to the total number of Single Business companies in our sample. Taking the counts in the upper portion of the exhibit and dividing by the total number of respondents in the corresponding diversification categories, we obtain the percentages appearing in the lower portion of the exhibit. These percentages tell us the frequency with which centralized operations occur for each function in each diversification category.

For all functions, centralized operations are more common in Single Business firms than in highly diversified firms. Furthermore, in each diversification category there is a clear ranking of functions with respect to frequency of centralization; centralized R&D is more common than centralized distribution, which in turn is more common than centralized selling.

Turning to the extent variables, we perform a cross-tabulation analysis involving them and the demographic variables. An overall summary of results appears in Exhibit C−11, and the next several exhibits present in detail some of the more interesting associations.

Our exploratory investigation found significant relationships between the extent variables and the diversification strategy categories. The cross-tabulation tables in Exhibits C−12 and C−15 present the associations that hold between diversification strategy and extent of corporate R&D, manufacturing, distribution, and selling, respectively. The negative correlation in each of these charts suggests that the more diversified firms tend to be less dependent on centralized operating functions. We see this same trend another way when we note how the average extent of each corporate operating function varies from one diversification category to the next. The average extents appear at the bottom of each exhibit. (We calculated them in the same manner as we found averages earlier.) The trends are quite clear. With few exceptions, centralized operations become less important in the more diversified firms. Centralized manufacturing and distribution drops some in importance, while centralized R&D and selling drop drastically.

Only one other significant association exists between the extent of corporate operating functions and the demographic variables, and we display that relationship in Exhibit C−16. For some reason, the extent of corporate R&D is positively related to the magnitude of profit center sales. The most likely explanation is that there is some intervening variable, such as company diversity, that is involved. One argument goes as follows: in a Single Business firm, R&D typically is highly centralized and since a small number of profit centers are required to handle the company's narrow product line, average revenues per profit center are quite high. Arguments of this kind may be an explanation of the observed relationship.

To sum up, we have found that the probability that a company has centralized operating functions, and the role played by these centralized operations, vary with the company's diversity. Usually there is greater dependence on corporate-level operations in the less diversified firms. No other major associations hold between the measures of extent and company demographics except for an anomalous relation between extent of corporate R&D and profit center sales.

CROSS-FUNCTIONAL ANALYSIS OF CORPORATE OPERATING FUNCTIONS

The six Exhibits C—17 through C—22 present cross-tabulations of pairs of extent variables against each other. In all cases, we note a strongly positive and significant relationship.

One major reason for these statistically significant relationships is simply that many firms do not have corporate-level functions; the largest number of respondents in any single category in the six tables is always in the upper left-hand corner. With that corner so heavily pegged down, it is almost inevitable that a statistically significant relationship will be observed.

In order to eliminate that bias in the analysis, we also examined the extent relationships among those firms which had no corporate operations for both of the functions displayed in each exhibit. When we eliminated the top row and the left-hand column of each table, only two relationships were significant at the .01 level: R&D versus selling, and manufacturing versus distribution. (The statistics are shown at the bottom of Exhibits C—17 through C—22.) These results tell us that when corporate-level operations exist in a company, centralized R&D usually plays as important a role as centralized selling. Furthermore, profit centers are as dependent on centralized manufacturing as they are on centralized distribution. The relation between distribution and manufacturing is not surprising since these functions are procedurally linked in the production cycle. The relation between R&D and selling, on the other hand, is a surprise. Further thought suggests that the relation may follow from the fact that a relatively undiversified firm probably has a relatively homogeneous product line and, in such circumstances, there may be significant economies of scale in centralizing both the R&D and the selling of that line of products.

FUNCTIONAL AUTHORITY INDICES FOR OPERATING FUNCTIONS

We have used extent variables as estimates of the importance of centralized operating functions, and thus they tell us the percentage of overall profit center needs that corporate-level groups fulfill. Now we ask who satisfies the remaining needs. For three of the four functions—R&D, distribution, and selling—we assume the profit centers themselves perform the remaining operations. We shall say that all operations performed by a profit center are a measure of the *functional authority* of the profit center manager. We thus calculate a "functional authority index" for each of these functions as:

$$\begin{array}{c} \text{Functional authority} \\ \text{index for R\&D,} \\ \text{distribution, and selling} \end{array} = 100\% - \begin{array}{c} \text{Extent of} \\ \text{corporate-level} \\ \text{operations} \end{array}$$

For manufacturing, the measurement of a profit center manager's functional authority is complicated by the transfer of goods between profit centers. It is not usually the case that a profit center's manufacturing operations together with corporate-level manufacturing operations meet all of that profit center's manufacturing needs because other profit centers play a role. Using the measure of extent of profit-center-to-profit-center transfers described in Section B, we calculate the functional authority index for manufacturing as:

$$\begin{array}{c} \text{Functional authority} \\ \text{index for} \\ \text{manufacturing} \end{array} = 100\% - \begin{array}{c} \text{Extent of} \\ \text{corporate-level} \\ \text{manufacturing} \end{array} - \begin{array}{c} \text{Percent of all} \\ \text{manufactured} \\ \text{goods transferred} \end{array}$$

A profit center is independent to the extent that it has functional authority over all the resources needed to design, manufacture, and sell its products. The functional authority indices, as calculated above, permit us to discuss meaningfully the notion of profit center independence. Exhibits C−23 and C−24 reinterpret the data from our sample of companies to show the observed variation in profit center independence. Exhibit C−23 summarizes the number of respondents in terms of their functional authority for each of four operating functions. The more authority a profit center has over all its required operations, the more independent it is of other parts of the company. Again we see that profit centers are customer-oriented; on average, profit center managers have a great deal of functional authority for selling and distribution but less functional authority over R&D and manufacturing. Exhibit C−24 displays cumulative frequency distributions for the percent of respondents versus the functional authority index for each of the four functions.

FINANCIAL RESPONSIBILITY INDICES FOR OPERATING FUNCTIONS

Now let us turn to the concept of financial responsibility. We shall say that a profit center manager has *financial responsibility* for all those activities whose associated costs appear iin the income statement for his or her profit center.

A profit center manager clearly is responsible for all functional operations performed under his direct authority. However, financial responsibility usually does not stop there. Usually a profit center manager is responsible for functions performed on his behalf by corporate groups and by other profit centers. These parties then charge the profit center for the costs associated with the services rendered. We make a distinction between nonlocal costs, which are all costs incurred outside a profit center on the profit center's behalf, and assigned costs, which are those portions of nonlocal costs that are charged to the profit center. Profit center managers have financial responsibility for the assigned portion of their nonlocal costs. For three functions (centralized manufacturing, distribution, and selling) assigned costs are the same as nonlocal costs because all nonlocal costs are charged to the profit center.[1] Furthermore, profit centers always charge each other for transferred manufactured goods. R&D is different, however, because there can be a difference between costs incurred outside a profit center (on the profit center's behalf) and the costs charged to that profit center. We recall from Exhibit C−8 that 42 firms in our sample do not assign centralized R&D costs to profit centers. With this fact in mind, we construct Exhibit C−25. It summarizes respondents' estimates of the portion of costs actually borne by the profit centers for R&D. The distribution of the R&D financial responsibility index appears in the first two columns. It was calculated using the information in the last three columns. First we examine those companies which do not assign corporate R&D costs to profit centers; they are categorized in the last column according to their extent of corporate R&D. Bearing in mind our assumption that all R&D not handled by headquarters must be handled by the profit center itself, for firms that do not assign costs we conclude that internal R&D costs are the only R&D costs that profit centers must face. That is, if corporate R&D costs are not assigned, the profit center is responsible for only its own R&D activity. Thus, if eight firms perform in corporate laboratories up to 30 percent of all R&D and they do not charge profit centers for this work, then these same eight firms are designated with a financial responsibility index in the range 70−99 percent. Any company that does assign costs for corporate-level work receives a financial responsibility index of 100 percent. The average for all companies, calculated using the midpoints of intervals as we did above, is 92 percent.

---

[1] There were a few exceptions to this statement. Six companies have some corporate-level selling whose costs are not charged to profit centers, but these anomalies are overlooked in this definition of a financial responsibility index.

Turning to the other operating functions, we know that, by our above assumptions all companies have financial responsibility indices for manufacturing, distribution, and selling of 100 percent.

Comparing these numbers with the averages for functional authority appearing in Exhibit C–23, we obtain the accompanying table:

Operating function	Average functional authority index	Average financial responsibility index
Research and development	64%	92%
Manufacturing	69	100
Distribution	79	100
Selling	82	100

These figures provide a succinct numerical representation showing how profit center financial responsibility often goes beyond profit center authority.

The introduction of two concepts in this and previous sections puts the survey results in broader light. The notion of profit center independence—once a vague descriptive term—now has definite meaning and measurable characteristics through the use of the concepts of a profit center manager's functional authority and financial responsibility. We have applied these terms here to our data on the operating functions, and in Section E they will serve as a backdrop to a more general discussion of profit center independence.

COST ASSIGNMENT METHODS FOR OPERATING FUNCTIONS

The structural questionnaire asked respondents to describe how they assign the costs associated with centralized operating functions to their profit centers. This information, we hoped, would demonstrate the wide range of cost assignment practices currently found in industry, and would lead to some new insights that might permit us to formulate guidelines for designing profit center measurement systems. Though our actual results are more modest, the data clearly demonstrate the richness of accounting methods currently used in decentralized manufacturing firms.

Exhibits C–26 through C–29 show the number of respondents using various cost assignment methods for each of the centralized operating functions—R&D, manufacturing, distribution, and selling. These exhibits display the counts in a format similar to the format of the original questions. They show that cost assignment methods vary widely, from the assignment of actual cost figures to the assignment of prorated amounts based on sales, profits, or some other factor.

Our primary interest in examining the cost assignment methods used by our respondents was to observe the relationship between (1) the design of the profit center measurement system (as defined by the cost assignment methods), and (2) the perceived autonomy of the profit center manager. The initial hypothesis (Figure 1—1 in Chapter 1) had been stated in terms of the "realism" of the profit measurement system. As our analysis of the data proceeded, however, we came to the realization that the selection of cost assignment methods was not an independent design decision but was dictated by corporate managers' determination of the intended autonomy of a profit center manager. Thus, we came to regard the selection of a cost assignment method as a signal to the profit center manager concerning the extent of his or her "control" over the utilization of resources that were located outside of the profit center.

If a profit center manager has a large amount of control, he can elect not to use a corporate-level service and hence will receive no charges. On the other hand, if he has no control, charges for a centralized operation will appear in his profit and loss statement without regard to the extent of his use of the centralized service. From another point of view, management control indicates the extent to which the costs charged to a profit center manager resemble the costs that an independent businessman might experience in a roughly similar situation.

We measure the management control dimension of a cost assignment method using a scale from 0 to 100, where 0 indicates no control and 100 indicates complete control. Values between these extremes indicate some degree of control, such as charges based on estimated usage.

For the three operating functions R&D, distribution, and selling, the cost assignment methods fall into three categories. We thus define the management control index for these functions based on these categories as follows:

R&D, distribution, and selling Method of cost assignment	*Management control index*
Prorated (on sales, costs, profits or assets)	0
Negotiated (estimated usage, other methods)	50
Metered (actual usage)	100

Note that the scales used here are quite arbitrary. Our aim here is simply to define ordinal variables that enable us to investigate statistical relationships between the measurement methods and other variables. The scales shown here serve that purpose.

All forms of proration clearly belong at one end of the scale, while methods that charge for metered use belong at the other. There is much ambiguity, however, surrounding the amount of control a profit center manager has over cost figures obtained by any other method, such as compromise between actual and prorated costs or negotiation. To simplify the analysis here, all these other methods are lumped together into one category that is assigned a control index falling between the two extremes, suggesting that firms which use these methods offer their profit center managers less control over costs for corporate operations than do firms which charge based on actual usage, but they offer more control than firms which simply prorate corporate costs.

For manufacturing, the management control index must weight together the profit center manager's control over both corporate manufacturing costs and transfer prices for goods from other profit centers. Considering corporate manufacturing charges first, we see that the wide variety of commonly used cost assignment methods fall into four categories:

Method of cost assignment	*Corporate manufacturing cost control index*
Variable cost	0
Full cost	33
Cost plus (including negotiation)	67
Market price	100

Here full cost methods earn a higher score than variable cost methods because they produce charges that more closely resemble the costs of marketplace transactions. All other methods, however, presumably lead to charges that are even more market-like in character so they are assigned higher scores. Again the group of miscellaneous and hybrid methods are lumped together into one category.

Now turning to transfer of goods pricing methods—the other component of a manufacturing management control index—we find it convenient to use the categories introduced in Section B (see Exhibit B−10). This scheme leads to a control index for transfer pricing policies:

Transfer pricing policy	Transfer of goods cost control index
Variable cost	0
Full cost	33
Cost plus	67
Negotiation	80
Market price	100

Note here that negotiation as a method is now separated from the cost plus and miscellaneous category because it is felt that a profit center manager who negotiates prices with several profit centers is more likely to control the charges he faces than if he negotiates with only a single party—namely, headquarters.

The management control index for manufacturing can now be defined as the weighted average of the two cost control indices introduced above. Formally,

$$\text{Manufacturing management control} = \frac{\left(\begin{array}{c}\text{Transfer of goods} \\ \text{cost control index}\end{array} \times \begin{array}{c}\text{Extent of} \\ \text{transfer of goods}\end{array}\right) + \left(\begin{array}{c}\text{Corporate} \\ \text{manufacturing} \\ \text{cost control index}\end{array} \times \begin{array}{c}\text{Extent of} \\ \text{corporate} \\ \text{manufacturing}\end{array}\right)}{\begin{array}{c}\text{Extent of} \\ \text{transfer} \\ \text{of goods}\end{array} + \begin{array}{c}\text{Extent of} \\ \text{corporate} \\ \text{manufacturing}\end{array}}$$

Each term is weighted by a measure of the importance of the charges that are passed on to the profit center through the cost assignment methods. There are some obvious serious difficulties with this measure. First of all, it treats the cost control indices as more than simple ordinal variables. By placing them in arithmetic expressions we ascribe an unwarranted significance to the values of the scale. Second, even though the terms are weighted, they are not quite weighted in the right way. For example, consider a profit center that performs intricate assembly of components produced by other profit centers and that buys all of its own manufactured pieces from corporate operations. It pays market prices for the transferred goods which amount to a full 25 percent of the total cost of the product, but pays prorated charges for the small amount of corporate manufacturing it requires. The manufacturing management control index by the above formula is

$$\frac{(100 \times 25\%) + (0 \times 100\%)}{25\% + 100\%} = 20$$

which is too low for a profit center manager who has a high degree of control over the major external manufacturing charges he faces, that is, the large costs of transferred goods. Because of these difficulties, several alternative definitions for a manufacturing management control index have been tried, but all yield the same sparce results as the one defined above.

Given these indices for cost assignment methods, we reinterpret the data on cost assignment methods from the survey. For each company, we first identify those operating functions that have some corporate-level operation and whose related costs are charged to the profit centers. Then for each of these functions, we examine the method used for charging these costs to determine its management control index or, for manufacturing, its cost control index. We complete the calculation of the management control index for manufacturing by weighing in the measures for management control over transfer prices, as described above. The next five exhibits, Exhibits C−30 through C−34, summarize the results. They display the distributions of the management control indices for the four operating functions, as well as the cost control index for corporate manufacturing. These exhibits reveal that:

a. Among companies that assign corporate-level R&D costs to their profit centers, the number of companies that base their charges on metered R&D costs is about the same as the number that prorate their R&D costs (Exhibit C− 30).

b. Less than one fifth of all companies surveyed that have centralized manufacturing operations and that charge profit centers for the associated costs actually handle their transactions in a market-like fashion. Usually *full manufacturing costs* determine the value of transactions from corporate plants to profit centers (Exhibit C−31).

c. Profit centers are charged for manufacturing performed by all other operating units of the firm (corporate and other profit centers) by a variety of methods, though a mixture of full-cost and cost-plus methods figure most importantly in one third of the firms (Exhibit C−32).

d. Most commonly, charges to profit centers for centralized distribution operations are based on *metered* usage of those operations by the profit centers (Exhibit C−33).

e. Charges to profit centers for centralized selling operations in well over half the companies surveyed are *prorated* figures (Exhibit C−34).

The indices introduced here reclassify the numerous cost assignment methods along a "management control" scale that permits us to make general statements about the accounting techniques commonly found in industry. Using the indices, it is clear that methods vary widely from firm to firm and from function to function.

DEMOGRAPHIC AND SITUATIONAL ANALYSIS OF THE MANAGEMENT CONTROL INDICES

The indices introduced in the previous section enable us to study the relationships between cost assignment methods for corporate-level operating functions and other characteristics of the firms in the survey. In this section, we carry out this analysis, examining the relations that exist:

1. Between the demographic variables and the management control indices (including the cost control index for manufacturing).
2. Between the functional authority indices and the management control indices.
3. Between the accounting methods for profit-center-to-profit-center dealings and the management control indices.
4. Among the management control indices themselves.

In each category there are very few significant correlations and consequently it is difficult to draw many inferences from the associations that emerge. In particular, we are unable to synthesize the results into guidelines for designing profit center measurement systems. Some interesting relations do emerge, however, and we illustrate them in the next exhibits of this section.

Regarding the demographic variables, there are two significant relationships between management control indices and the demographic measures. Exhibit C− 35 summarizes the results of this investigation, showing the sign and the significance of all tested associations. First, the manufacturing management control index is positively correlated with the number of profit centers. Exhibit C–36 reveals that the larger the number of profit centers in a firm, the less likely the use of variable or full-cost based methods; in firms with many profit centers, market or negotiated prices tend to predominate for all internal exchanges of manufactured goods. Second, the selling management control index is positvely correlated with company sales revenues. Exhibit C–37 illustrates this relation. Nearly all firms with large revenues grant their profit center managers a good deal of control over the selling costs charged to them, while in smaller firms profit center managers often have less control. We note in Exhibit C–35 that actually all management control indices have positive relationships with sales revenue. This pattern indicates that, at least for the companies in our sample, most large firms offer profit centers some degree of control over their burden of costs for operating functions performed on their behalf. Small firms, on the other hand, usually offer less control.

Regarding the functional authority indices for the four operating functions, we find the two relationships displayed in Exhibits C–38 and C–39. The manufacturing management control index is positively correlated with the manufacturing functional authority index. Also, the selling management control index is positively correlated with the selling functional authority index. Let us interpret these results. When profit centers have direct authority over most of their requisite manufacturing and selling operations, they exercise a high degree of control over the costs assigned to them for meeting their remaining manufacturing and selling requirements. On the other hand, when profit centers have little functional authority over manufacturing and selling, profit centers tend to have less control over the amounts they are charged. These exhibits tell us, in other words, that cost assignment methods for manufacturing and selling more accurately reflect actual use of operations outside the profit center when only a small portion of the operations is performed outside the profit center. For highly decentralized firms with limited inter-profit center transfers, the typical profit center manager has a high degree of control over all the manufacturing and selling costs in his income statement; most of his costs are associated with functions performed within his profit center, while the remaining costs are assigned by other units on the basis of their actual use of resources (usually priced at their market value). In highly centralized firms, the profit center manager has much less control over manufacturing and selling costs; he incurs fewer costs locally, bears prorated charges for corporate selling, and is assigned costs below market price for manufactured goods.

Regarding the accounting methods for profit-center-to-profit-center dealings, there are two significant relationships. In Exhibit C−40 we find a relationship between the R&D management control index and the methods used for assigning the costs of shared facilities. A profit center manager apparently has about the same degree of control over the charges for corporate-level R&D as he has over the charges for shared facilities. Both sets of charges usually are determined using analogous methods. Another similar relation exists between the corporate manufacturing cost control index and transfer price methods, presented in Exhibit C−41. Here we find that profit center managers usually experience similar degrees of control over both the costs of corporate-level manufacturing and the costs for the transfer of goods. (That is, costs levied by corporate-level manufacturing often are assigned on the same basis as the costs associated with the transfer of goods among profit centers.) Since the correlation in the table is so strong, it appears that management decided to use methods that give profit centers the same degree of control over either source of manufactured products.

Finally, regarding the interrelations between the management control indices themselves, there is one significant relationship. The corporate manufacturing cost control index is negatively correlated with the R&D management control index. Cross-tabulation results appear in Exhibit C−42. According to the table, when a profit center manager has a large amount of control over charges for corporate-level manufacturing he usually has much less control over corporate R&D charges. Similarly, when he has little control over manufacturing costs he usually has much control over R&D costs. These results are surprising, even paradoxical. They tell us that a company's cost assignment method for manufacturing usually diverges from the cost assignment methods for R&D. Management's line of reasoning when they selected cost assignment methods led them to treat the two functions in opposite manners.

The relations enumerated above are all the associations that our exploratory study identified involving the management control indices. The indices have relationships with some of the financial performance measures, with some measures of extent of the corporate operating functions, with some measures of accounting methods for profit-center-to-profit-center dealings, and with each other. Though some interesting correlations exist, as a whole, the results are too sparse to lead to the development of useful guidelines for the design of profit center measurement systems.

Exhibit C– 1
Existence of corporate operating functions

Operating function shared by profit centers	Number of respondents with such corporate functions	Percent of total sample (291)
Research and development	169	58%
Manufacturing	134	46
Distribution*	118	41
Selling	91	31

* For distribution, two questionnaires showed no response. Thus a corporate distribution function exists for 118 companies out of a sample of 289.

Exhibit C– 2
Extent of operating functions performed at the corporate level (number of respondents)

Operating function	Percent performed at corporate level					Total respondents
	None	1–30%	30–70%	70–99%	100%	
Research and development ..	122	29	31	35	45	262
Manufacturing	157	62	36	21	15	291
Distribution	171	34	42	24	14	285
Selling	200	21	24	22	17	284

Exhibit C– 3
Extent of the R&D function performed at the corporate level

Percent of R&D performed at corporate level	Number of respondents	Frequency distribution for all respondents	Frequency distribution for respondents with corporate R&D
0	122	47%	—
1–30	29	11	21%
30–70	31	12	22
70–99	35	13	25
100	45	17	32
Total	262	100%	100%
Mean extent of corporate R&D		36%	68%

Exhibit C– 4
Extent of the manufacturing function performed at the corporate level

Percent of manufacturing performed at corporate level	Number of respondents	Frequency distribution for all respondents	Frequency distribution for respondents with corporate manufacturing
0	157	54%	—
1–30	62	21	46%
30–70	36	13	27
70–99	21	7	16
100	15	5	11
Total	291	100%	100%
Mean extent of corporate manufacturing ...	21%		45%

Exhibit C– 5
Extent of the distribution function performed at the corporate level

Percent of distribution performed at corporate level	Number of respondents	Frequency distribution for all respondents	Frequency distribution for respondents with corporate distribution
0	171	60%	—
1–30	34	12	30%
30–70	42	15	37
70–99	24	8	21
100	14	5	12
Total	285	100%	100%
Mean extent of corporate distribution	21%		53%

Exhibit C– 6
Extent of the selling function performed at the corporate level

Percent of selling performed at corporate level	Number of respondents	Frequency distribution for all respondents	Frequency distribution for respondents with corporate selling
0	200	70%	—
1–30	21	7	25%
30–70	24	9	29
70–99	22	8	26
100	17	6	20
Total	284	100%	100%
Mean extent of corporate selling		18%	61%

Exhibit C– 7
Cumulative frequency distributions of the extent of corporate-level operating functions (cumulative percent of respondents versus extent of corporate operations)

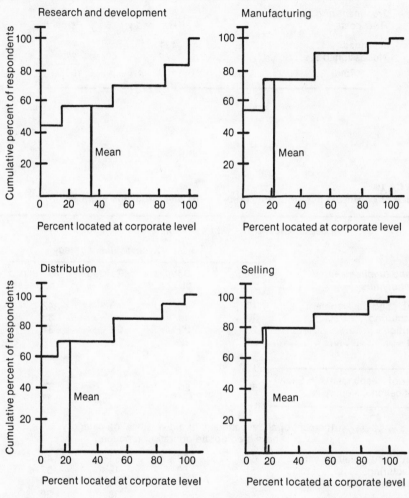

Exhibit C– 8
Research and development as a profit center (number of respondents)

Treatment of R&D department	Number of respondents	Percent
Profit center for all activities	10	8%
Profit center for some projects	8	6
Not a profit center	112	86
Total	130	100%

Exhibit C– 9
Assignment of the costs of corporate research and development to the profit centers

Treatment of corporate R&D costs	Number of respondents	Percent
Assigned	111	73%
Not assigned	42	27
Total	153	100%

Exhibit C– 10
Existence of corporate operating functions versus diversification strategy

(number of respondents with a corporate operating function.)

| Operating function shared by profit centers | Diversification strategy | | | | |
	Single business	Dominant business	Related businesses	Unrelated businesses	Total
Research and development	40	47	40	42	169
Manufacturing	30	40	32	32	134
Distribution	26	29	32	31	118
Selling	25	22	25	19	91
Number of Respondents in Each Diversification Category	59	80	65	87	291

(percent of all respondents in a diversification category that have a corporate operating function.)

	Single business	Dominant business	Related businesses	Unrelated businesses	Total
Research and development	68%	59%	62%	48%	58%
Manufacturing	51	50	49	37	46
Distribution	44	36	49	36	41
Selling	42	28	38	22	31

Exhibit C-11
Correlation matrix of the seven demographic variables and the extent of corporate operating functions

	Extent of corporate-level operations											
	R&D			Manufacturing			Distribution			Selling		
Demographic variable	Sign of Kendall's Tau	Significance at 1% level	Detailed exhibit	Sign of Kendall's Tau	Significance at 1% level	Detailed exhibit	Sign of Kendall's Tau	Significance at 1% level	Detailed exhibit	Sign of Kendall's Tau	Significance at 1% level	Detailed exhibit
Diversification strategy	Neg.	Yes	C-12	Neg.	No	C-13	Neg.	No	C-14	Neg.	Yes	C-15
Sales revenue	Pos.	Yes		Pos.	No		Pos.	No		Neg.	No	
Profit margins	Pos.	No		Neg.	No		Neg.	No		Neg.	No	
EPS growth rate	Pos.	No		Neg.	No		Neg.	No		Neg.	No	
Return on investment	Pos.	No		Neg.	No		Pos.	No		Neg.	No	
Profit center sales	Pos.	Yes	C-16	Pos.	No		Pos.	No		Pos.	No	
Number of profit centers	Pos.	Yes		Pos.	No		Neg.	No		Pos.	No	

Exhibit C– 12
Extent and assignment of corporate R&D versus diversification strategy
(number of respondents)

Extent of corporate R&D	Diversification strategy				
	Single business	Dominant business	Related businesses	Unrelated businesses	Total
All at profit center	19	33	25	45	122
1–30%	1	5	12	11	29
30–70	7	6	7	11	31
70–99	7	15	4	9	35
All at corporate level	18	15	9	3	45
Total	52	74	57	79	262

Statistics for cross-tabulation with four diversity categories
Kendall's Tau $C = -0.19754$ Significance $= 0.00000$

Mean extent of corporate R&D					
All respondents	53%	43%	31%	23%	36%
Respondents with corporate R&D	84%	77%	55%	52%	68%

Assignment of corporate R&D costs	(number and percent of respondents)				
Profit center charged	25 (71%)	31 (74%)	28 (76%)	27 (69%)	111 (73%)
Profit centers not charged	10 (29%)	11 (26%)	9 (24%)	12 (31%)	42 (27%)
Total	35(100%)	42(100%)	37(100%)	39(100%)	153(100%)

Exhibit C– 13
Extent of corporate manufacturing versus diversification strategy
(number of respondents)

	Diversification strategy				
Extent of corporate manufacturing	Single business	Dominant business	Related businesses	Unrelated businesses	Total
All at profit center	29	40	33	55	157
1–30%	12	18	17	15	62
30–70	5	13	9	9	36
70–99	7	5	4	5	21
All at corporate level	6	4	2	3	15
Total	59	80	65	87	291

Statistics for cross-tabulation with four diversity categories
Kendall's Tau $C = -0.09712$ Significance = 0.0173

Mean extent of
corporate
manufacturing

All respondents	28%	22%	19%	16%	21%
Respondents with corporate manufacturing	54%	44%	39%	44%	45%

Exhibit C– 14
Extent of corporate distribution versus diversification strategy
(number of respondents)

	Diversification strategy				
Extent of corporate distribution	Single business	Dominant business	Related businesses	Unrelated businesses	Total
All at profit center	33	51	32	55	171
1–30%	7	6	9	12	34
30–70	7	12	12	11	42
70–99	7	8	4	5	24
All at corporate level	4	2	7	1	14
Total	58	79	64	84	285

Statistics for cross-tabulation with four diversity categories
Kendall's Tau $C = -0.04337$ Significance = 0.1674

Mean extent of
corporate
distribution

All respondents	25%	20%	28%	15%	21%
Respondents with corporate distribution	58%	56%	55%	43%	53%

Exhibit C–15
Extent of corporate selling versus diversification strategy (number of respondents)

Extent of corporate selling	Diversification strategy				
	Single business	Dominant business	Related businesses	Unrelated businesses	Total
All at profit center	34	58	40	68	200
1–30%	4	2	9	6	21
30–70	5	6	3	10	24
70–99	6	9	6	1	22
All at corporate level	7	4	5	1	17
Total	56	79	63	86	284

Statistics for cross-tabulation with four diversity categories
Kendall's Tau $C = -0.09753$ Significance $= 0.0088$

Mean extent of corporate selling					
All respondents	27%	19%	21%	9%	18%
Respondents with corporate selling	69%	71%	56%	43%	61%

Exhibit C–16
Extent of corporate R&D versus profit center sales (number of respondents) [

Extent of corporate R&D	Profit center sales*			
	$0–24 million	$25–74 million	$75 million or more	Total
All at profit center	19	18	9	46
1–30%	2	5	4	11
30–70	4	5	9	18
70–99	3	9	7	19
All at corporate level	5	1	9	15
Total	33	38	38	109

Kendall's Tau $C = 0.23293$ Significance $= 0.0011$

* The categories for profit center sales are condensed here to simplify the display.

Exhibit C–17
Extent of corporate R&D versus extent of corporate manufacturing
(number of respondents)

Extent of corporate R&D	Extent of corporate manufacturing					Total
	None	*1–30%*	*30–70%*	*70–99%*	*All*	
0%	85	17	10	5	5	122
1–30	13	9	4	0	3	29
30–70	14	9	6	1	1	31
70–99	15	8	7	4	1	35
100	17	12	7	7	2	45
Total	144	55	34	17	12	262

Statistics for cross-tabulation—full array
Kendall's Tau B = 0.22460   Significance = 0.0000

Statistics for cross-tabulation—array without first row and first column
Kendall's Tau B = 0.10559   Significance = 0.1348

Exhibit C–18
Extent of corporate R&D versus extent of corporate distribution
(number of respondents)

Extent of corporate R&D	Extent of corporate distribution					Total
	None	*1–30%*	*30–70%*	*70–99%*	*All*	
0%	86	10	14	5	3	118
1–30	17	5	4	1	1	28
30–70	15	4	7	1	4	31
70–99	16	7	5	7	0	35
100	28	3	7	2	5	45
Total	162	29	37	16	13	257

Statistics for cross-tabulation—full array
Kendall's Tau B = 0.15114   Significance = 0.0024

Statistics for cross-tabulation—array without first row and first column
Kendall's Tau B = 0.14967   Significance = 0.0810

Exhibit C-19
Extent of corporate R&D versus extent of corporate selling
(number of respondents)

Extent of corporate R&D	Extent of corporate selling					Total
	None	1–30%	30–70%	70–99%	All	
0%	96	5	12	1	5	119
1–30	24	2	2	0	0	28
30–70	18	3	3	5	2	31
70–99	23	2	2	6	2	35
100	28	1	2	7	6	44
Total	189	13	21	19	15	257

Statistics for cross-tabulation—full array
    Kendall's Tau B = 0.17651   Significance = 0.0006

Statistics for cross-tabulation—array without first row and first column
    Kendall's Tau B = 0.35912   Significance = 0.0025

Exhibit C-20
Extent of corporate manufacturing versus extent of corporate distribution
(number of respondents)

Extent of corporate manufacturing	Extent of corporate distribution					Total
	None	1–30%	30–70%	70–99%	All	
0%	111	12	18	8	2	151
1–30	35	11	8	6	2	62
30–70	18	7	8	1	2	36
70–99	4	3	4	6	4	21
100	3	1	4	3	4	15
Total	171	34	42	24	14	285

Statistics for cross-tabulation—full array
    Kendall's Tau B = 0.31967   Significance = 0.0000

Statistics for cross-tabulation—array without first row and first column
    Kendall's Tau B = 0.27180   Significance = 0.0029

Exhibit C–21
Extent of corporate manufacturing versus extent of corporate selling
(number of respondents)

Extent of corporate manufacturing	Extent of corporate selling					Total
	None	1–30%	30–70%	70–99%	All	
0%	116	9	12	7	8	152
1–30	44	7	5	5	1	62
30–70	18	1	4	8	5	36
70–99	12	2	2	2	1	19
100	10	2	1	0	2	15
Total	200	21	24	22	17	284

Statistics for cross-tabulation—full array
  Kendall's Tau B = 0.13988   Significance = 0.0038

Statistics for cross-tabulation—array without first row and first column
  Kendall's Tau B = 0.16294   Significance = 0.0947

Exhibit C–22
Extent of corporate distribution versus extent of corporate selling
(number of respondents)

Extent of corporate distribution	Extent of corporate selling					Total
	None	1–30%	30–70%	70–99%	All	
0%	131	11	10	7	9	168
1–30	22	5	2	4	1	34
30–70	21	2	8	5	3	39
70–99	12	2	3	4	2	23
100	9	1	0	2	2	14
Total	195	21	23	22	17	278

Statistics for cross-tabulation—full array
  Kendall's Tau B = 0.19615   Significance = 0.0001

Statistics for cross-tabulation—array without first row and first column
  Kendall's Tau B = 0.20788   Significance = 0.0497

Exhibit C– 23
Functional authority indices for operating functions (number of respondents)

Operating function	Functional authority index					Total respondents	Mean index
	None	1–30%	30–70%	70–99%	All		
Research and development*	45	35	31	29	122	262	64%
Manufacturing†	24	23	55	153	24	279	69
Distribution*	14	24	42	34	171	285	79
Selling*	17	22	24	21	200	284	82

* The figures for R&D, distribution, and sales are the same as those appearing in Exhibit C–2 on extent of corporate-level functions, but with the sequence reversed.

† The functional authority index for manufacturing is a multivalued variable, but it is collapsed into the five intervals above to simplify the comparison with the other indices that have only five possible values each.

Exhibit C– 24
Cumulative frequency distributions of the functional authority index for four operating functions (cumulative percent of respondents versus index)

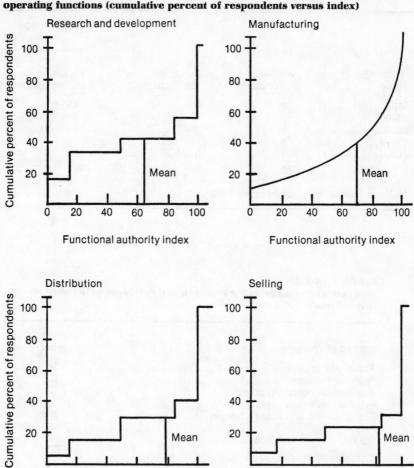

Exhibit C–25
Financial responsibility index for research and development

Financial responsibility index	Number of respondents	Extent of corporate R&D	Number of respondents	
			Reporting this extent	Not assigning costs
0%	8	All	45	8
1–30	9	70–99%	35	9
30–70	6	30–70	31	6
70–99	8	1–30	29	8
100	231	None	122	0
Total	262	Total	262	31

Mean financial responsibility index = 92%

Exhibit C–26
Cost assignment methods for research and development (number of respondents)

Method of charging	Number of respondents
Actual usage	34
Prorated on sales	13
Prorated on operating costs	12
Prorated on assets	2
Both prorated and actual charges	36
Negotiation	3
Combination of methods	4
Subtotal	104
Common R&D function—costs not assigned	42
No common R&D function	122
Not applicable	23
Total	291

Exhibit C-27
Cost assignment methods for manufacturing (number of respondents)

Basis of charge	Method	Number of respondents
Market price		23
Variable cost	Standard	4
	Actual	6
Full cost	Standard	32
	Actual	43
Full cost plus defined profit	Sales basis	2
	Investment basis	2
	Standard markup basis	10
Negotiation		7
Other method		2
Subtotal		131
Common manufacturing—no response on method		3
No common manufacturing		157
Total		291

Exhibit C-28
Cost assignment methods for distribution (number of respondents)

Method of charging	Number of respondents
Actual use of resources	79
Budgeted time	9
Prorated on sales	7
Prorated on operating costs	1
Prorated on profit	1
Both prorated and actual charges	15
Negotiation	1
Combination of methods	5
Subtotal	118
No common distribution	171
Not applicable	2
Total	291

Exhibit C– 29
Cost assignment methods for selling (number of respondents)

Method of charging	Number of respondents
Actual time	13
Budgeted time	9
Prorated on sales	40
Prorated on operating costs	5
Prorated on profit	—
Negotiation	11
Other method	5
Subtotal	83
Common selling—costs not assigned	6
Common selling—no response on method	2
No common selling	200
Total	291

Exhibit C– 30
Management control index for research & development

Management control index for the cost assignment method	Number of respondents	Percent
Prorated (0)	27	26%
Negotiated (50)	43	41
Metered (100)	34	33
Total	104	100%

Exhibit C– 31
Cost control index for corporate manufacturing

Cost control index for the cost assignment method	Number of respondents	Percent
Variable cost (0)	10	8%
Full cost (33)	75	58
Cost plus (67)	21	16
Market price (100)	23	18
Total	129	100%

Exhibit C–32
Management control index for manufacturing

Management control index for the cost assignment method*	Number of respondents	Percent
Variable cost—Full cost (0–32)	13	6%
Full cost—Cost plus (33–66)	74	33
Cost plus—Negotiation (67–79)	43	19
Negotiation—Market price (80–99)	41	19
Market price (100)	51	23
Total.................................	222	100%

* The manufacturing management control index is defined in a manner that makes it a continuous variable, but its distribution is presented here using categories that are easily interpretable. The labels for the categories should not be construed literally; they merely suggest types of cost assignment methods that may predominate in any firm.

Exhibit C–33
Management control index for distribution

Management control index for the cost assignment method	Number of respondents	Percent
Prorated (0)	9	8%
Negotiated (50).............................	30	25
Metered (100)	79	67
Total.................................	118	100%

Exhibit C–34
Management control index for selling

Management control index for the cost assignment method	Number of respondents	Percent
Prorated (0)	45	54%
Negotiated (50).............................	25	30
Metered (100)	13	16
Total.................................	83	100%

Exhibit C-35
Correlation matrix of the seven demographic variables and the management control indices for corporate operating functions

	Management control index									
	R&D		Manufacturing			Distribution		Sales		
Demographic variables	Sign of Kendall's Tau	Signifi- cance at 1% level	Sign of Kendall's Tau	Signifi- cance at 1% level	Detailed exhibit	Sign of Kendall's Tau	Signifi- cance at 1% level	Sign of Kendall's Tau	Signifi- cance at 1% level	Detailed exhibit
Diversification strategy	Pos.	No	Pos.	No		Pos.	No	Neg.	No	
Sales revenue	Pos.	No	Pos.	No		Pos.	No	Pos.	Yes	C–37
Profit margins	Pos.	No	Pos.	No		Neg.	No	Zero	No	
EPS growth rate	Pos.	No	Pos.	No		Pos.	No	Pos.	No	
Return on investment	Pos.	No	Pos.	No		Pos.	No	Neg.	No	
Profit center sales	Pos.	No	Pos.	No		Pos.	No	Pos.	No	
Number of profit centers	Neg.	No	Pos.	Yes	C–36	Neg.	No	Neg.	No	

Exhibit C– 36
Manufacturing management control index versus number of profit centers (number of respondents)

Manufacturing management control index*	Number of profit centers*				Total respondents
	5 or less	6 to 10	11 to 20	Over 20	
0–32	2	2	0	1	5
33–66	11	8	10	2	31
67–79	6	5	9	5	25
80–99	4	6	3	6	19
100	3	6	8	4	21
Total	26	27	30	18	101

Kendall's Tau C = +0.18257   Significance = 0.0084

* The categories for both the management control index and the number of profit centers are condensed here to simplify the display.

Exhibit C– 37
Selling management control index versus sales revenue (number of respondents)

Selling management control index	Sales revenue (in $ millions)*			Total
	$0–200	$200–600	$600 or more	
Prorated (0)	18	17	6	41
Negotiated (50)	4	5	13	22
Metered (100)	3	5	5	13
Total	25	27	24	76

Kendell's Tau C = 0.27735   Significance = 0.0034

* The categories for sales revenue are condensed here to simplify the display.

Exhibit C– 38
Manufacturing management control index versus manufacturing functional authority index (number of respondents)

Manufacturing management control index*	Manufacturing functional authority index*					
	0–40%	40–75%	75–85%	85–97%	97–100%	Total
0–32	4	3	3	3	0	13
33–66	27	19	16	9	3	74
67–79	7	8	12	10	6	43
80–99	1	6	5	19	10	41
100	6	15	10	12	8	51
Total	45	51	46	53	27	222

Kendall's Tau C = 0.18540   Significance = 0.0000

* The categories for both the management control index and the functional authority index are condensed here to simplify the display.

Exhibit C– 39
Selling management control index versus selling functional authority index (number of respondents)

Selling management control index	Selling functional authority index				
	1–30%	30–70%	70–99%	All	Total
Prorated (0)	9	11	13	7	40
Negotiated (50)	0	8	6	9	23
Metered (100)	3	2	3	5	13
Total	12	21	22	21	76

Kendall's Tau C = +0.17867   Significance = 0.0383

Exhibit C– 40
R&D management control index versus accounting method for shared facilities (number of respondents)

R&D management control index	Accounting method for shared facilities			
	Prorated	Negotiated	Metered	Total
Prorated (0)	5	3	11	19
Negotiated (50)	2	6	29	37
Metered (100)	0	6	25	31
Total	7	15	65	87

Kendall's Tau B = 0.14665   Significance = 0.0273

Exhibit C– 41
Corporate manufacturing cost control index versus transfer pricing policy for goods (number of respondents)

Corporate manufacturing cost control index	Transfer of goods pricing policy					
	Variable cost 0	Full cost 33	Cash and profit 67	Negotia- tion 80	Market price 100	Total
Variable cost (0)	2	0	2	0	5	7
Full cost (33)	3	37	2	7	12	61
Cost plus (67)	0	1	9	7	1	18
Market price (100)	1	2	1	2	14	20
Total	6	40	14	16	32	108

Kendall's Tau B = 0.29899   Significance = 0.0002

Exhibit C– 42
Corporate manufacturing cost control index versus R&D management control index (number of respondents)

Corporate manufacturing cost control index	R&D management control index			
	Prorated	Negotiated	Metered	Total
Variable cost (0)	0	2	1	3
Full cost (33)	6	17	13	36
Cost plus (67)	5	5	1	11
Market price (100)	2	4	1	7
Total	13	28	16	57

Kendall's Tau C = −0.22899   Significance = 0.0152

Section D

Corporate administrative services and other expenses*

* This Section was prepared by Lee E. Buddrus.

SUMMARY

This section describes and analyzes the respondent answers to the following questions in the structural questionnaire (Section H):

First, this section displays the extent of administrative services performed at the corporate level and then explores the relationship between this variable and the demographic variables (Section A). The extent measure summarizes the importance of corporate-level activity, but only for those administrative services that sometimes occur outside the corporate level.

Second, measures of functional authority and financial responsibility for administrative services are introduced. The distributions of these measures demonstrate that the companies in the survey vary widely in their treatment of profit centers and that profit centers typically have greater financial responsibility for administrative services than functional authority.

Third, the cost assignment methods that are used to charge profit centers for corporate-level administrative services are described. A new variable is created that represents a profit center manager's control over his or her portion of corporate administrative services costs. Using this management control index, the text explores its relationships with (1) the demographic variables, (2) the functional authority measure for administrative services, and (3) the management control indices for transfers of goods and services and the corporate operating functions.

Finally, this section displays our data on cost assignment methods for interest expense, income taxes, and miscellaneous income, along with the results from our analyses of these data.

EXTENT OF CORPORATE ADMINISTRATIVE SERVICES

For each of the corporate administrative services listed in Exhibit D−1, the percentages shown across the top of the table give the estimated cost of a service performed at the corporate level as a percent of the total domestic cost of that service performed throughout the company. Exhibit D−1 indicates that the amount of service performed at the corporate level versus the profit center level depends to some degree on the type of service.

To shed more light on the patterns which firms follow in locating the various administrative services, we calculate the mean extent to which each administrative service appears at the corporate level. We construct the accompanying scale to recode the respondents' estimates of the extent of corporate activity for each service:

Range of extent of a corporate-level administrative service	Assigned value
None	0%
1–30%	15
30–70	50
70–99	85
All	100

Using the assigned value on the right for each interval on the left, we find averages by adding up all assigned values and dividing by the number of respondents. The rightmost column in Exhibit D−1 displays the results. Legal services are nearly always performed at the corporate level, whereas various marketing services, operations research, and purchasing services tend to be decentralized to the profit center level.

Usually when administrative services are performed at the corporate level, profit centers are charged for all or part of the costs. To learn more about these practices, we asked respondents to estimate what percent of corporate-level administrative costs are assigned to profit centers. The results are reproduced in Exhibit D−2. A quick glance reveals that most companies assign either all or none of their corporate administrative service costs. In Section E we shall make use of this observation and assume that all companies either assign all or none of the costs associated with each corporate administrative service.

To summarize the data on the magnitude of the corporate role in performing administrative services, we calculate for each company an average extent of all administrative services performed at the corporate level. This new variable takes on a value for each company that is the average of the separate administrative service extent measures; the scores for each of the 12 administrative service categories are summed and divided by 12 (president's office and the corporate planning department are excluded because we assume that, by definition, these functions are always performed entirely at the corporate level). In a few instances, respondents failed to answer all parts of the question. If the respondent answered the question for 6 or fewer of the 12 categories, the observation is treated as a missing value. If the respondent reported data for seven or more services, the categories are summed and then divided by a denominator equaling the number of services reported. This procedure defines a new variable—the extent of corporate administrative services averaged for 12 services—for each corporation in the sample.

This summary variable is, admittedly, crude in several respects. First, the "percent" levels of administrative services are broad. We wanted our respondent to be able to answer this complex, multipart question without leaving his desk. The five percentage categories are essentially "none," "some," "about half," "most," and "all." Second, we weigh each of the 12 administrative services equally in calculating the summary variable. Some services are obviously more important than others both in terms of cost and in effect on a profit center manager's autonomy. Further, the relative importance of some services—advertising, for example—varies greatly from one corporation to another. Nonetheless, the measure is a useful summary of the data.

Exhibit D—3 shows that the location of administrative costs is slightly skewed toward the profit center level. Half of the firms in our sample incur 44 percent or less of their administrative costs at the corporate level; thus half the firms have 56 percent or more of the cost located at the profit center level. On the whole, though, there is a fairly even spread of companies according to their degree of decentralization of administrative services.

The data producing Exhibit D—3 represent an almost continuous range of points from 0 percent to 100 percent. In their current form, they can be used to produce scattergrams with other variables, but for tabular displays it is more convenient to consolidate the data as shown in Exhibit D−4. This exhibit presents the same variable as shown in Exhibit D−3 but with cutpoints defined to produce roughly equal numbers of companies in each defined interval. The variable in its cutpoint version is used in the analysis below.

DEMOGRAPHIC ANALYSIS OF CORPORATE ADMINISTRATIVE SERVICES

We now test for relationships between the extent of corporate administrative services and the seven demographic variables defined in Section A. The results are summarized in Exhibit D−5. Not surprisingly, none of the financial performance measurements—profit margins, EPS growth rate, and return on investment—have a significant relationship to the extent of corporate administrative services. Also neither sales revenue of a company nor the number of profit centers make a difference in the amount of administrative service at the profit center level versus the corporate level.

We do obtain a strong negative correlation between the diversification strategy of a firm and the extent of corporate administrative services, as displayed in Exhibit D−6. This exhibit shows that the more diverse a firm, the more administrative services are performed at the profit center level. The less diverse Single and Dominant Business firms tend to centralize administrative costs because their profit centers usually contain only product management activities; administrative services such as financial analysis and accounting are centralized at the corporate level so as to serve all the profit centers in the firm. Firms that combine Unrelated Businesses under one roof tend to decentralize administrative services, however, allowing each profit center to heavily participate in administrative tasks such as finance and accounting; each company's headquarters maintains a small corporate staff simply to perform consolidations and assist in control and planning. The figures at the bottom of the exhibit show quite clearly how the average extent of corporate activity varies monotonically from 56 percent to 34 percent across the diversification categories.

There is a positive correlation between the return on investment and the extent of corporate administrative services, Exhibit D−7 presents this interesting result. Apparently the companies in our survey that earn a high return tend to locate more administrative services at the corporate level. They no doubt benefit from the economies of centralizing administrative activities, but the real reasons behind this observed relation remain unknown. We note in Exhibit D−5 that several other of the financial performance measures are also positively correlated with the extent of corporate administrative services. Though these relations are not highly significant, they lend further credence to the claim that successful companies have highly centralized administrative support functions.

The extent of corporate administrative services thus appears to be greater in the less diversified firms and greater in companies with higher ROI. These associations are noteworthy, but further research is required before we can confidently suggest an explanatory causal link.

COST ASSIGNMENT METHODS FOR ADMINISTRATIVE SERVICES

Exhibit D−8 reproduces a tally of the answers we received for the question on cost assignment methods for administrative services. It shows the number of respondents who charge profit centers for these costs and details both the bases and the methods they employ for each type of administrative service. Exhibit D−9 then recasts much of these data on a percentage basis, showing for each administrative service category the fraction of respondents who charge their profit centers for corporate services and the percent of respondents who, if they do charge, use a "usage" method versus a "proration" method. These exhibits present data on 14 administrative services; to the 12 categories discussed above we have added two functions—top corporate overhead and corporate planning—which occur only at a corporate level but whose costs often are charged to profit centers.

The data presented in these exhibits reveal that the great majority of the respondents—60 percent to 70 percent—charge profit centers for administrative services performed at the corporate level. Because Exhibit D−2 showed that most companies charge either all of the cost or none of it, it is safe to say that well over half the companies are willing to assign nearly all the corporate-level administrative costs to their profit center managers.

Exhibit D−9 also indicates that the decision to charge profit centers varies, depending upon the type of administrative service provided. For example, 87 percent of the companies in the sample charge their profit centers for corporate-level electronic data processing costs, whereas only around 60 percent of the companies surveyed charge profit centers for services such as public relations, real estate, operations research, top corporate management, and the corporate planning department. One possible explanation for not assigning these costs might be the difficulty of measuring the cost and/or benefits of these services to the profit centers.

For any particular corporate administrative service, the decision to charge profit centers varies from company to company. To investigate this variation further, we categorize the companies in our sample according to their diversification strategies and then examine how the decision to assign costs varies across categories. Exhibit D−10 presents the results. It tells us for each type of administrative service what fraction of companies in each diversification category charge profit centers for corporate activity. For most services, costs are charged as commonly in one category as another. For some services, though, assignment of costs varies considerably from one category to the next. The fluctuations are most noticeable for operations research and advertising.

Our survey yielded additional information about special kinds of administrative services. We asked respondents (1) to list any other significant services, (2) to tell us if their electronic data processing department was treated as a profit center, and (3) to list any significant administrative services which were treated as profit centers. The results of these questions are displayed in Exhibits D−11 and D−12. (The information appears in the exhibits but is not used for any of the subsequent analysis presented in this section.)

Turning now to the various approaches followed to charge profit centers for administrative services, we examine in more detail the information in Exhibits D−8 and D−9 about the bases and the methods used for charging for corporate administrative activity. We first note that charges may reflect either market figures, budgeted or standard costs, or actual costs. The survey revealed that only one or two firms in the entire sample base their charges on some form of market price; all the rest base their charges on costs. Furthermore, for each administrative service, a slightly higher number of companies base their cost figures on actual costs rather than on budgeted or standard costs.

Given the predominance of cost-based charging for administrative services, most firms must contend with the problem of assigning administrative costs to individual profit centers. The survey revealed that a wide variety of methods are currently employed by manufacturing firms to determine a profit center's portion of assigned corporate administrative costs. The set of columns in Exhibit D−8B present data on the most common of these: actual usage, estimated usage, negotiations, or a proration based on sales, on costs, or on profits (the format of the question is displayed in Section H). If a company uses a method other than the six standard methods listed, we provided space for the respondent to explain what the "other method" is. Most of the other methods described are either a proration method based on assets or some combination of the standard methods listed above.

Only a very few of the companies surveyed use negotiations as a method for determining the assigned costs of administrative services. This contrasts markedly with the common use of negotiation for determining a profit center's share of the cost of corporate-level operating functions (illustrated in Exhibits C−26 through C−29). It also differs notably from the common use of negotiation in the setting of transfer prices for the exchange of goods between profit centers (illustrated in Exhibit B−10).

Exhibit D−8 indicates most companies tend to use either a "usage" type or a "proration" type of cost assignment method. More companies tend to estimate the usage of administrative services than companies that actually meter such usage, but data processing and advertising are exceptions to that rule. In prorating costs, most companies—50 percent to 60 percent—use sales revenue as a basis for the proration, while the remainder use a cost basis or an asset basis. Only a few companies prorate administrative costs on the basis of profit center profits. Companies which charge for such services as public relations, top corporate management overhead, real estate, and corporate planning are more likely to prorate such costs than attempt to meter or estimate usage.

The few exhibits discussed above present in all their complexity the patterns observed among manufacturing firms in the assigning of costs for corporate administrative services to profit centers. Sometimes the costs are assigned; when they are assigned several bases may be used to determine how much must be charged; the total amount to be charged may be assigned according to various methods. By analogy, our analysis asked first if each administrative cost "pie" is to be divided, then asked how the size of the pie is decided, and finally queried by what rule the pie is commonly divided. In the next several parts of this section, the mass of data available from this analysis is consolidated into a few summary measures that describe in concise form some key features about the way decentralized companies handle administrative services.

FUNCTIONAL AUTHORITY INDEX FOR ADMINISTRATIVE SERVICES

The questionnaire asked each company about the extent of corporate involvement in the administrative services. If we now take the perspective of profit center managers, we infer that they have direct authority over the remaining portions of the administrative services performed in their company. For example, in a company whose headquarters handles 65 percent of the firm's purchasing, we note that the profit centers perform the remaining 35 percent. Furthermore, we say that each "typical" profit center handles 35 percent of its own purchasing requirements. Interpreting our data in this way leads to a measure of profit center authority over administrative services.

The *functional authority index* for administrative services is an average of 12 measures of extent-of-profit-center involvement in the 12 categories of administrative services. For each category, a profit center's involvement is taken as simply:

100% − Extent performed at the corporate level.

Adding these values up and dividing by 12 yields for each company an index whose distribution over all companies appears in Exhibit D − 13. The curve is a smooth cumulative frequency distribution that ranges from a little more than 1 percent to 100 percent. Since the median is close to 56 percent, the profit centers in over half of the companies surveyed perform the majority of their own administrative tasks.

The functional authority index as defined here is a simple average of 12 measures of profit center activity, and thus it is directly related to the average of 12 measures of corporate-level activity—namely, the extent of corporate administrative services. We saw this latter variable in Exhibit D − 3. The curve pictured there is really just a mirror image of the curve in Exhibit D − 13 since the definitions of these measures imply that

$$
\begin{array}{c}
\text{Functional authority} \\
\text{index} \\
\text{for administrative services}
\end{array} = 100\% - \begin{array}{c}
\text{Extent of corporate} \\
\text{administrative services}
\end{array}
$$

We nevertheless include the distribution for the functional authority index so that it can be readily compared with the next measure introduced below.

FINANCIAL RESPONSIBILITY INDEX FOR ADMINISTRATIVE SERVICES

Corporate-level activities are often charged to profit centers, making profit center managers financially responsible for more costs than simply those they incur inside their own ranks. Their income statements reflect charges for administrative work performed both within their profit center and at headquarters. To gather some insight into the magnitude of profit center managers' total financial responsibility for all administrative activities, we rearrange and recombine the data discussed thus far to create a financial responsibility index for each company.

The index is constructed in a straightforward manner. First, we determine a financial responsibility measure for each of 12 administrative services.

From the survey, we know for each administrative service what portion of all costs is incurred at the corporate level as well as what (complementary) portion is incurred at the profit center level. Profit centers are always financially responsible for the costs they themselves incur, but their responsibility for corporate-level costs depends on the cost assignment policies and procedures currently in place in their firm. If only a fraction of corporate-level costs are assigned, the income statements of all the profit centers collectively include charges for only a portion of all administrative costs: all the local profit center costs plus the assigned fraction of corporate costs. The financial responsibility index for any one administrative service is this portion of companywide costs which appears in the income statements of profit centers. In other words,

$$
\begin{aligned}
&\text{Financial responsibility} \\
&\qquad \text{index} \qquad\qquad = \qquad \text{Local costs + assigned costs} = \\
&\text{for administrative service}
\end{aligned}
$$

$$
\left\{
\begin{array}{c}
\text{Extent performed} \\
100\% - \text{at the} \\
\text{corporate level}
\end{array}
\right\}
+
\left\{
\begin{array}{c}
\text{Fraction of} \\
\text{corporate costs} \\
\text{assigned}
\end{array}
\times
\begin{array}{c}
\text{Extent performed} \\
\text{at the} \\
\text{corporate level}
\end{array}
\right\}
$$

Appealing again to the notion of a "typical" profit center, we can say that the financial responsibility index for an administrative service is the portion of all costs incurred on behalf of a "typical" profit center for which that profit center is ultimately charged.

The 12 financial responsibility measures are then averaged by summing and dividing by 12. The result is called the *financial respon-*

sibility index for administrative services. Note that this unweighted average does not reflect the varied importance of services within each firm and from firm to firm.

When we calculate this financial responsibility index for each company in our sample, we obtain the cumulative frequency distribution pictured in Exhibit D—14. The sharply peaked curve reveals that over half the firms make their profit center managers completely responsible for all the costs of the 12 administrative services. (Remember that top management overhead and corporate planning are not included in this list of 12.) In less than 7 percent of the firms, profit centers bear a minor share of the administrative service costs, but one firm has profit centers whose income statements show only 5 percent of all administrative costs.

MANAGEMENT CONTROL INDEX FOR ADMINISTRATIVE SERVICES

Earlier in this section we discussed the cost assignment methods employed by U.S. manufacturing firms for charging profit centers for the costs of corporate administrative services. The data on these methods is complex, though, and consolidation of the data is desirable in order to clarify the patterns underlying company cost assignment practices. Using the concept of management control and averaging together management control indices for 14 administrative service categories we create a new summary measure that alone can describe cost assignment practices for all corporate administrative services activity.

We saw in Section C that the concept of management control is a useful aid for classifying cost assignment practices. To apply the concept here, we recall that for each administrative service some methods assign profit centers charges that accurately reflect actual use of the corporate service. Other methods simply prorate costs on a systematic basis. The management control index groups these methods according to the degree of control they grant a "typical" profit center manager over the costs he is assigned. Operationally, we first assign a score to each of the cost assignment methods by using the same management control scale that we used in scoring the cost assignment methods in Section C. This scoring is given below.

Most common method	Management control index
Prorated (on sales, costs, profits, or assets)	0
Estimated usage, negotiated, other methods (excluding asset prorations)	50
Actual usage	100

We then exclude all observations which have six or more missing values for the 14 administrative service categories. We also exclude observations for which either (1) none of the corporate administrative service costs are assigned, or (2) there are no corporate-level administrative services. The scores for all of the remaining observations are then summed and divided by the total number of administrative service categories whose cost assignment method is given. This procedure produces a variable called the *management control index for administrative services*. A cumulative frequency distribution for this variable is shown in Exhibit D–15.

The distribution is somewhat erratic with steep rises in the curve at the points 0, 50, and 100. These values are the numbers we assigned to cost assignment methods for individual administrative services, and now we find these same values appearing after averaging over 14 administrative services. Thus, for many companies the 14 separate indices are all the same, indicating that many companies tend to select a cost assignment method and apply it to all corporate administrative services. Examining the magnitude of the peaks in the curve, we note first of all that 29 percent of the sample prorate all of the costs for the 14 administrative services. Seventeen percent of the components which assign administrative service costs use either negotiation, estimated usage, or some other method for all 14 of the administrative service centers, and 13 percent measure the actual usage of all 14 service centers. Analysis of individual company responses confirms these observations. One should also note that 28 of the companies either have no administrative costs above the profit center level or, if they do, they do not assign such costs to profit centers for any of the 14 administrative service center categories.

The mean of the distribution shown in Exhibit D–15 is 38 and the median is 41. This indicates that, on a somewhat arbitrary scale, our sample companies are slightly weighted toward cost assignment methods which grant profit center managers a diminished sense of control over the administrative costs that are charged to their profit centers.

The management control index for administrative services is used to perform scattergram analyses. In order to have an index variable in a more convenient form for cross-tabulation purposes, we establish the cutpoints shown in Exhibit D−16. The cutpoints are chosen to produce roughly equal numbers of respondents in the high and low categories.

DEMOGRAPHIC ANALYSIS OF MANAGEMENT CONTROL INDEX FOR ADMINISTRATIVE SERVICES

The management control index for administrative services characterizes succinctly some key features of any company's corporate administrative cost policies. Let us now see how this measure is related to company demographic data. Using cross-tabulation studies, we obtain the results displayed in Exhibit D−17.

A firm's diversification strategy apparently plays some role in the degree of management control that profit center managers have over corporate administrative services. The cross-tabulation analysis displayed in Exhibit D−18 indicates a positive correlation between the diversification strategy of the firm and the management control index for administrative services. The more diversified firms tend to use cost assignment methods that charge profit centers for their actual use of corporate administrative services.

We also find a somewhat less significant relationship between sales revenue and the management control index for administrative services, as displayed in Exhibit D−19. Profit center managers tend to have somewhat greater control over these costs in larger companies. The other five demographic variables—profit margins, EPS growth rate, return on investment, profit center sales, and number of profit centers—are not significantly related with the index.

SITUATIONAL ANALYSIS OF MANAGEMENT CONTROL INDEX FOR ADMINISTRATIVE SERVICES

One question of considerable interest is whether or not there is any relationship between the functional authority index for administrative services and the management control index for administrative services. Analogous correlations were found in Section C for selling and manufacturing, leading to our claim that more decentralized firms offer their profit center managers greater control over their share of corporate-level selling and manufacturing costs. For administrative services, our study reveals that no such relationship exists.

Another point of interest concerns the relations between the management control index for administrative services and the management control indices for other functions, as defined in Sections B and C. Exploring these relationships, we find only one significant correlation. Exhibit D−20 indicates a strong positive relationship between the management control index for administrative services costs and the analogous index for the research and development function. We noted above while discussing the administrative services cost assignment methods for the 14 categories that, once a method is chosen by a company, it is usually applied across the board to all of the administrative services. Apparently many companies regard corporate R&D services as another type of administrative service. Thus if EDP or public relations services are prorated, so also will firms tend to prorate corporate R&D services. This is not true of the primary operating functions of sales, distribution, and manufacturing; we found no correlation between the management control indices for these functions and the index for administrative services.

INTEREST EXPENSE, INCOME TAXES, AND MISCELLANEOUS INCOME

When designing the questionnaire, we had great difficulty in constructing an instrument for capturing the method used to assign interest expense and/or a capital charge to profit centers. The final design of our question really consists of three separate questions, the responses to which are displayed in Exhibits D−21, D−22, and D−23.

We first asked the respondent to tell us whether or not the company charged the profit center for interest, capital employed, both interest and capital employed, or did not charge the profit center for either interest or capital employed. Of course, we realized that an interest charge is a type of charge for capital employed, but we wanted to distinguish between a methodology which started with corporate interest expense as a basis for charging profit centers versus a methodology which started with assets (or capital) employed in the profit center. Most companies use one methodology or the other (or neither); only 9 percent use both methods, probably to serve two different purposes.

As illustrated in Exhibit D—22 we next asked respondents who allocate corporate interest to tell us the basis for that allocation: either proration of some sort, or use of some kind of simulated capital structure. To use a simulated capital structure, the corporate financial manager constructs a hypothetical balance sheet for each profit center. The debt portion of the balance sheet multiplied by an interest rate is then the profit center interest charge. As Exhibit D—22 shows, two thirds of the companies prorate interest expense on the basis of capital employed in the profit center.

Finally we asked all companies which either assigned a charge for capital used in the profit center or allocated interest on the basis of a simulated capital structure to tell us how they determined the interest rate used. Their responses are shown in Exhibit D—23. As seen there, we gave those respondents who use different rates for different maturity dates the opportunity to specify the rate by maturity date. Most of the cells of the matrix of Exhibit D—23 contain too few responses to permit extensive analysis.

Through a study of the correlations between all these data on interest expense and other variables in our study we find no significant relationships.

Income taxes

Forty-four percent of the 291 companies calculate income taxes for each profit center. Of this 44 percent, 55 percent uses a proration method based on either an effective rate or a nominal rate. The others treat their profit centers as if they were separate corporations, using the tax regulations as if they were directly applicable. None of the companies prorate income taxes on the basis of sales or operating costs. These results are displayed in Exhibit D—24.

We also asked respondents to tell us if they included as an element of tax expense any special taxes which one profit center might incur but which another profit center might not incur (for example, state taxes). Furthermore, we asked respondents if they reflected investment tax credits in their calculation of profit center income taxes. In both cases, two thirds of the respondents answered in the affirmative, as reported in Exhibit D—25.

As with corporate interest expense, we look for relationships between these data on assigned income tax expenses and other variables in our study. Again, we find no significant relationships.

Miscellaneous ("other") income

Half the 291 companies in our sample (145) had significant amounts of miscellaneous corporate income (2 percent or more of net corporate profit) in 1974. We asked these respondents to tell us whether or not this income was assigned to profit centers and if so, how it was assigned. The results are displayed in Exhibit D—26. Most of the respondents (63 percent) do not assign miscellaneous corporate income. We find no significant relationships between these data and other variables in our study.

Corporate assignments and diversification

To complement the discussions above about how the decision to assign costs of corporate administrative services varies across diversification categories, we present a similar analysis here for the special items. Just as Exhibit D—10 shows the fraction of companies in each category which charge their costs to profit centers, Exhibit D—27 displays the fraction of companies in each category which assign interest expenses, income taxes, and miscellaneous income to profit centers. We find a much wider spread across categories for these items than we do for most administrative services. Income taxes in particular are assigned in only 29 percent of the Single Business firms, but in 52 percent of firms with Unrelated Businesses. Thus the highly diversified firms are more inclined to assign these corporate costs and income than the undiversified firms.

Exhibit D—1
Extent of administrative services performed at the corporate level (number of respondents)

Administrative services	Extent of service performed at corporate level					Total respondents reporting	Mean extent of administrative service
	None	1–30%	30–70%	70–99%	All		
1. Finance and accounting	2	160	52	52	18	284	36%
2. Legal	8	30	34	84	127	283	78
3. Electronic data processing	41	40	64	95	44	284	57
4. General marketing services	112	85	16	29	39	281	30
5. Advertising	91	79	30	36	46	282	37
6. Market research services	102	66	13	41	56	278	39
7. Public relations	19	54	25	84	102	284	68
8. Industrial relations	33	93	55	51	48	280	47
9. Personnel	26	124	66	51	13	280	39
10. Real estate	76	44	19	47	91	277	53
11. Operations research department	144	26	9	31	60	270	35
12. Purchasing department	84	93	48	38	17	280	31

Exhibit D–2
Percent of administrative service costs assigned to profit centers (number of respondents)

Administrative service	Percent of assigned cost						Total respondents reporting
	None	1–30%	30–70%	70–99%	All	N/A*	
1. Finance and accounting	75	19	20	26	142	1	284
2. Legal	75	15	16	28	135	10	277
3. Electronic data processing	30	12	23	39	140	40	285
4. General marketing services	47	6	6	24	96	103	282
5. Advertising	49	10	10	22	105	86	282
6. Market research services	54	6	5	21	99	96	281
7. Public relations	90	11	6	18	136	20	281
8. Industrial relations	72	8	7	29	129	36	281
9. Personnel	75	13	12	23	132	26	281
10. Real estate	69	8	9	20	95	80	281
11. Operations research department	50	5	5	11	66	141	278
12. Purchasing department	54	8	5	25	113	79	284
13. Top corporate management overhead (i.e., President's Office)†	97	5	4	24	141	—	271
14. Corporate planning department†	95	5	5	17	131	28	281

*N/A (not applicable): Respondents which had no corporate level administrative cost, therefore, no costs are assigned. For the last category (Corporate Planning Department) this can be taken to mean that there is no such department. There are some small discrepancies in this column and the "None" column of Exhibit D–1. Some respondents failed to respond to the question on extent of administrative services, and hence were treated as missing values, but did respond to the question on the amount of cost assigned by checking "not applicable." Thus they were *not* treated as missing values for this question. This discrepancy is very small and does not affect the interpretation of the data.

† These categories did not appear on Exhibit D–1 because by definition these services are performed entirely at the corporate level.

Exhibit D–3
Cumulative frequency distribution of the extent of corporate administrative services averaged for twelve administrative services (283 respondents)

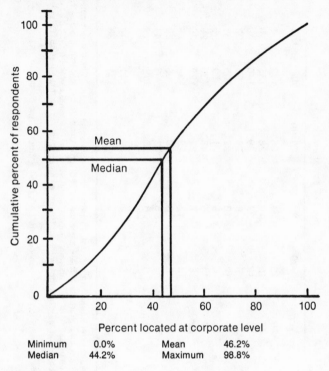

Minimum   0.0%   Mean   46.2%
Median   44.2%   Maximum   98.8%

Exhibit D–4
Extent of corporate administrative services averaged for twelve services with cutpoints defined (283 respondents)

Average percent of administrative services performed at corporate level	Number of respondents	Percent
0–15%	34	12%
15–20	19	7
21–28	30	11
29–35	28	10
36–43	28	10
44–50	26	9
51–60	33	12
61–70	29	10
71–85	35	12
86–100	21	7
Total	283	100%

Exhibit D–5
Correlation matrix of the seven demographic variables and the extent of corporate administrative services

Demographic variable	Sign of Kendall's Tau	Significance at 1% level	Detailed exhibit
Diversification strategy	Negative	Yes	D–6
Sales revenue	Negative	No	
Profit margins......................	Positive	No	
EPS growth rate	Positive	No	
Return on investment	Positive	No	D–7
Profit center sales	Positive	No	
Number of profit centers	Negative	No	

Exhibit D–6
Extent of corporate administrative services versus diversification strategy (number of respondents)

Extent of corporate administrative services*	Diversification strategy				
	Single business	Dominant business	Related businesses	Unrelated businesses	Total
0–20%	10	8	14	21	53
21–35	3	14	15	26	58
36–50	9	18	11	16	54
51–70	15	19	10	18	62
71–100	19	20	14	3	56
Total	56	79	64	84	283

Statistics for cross-tabulation with four diversity categories
Kendall's Tau $C = -0.26867$ Significance = 0.0000

Distribution of corporate administrative services

First quarter	38%	32%	23%	19%	25%
Median	57	50	39	30	44
Mean	56	53	45	34	46
Third quarter	76	71	67	49	66

* The categories for extent of corporate administrative services with cutpoints are condensed here to simplify the display.

Exhibit D–7
Extent of corporate administrative services versus return on investment
(number of respondents)

Extent of corporate administrative services*	Return on investment*				
	4% or less	5 to 6%	7 to 9%	10% and over	Total
0–20%	15	14	9	5	43
21–35	22	12	11	8	53
36–50	12	18	15	5	50
51–70	14	11	15	10	50
71–100	14	11	10	10	45
Total	77	66	60	38	241

Kendall's Tau C = 0.10300   Significance = 0.0148

* The categories for extent of corporate administrative services with cutpoints and return on investment are condensed here to simplify the display.

Exhibit D–8A
Cost assignment methods for administrative services (number of respondents)

Administrative service category	Is profit center charged?				Basis of charge			
	Yes	No	N/A*	Total	Budgeted or standard cost	Actual cost	Market price or cost plus defined profit	Total
1. Finance and accounting	206	76	1	283	81	112	1	194
2. Legal	189	82	11	282	65	110	1	176
3. Electronic data processing	215	31	39	285	81	117	2	200
4. General marketing services	129	47	107	283	41	81	1	123
5. Advertising	139	55	89	283	37	93	0	130
6. Market research services	124	52	107	283	39	77	1	117
7. Public relations	165	97	22	284	61	93	0	154
8. Industrial relations	173	75	36	284	64	97	1	161
9. Personnel	179	77	25	281	68	97	1	166
10. Real estate	125	76	83	284	51	65	1	117
11. Operations research department	79	52	154	285	37	38	0	75
12. Purchasing department	146	56	83	285	54	80	2	136
13. Top corporate overhead	176	102	4	282	63	99	1	163
14. Corporate planning department	153	96	34	283	60	82	1	143

* N/A = not applicable.

Exhibit D–8B
Cost assignment methods for administrative services (number of respondents)

Service category number	Actual usage	Estimated usage	Negotiations	Prorated on sales	Prorated on cost	Prorated on profit	Prorated on assets	Other methods	Total
				Most common method of charging for administrative services					
1.	13	59	1	56	29	2	22	21	203
2.	29	37	0	57	28	0	18	17	186
3.	83	48	5	29	17	0	14	13	209
4.	14	30	0	42	11	1	15	11	124
5.	43	25	1	28	12	1	15	12	137
6.	18	25	0	39	12	1	13	12	120
7.	8	31	0	48	29	1	22	22	161
8.	11	43	2	43	30	2	18	20	167
9.	14	46	0	40	32	0	20	19	173
10.	15	31	0	30	22	2	12	13	125
11.	12	25	0	17	9	1	6	0	79
12.	18	39	0	40	22	1	10	13	143
13.	3	19	0	65	32	4	24	27	174
14.	6	25	0	55	24	2	19	21	152

Exhibit D–9
Percent of firms which charge for administrative services and percent employing the major types of cost assignment methods

Administrative service category	Percent of firms which charge*	Percent by method		
		Usage (actual or estimated)	Prorated	Other, (Neg., other methods)
1. Finance and accounting	73%	35%	54%	11%
2. Legal	70	35	55	10
3. Electronic data processing	87	63	29	8
4. General marketing services	73	35	56	9
5. Advertising	72	50	41	9
6. Market research services	70	36	54	10
7. Public relations	63	24	62	14
8. Industrial relations	70	32	56	12
9. Personnel	70	35	53	12
10. Real estate	62	37	53	10
11. Operations research department	60	47	42	11
12. Purchasing department	51	40	51	9
13. Top corporate management overhead	63	13	72	15
14. Corporate planning department	61	20	66	14

* The total for the denominator includes only respondents who answered "yes" or "no" and excludes missing values and respondents who answered "not applicable."

Exhibit D–10

Assignment of corporate administrative service costs versus diversification strategy (percent of respondents in each category that assign costs to profit centers)

Administrative service category	Diversification strategy					Total number of respondents
	Single business	Dominant business	Related businesses	Unrelated businesses	All respondents	
1. Finance and accounting	74%	71%	74%	73%	73%	282
2. Legal	66	67	71	72	70	271
3. Electronic data processing	82	83	90	95	87	246
4. General marketing services	76	71	74	72	73	176
5. Advertising	76	70	80	62	72	194
6. Market research services	75	69	78	62	70	176
7. Public relations	74	58	61	62	63	262
8. Industrial relations	75	66	68	71	70	248
9. Personnel	75	65	69	71	70	256
10. Real estate	62	59	65	63	62	201
11. Operations research department ..	57	49	72	70	60	131
12. Purchasing department	78	72	76	64	72	285
13. Top corporate overhead	66	59	65	65	63	278
14. Corporate planning department ...	63	61	61	61	61	249

Exhibit D–11
Examples of other significant administrative services

Agricultural services
Architectural services
Communications services
Credit services
Engineering services
Facilities services
Flight services
Forestry services
Health services
Insurance services

Inventory control services
Laboratory services
Manufacturing services
Metalurgical services
Printing services
Quality control services
Securities services
Supply services
Traffic services

Exhibit D–12
Administrative services treated as profit centers

Is EDP department treated as a profit center?

	Number of respondents	Percent
Yes	25	9%
No	260	91
Total	285	100%

Other administrative services treated as profit centers

	Number of respondents
Corporate traffic services	5
Canteen services	3
Product development services	3
Real estate	1
General services	1

Exhibit D– 13
Cumulative frequency distribution of the functional authority
index for administrative services (283 respondents)

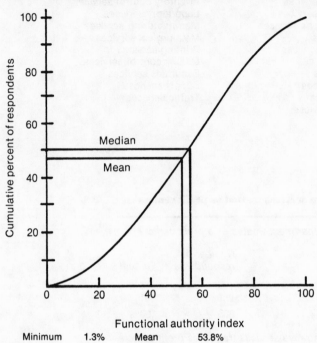

Functional authority index

Minimum	1.3%	Mean	53.8%
Median	55.8%	Maximum	100.0%

Exhibit D–14
Cumulative frequency distribution of the financial responsibility index for administrative services (283 respondents)

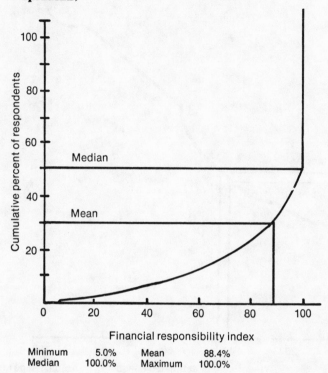

| Minimum | 5.0% | Mean | 88.4% |
| Median | 100.0% | Maximum | 100.0% |

Exhibit D-15
Cumulative frequency distribution of the percent of respondents versus the management control index for administrative services (253 respondents)

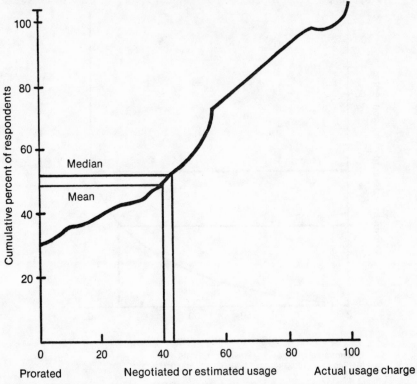

Note: Twenty-eight of the respondents reported all local cost for all 12 administrative service categories of Exhibit D-1 and were not included in method calculations.

Minimum	0.0	Median	40.9
Mean	38.4	Maximum	100.0

Exhibit D-16
Management control index for administrative services with cutpoints defined (253 respondents)

Management control index	Number of respondents	Percent
0	73	29%
1–50	106	42
51–100	74	29
Total	253	100%

Exhibit D–17

Correlation matrix of the seven demographic variables and the management control index for administrative services

Demographic variable	Sign of Kendall's Tau	Significance at 1% level	Detailed exhibit
Diversification strategy	Positive	Yes	D–18
Sales revenue	Positive	Yes	D–19
Profit margins	Negative	No	
EPS growth rate	Negative	No	
Return on investment	Negative	No	
Profit center sales	Positive	No	
Number of profit centers	Negative	No	

Exhibit D–18

Management control index for administrative services versus diversification strategy (number of respondents)

Management control index	Diversification strategy				
	Single business	Dominant business	Related business	Unrelated business	Total
0	22	24	10	17	73
1–50	22	20	30	34	106
51–100	8	20	20	26	74
Total	52	64	60	77	253

Kendall's Tau C = 0.16873   Significance = 0.0015

Exhibit D–19
Management control index for administrative services versus sales revenue
(number of respondents)

Management control index	Sales revenue (in $ millions)*			
	$0–200	$200–600	$600 or more	Total
0	23	26	20	69
1–50	29	30	37	96
51–100	17	11	41	69
Total	69	67	98	234

Kendall's Tau $C = 0.15061$ Significance $= 0.0063$

Scattergram statistics for sales revenue versus management control index for administrative services (no cutpoints):
$R^2 = 0.01913$ Significance $= 0.01722$

* The categories for sales revenue are condensed here to simplify the display.

Exhibit D–20
Management control index for administrative services versus management control index for research and development (number of respondents)

Management control index for administrative services	Management control index for research and development			
	0	50	100	Total
0	12	10	4	26
1–50	14	21	13	48
51–100	1	11	11	23
Total	27	42	28	97

Kendall's Tau C $= 0.29844$ Significance $= 0.0003$

Exhibit D-21
Assignment of corporate interest expense and/or a capital charge to profit centers (288 respondents)

Interest and/or capital charge assigned	Number of respondents	Percent
Allocate actual corporate Interest	80	28%
Assign charge for capital invested in profit center	72	25
Both allocate interest and assign a capital charge	26	9
Do not charge profit centers for interest or capital employed	110	38
Total	288	100%

Exhibit D-22
Basis for assigning corporate interest expense (105 respondents*)

Basis for assignment	Number of respondents	Percent
Prorate on profit center sales	12	11%
Prorate on profit center profits	2	2
Prorate on percent of capital employed by profit center	70	67
Calculated using simulated capital structure for profit center†	19	18
Combination of above methods	2	2
Total	105	100%

* Number of respondents who charge for interest should be the total of 80 respondents who allocate interest and 26 respondents who both allocate interest and assign a charge in Exhibit D–21. There is one missing value.

† Breaking the total investment into debt and equity components and multiplying the debt component by an interest rate.

Exhibit D-23
Type of rate used for interest charge and/or charge for capital employed (number of respondents)

| Type of rate | For assignment of actual corporate interest | | | For assigning charge for use of capital employed in profit centers |
| | If debt split by maturity date | | If not split | |
	Short term	Long term	Total debt	
Historical average rate	1	5	2	11
Current corporate rate	15	12	19	23
Prime rate	4	1	5	7
Corporate cost of capital	1	1	13	17
Some other computed rate	3	6	13	40
Total respondents	24	25	52	98

Exhibit D-24
Assignment of income taxes

	Number	Percent
Respondents calculating taxes	129	44%
Respondents not calculating taxes	162	56
Total	291	100%

Methods used by respondents which calculate profit center taxes	Number	Percent
Actual calculation treating profit center as if separate corporation	57	45%
Proration of corporate taxes based on effective rate	46	37
Proration of corporate taxes based on nominal rate	23	18
Total	126*	100%

* Does not total 129 because there are three missing observations.

Exhibit D-25
Special taxes and investment tax credits

Special taxes	Number	Percent
Respondents including special taxes	85	66%
Respondents not including special taxes	44	34
Total	129	100%

Investment tax credits	Number	Percent
Respondents including investment tax credit	86	67%
Respondents not including investment tax credit	43	33
Total	129	100%

Exhibit D-26
Assignment of miscellaneous income

Method	Number of respondents	Percent
Do not assign	91	63%
Prorated on basis of profit center sales revenue	5	3
Prorated on basis of profit center operating cost (or some cost basis)	5	3
Prorated on basis of profit center profit	1	1
Prorated based on profit center assets	6	5
All miscellaneous income is directly identifiable with profit center and included in profit center measurement	32	22
Combination of above methods	5	3
Total	145	100%

Exhibit D–27

Allocation of corporate costs and income versus diversification strategy (percent of respondents in each category that allocate cost or income to profit centers)

Type of corporate cost or income	Diversification strategy					Total number of respondents
	Single business	Dominant business	Related businesses	Unrelated businesses	All respondents	
Interest expenses and/or capital charges	56%	61%	55%	71%	62%	288
Income taxes	29	44	49	52	44	291
Miscellaneous income	27	40	39	39	37	145

Summary measures of functional authority and financial responsibility*

---

* This Section was prepared by Richard G. Linowes and Srinivasan Umapathy.

SUMMARY

Section E develops and explores some summary measures of profit center structural characteristics. The summary measures are constructed using the data and analyses presented in Sections B, C, and D because transfers between profit centers (discussed in Section B), corporate-level operating functions (discussed in Section C), and corporate-level administrative services (discussed in Section D) all play an important role in the relation between a "typical" profit center and other parts of a company.

The first summary measure is the functional authority index, which indicates the extent to which a profit center is self-sufficient in providing the goods and services required for its operations. The index, in other words, tells what percent of all costs expended on a profit center's behalf actually are incurred within the profit center. The relations between this index and the demographic variables are explored.

The second summary measure is the financial responsibility index, which indicates the extent to which a profit center is charged for all the goods and services it utilizes in its operations. This index tells what percent of all costs expended on a profit center's behalf actually show up in the profit center's income statement. The relations between this index and the demographic variables also are investigated.

Finally, the third summary measure is the management control index. This measure attempts to depict the degree of control that a profit center manager has over all the costs assigned to him from other operating units in the firms.

FUNCTIONAL AUTHORITY INDEX

Sections C and D discussed functional authority with respect to specific functions, such as research and development. In this section, we combine those data to develop an overall functional authority index. It is basically the numerical average of the five functional authority indices that we previously considered separately.

Before proceeding further, though, we turn to Exhibit E−1 to see the data pertaining to a hypothetical company. Throughout this section we shall use these data to illustrate the calculation of the summary measures, and in this section we use it to describe the calculation of the functional authority index, in particular. The second column of numbers lists the functional authority indices for the five functions of selling, distribution, manufacturing, R&D, and administrative services. We remember that each of the numbers represents the percent of all function-related costs expended on behalf of the profit center that are incurred within the profit center itself. The overall functional authority index for the sample company is simply the mean of these five values, shown at the bottom of column two.

Formally, the *functional authority index* of a company is the mean extent to which functions are performed at the typical profit center. It is the (unweighted) average of the five functional authority indices developed for the five operating functions. Note that whereas a weighted average of the five indices, reflecting the relative importance of the functions in the eyes of a typical profit center manager, would make a more desirable overall index, information required for computing such a measure was not collected in the survey.

Exhibit E−2 displays how the summary functional authority index varies for the companies in our sample. The results appear graphically in Exhibit E−3. Our overall measure clearly demonstrates that the companies surveyed differ greatly in the extent to which their profit centers have physical custody of the functional resources required for their operations. On average, a typical profit center is self-contained to the extent of having functional authority for 70 percent of such resources. (One should exercise caution in interpreting this statement because the index is a "blind" average; no weights enter into the calculation and, hence, functions that are relatively unimportant for the business influence the final outcome as much as important functions.) Returning to Exhibit E−1, we find a functional authority index of 66 percent in our sample company.

DEMOGRAPHIC ANALYSIS OF THE FUNCTIONAL AUTHORITY INDEX

In this section we examine the relationships between the functional authority index and the seven demographic variables introduced in Section A. On the whole, cross-tabulations show very few significant correlations. Exhibit E−4 summarizes the results of the analysis.

A significant relationship exists between the functional authority index and diversification strategy. As seen in Exhibit E−5, highly diversified firms are likely to have very high functional authority indices. Profit centers in these firms are relatively independent of other operating units in the firm. In less diversified firms, however, a larger portion of all functions are performed centrally and interdivisional transfers are greater, so profit centers have less functional authority over the resources they require. This result merely states for all functions at once a relation that we saw in earlier sections for each function separately.

The functional authority index also has negative relationships with all financial performance measures appearing in this study. Though the results are not highly significant, Exhibit E−4 suggests that extensive decentralization of all functions is not an earmark of financial success for the companies in our survey. Lest we interpret this pattern too broadly, however, it is instructive to review Exhibits C−11 and D−5 displaying widely varying results for each of the measures of extent of corporate functions—largely the complements of the component functional authority indices. These exhibits reveal that functional authority indices have both positive and negative relationships with financial performance variables. An overall functional authority index may be negatively related to successful performance (suggested by Exhibit E−4), but arguments built on this (not highly significant) result might be fallacious since functional authority indices for individual functions do not show the same pattern.

Only diversification strategy then is significantly correlated with the functional authority index. This relation illustrates how a company's strategy of diversification is connected with the independence of its profit centers. Other company demographic measures, and in particular the company financial performance measures, have no highly significant relations with the functional authority index based on the data in the study. These results diminish the hope that there is some ideal extent of profit center independence that ensures the financial success of a decentralized enterprise.

FINANCIAL RESPONSIBILITY INDEX

The next summary measure addresses the comprehensiveness of a typical profit center's income statement. Of all the costs incurred on a profit center's behalf, only some are actually charged to the profit center. The financial responsibility index measures the extent to which these costs are charged to it.

The financial responsibility index owes its name to its link with profit center income statements. Such an income statement high-lights all the costs for which a profit center manager is responsible, and these include (a) the cost of all functions performed at the profit center, and (b) the cost of all functions performed elsewhere in the company that provide goods and services required by the profit center and that are assigned to the profit center. Data collected in the study permit us to construct a picture of what charges reach the income statement of each company's typical profit center. We know the extent to which functions are performed at the profit center level. We also know whether or not costs of centralized operations are assigned to profit centers. By combining these several measures of each company as a whole, we obtain a measure that summarizes the financial responsibility of a company's typical profit center manager.

The financial responsibility index is defined separately from the functional authority index introduced above because the data suggest that profit center managers often are held responsible for operations over which they have no direct authority. That is, responsibility and authority do not exist in equal proportion.

In Exhibit E−1 we see how the financial responsibility index is calculated for our hypothetical company. Each function's total cost appears in the income statement as the sum of the local cost and the assigned cost. For the manufacturing, distribution, and sales func-tions, any costs incurred outside the profit center are always assigned to the profit centers; total costs reported in the income statement are 100 percent of the costs of those functions. For R&D, however, the situation is different in this example; half of the profit-center-related R&D costs are incurred at the corporate level and they are not as-signed to the profit centers. Corporate-level administrative costs, on the other hand, are assigned to the profit center in this example. The financial responsibility index is the average of the five total cost figures, and for this company its value is 90 percent.

Exhibit E−6 displays in summarized form the distribution of the financial responsibility index for the companies in the survey. The majority of firms charge *all* profit-center-related costs to the profit centers, while overall an average of 96 percent of the costs are charged. The example in Exhibit E−1 thus is below average for the companies in the study.

The financial responsibility index is a summary measure that esti-mates the extent to which a profit center is charged for all the goods and services it utilizes in its operations. The survey revealed that most firms charge nearly all appropriate costs to their profit centers. Since the distribution of the financial responsibility index differs so markedly from the distribution of the functional authority index, we conclude that many profit center managers have responsibility for functions over which they have no direct authority.

DEMOGRAPHIC ANALYSIS OF THE FINANCIAL RESPONSIBILITY INDEX

The relationships between the financial responsibility index and the demographic variables are explored here. As we saw above, the financial responsibility index estimates how completely a profit center's income statement reports all profit-center-related costs. We saw that nearly all firms charge most of their profit-center-related costs to their profit centers, and thus all firms have very similar values for their financial responsibility indices. As a result, the financial responsibility index does not permit consequential distinctions between firms, so we do not expect to find revealing relationships between a company's financial responsibility index and its demographic data.

Exhibit E−7 distills the results of several cross-tabulations. We see that in most situations the financial responsibility index is not related to demographic variables. There is one exception to the rule; the index shows a significant correlation with company profit margins.

Let us first look closer at the relationship between this new index and diversification strategy. Throughout Part Two we have introduced measures and then examined how they vary across company diversity categories, and so we do the same here in Exhibit E−8. The table displays the positive correlation between the measure of financial responsibility and company diversity, and the distribution information at the bottom of the page summarizes concisely how average profit center financial responsibility is higher in the more diversified companies.

The statistically significant cross-tabulation of the financial responsibility index with company profit margins is displayed in Exhibit E−9. The statistics show a negative correlation, implying that with higher financial responsibility (more complete reporting of costs in the profit center income statement), there is lower corporate-wide profit margins. The gist of this analysis is questionable, however, since the bulk of the respondents have a financial responsibility index with a value of 100 percent, and nearly all others have values close to that. With so many observations clustered around so few values, the statistics for the cross-tabulation have limited meaning.

An interesting relationship appears in Exhibit E−10, and it is included here for its suggestive value. We find an increasing financial responsibility as the number of profit centers increases. Again, we may question inferences from the table since half of the respondents have the 100 percent value for the financial responsibility index. If we ignore this objection momentarily, though, the exhibit suggests that profit-center-related costs are more completely assigned to the profit centers in firms with multiple profit centers than in firms with few profit centers. This proposition is plausible, but it loses its power when we remember that only costs for corporate-level R&D and administrative services sometimes are not assigned to profit centers. Costs for all other corporate functions always are assigned. Thus, the relation does not say as much as it appears to say because the distribution of the financial responsibility index is lopsided and because the list of costs that sometimes are not assigned is limited.

Thus, the relations between the financial responsibility index and the demographic variables are few and somewhat spurious. The index is related statistically to company profit margins and to the number of profit centers, but for several reasons we refrain from making inferences from these reported correlations.

MANAGEMENT CONTROL INDEX

The third and final variable defined in this section measures the degree of control the profit center manager has over the assigned costs of centralized operations. The variable is called the management control index, and it is constructed from the management control indices previously introduced for the four operating functions and administrative services.

The new index is an overall measure of the realism of a company's cost assignment methods. We use it to portray how charges levied on a typical profit center approximate the market value of the goods and services provided to that profit center since market-like prices provide the proper setting for profit centers to act independently. Ultimately, we hope to employ the index to identify how cost assignment methods are related to other key organizational issues, such as the profit center manager's sense of independence. Section F addresses these more general issues, while in this section we describe the calculation of the management control index and its distribution over the companies in our study.

The management control index is a weighted average of the management control indices for the four operating functions plus administrative services. We recall that the management control index for each of these functions was defined in Sections C and D as a mapping that assigns values between 0 and 100 to each cost assignment method. The higher the value, the more accurate the cost assignment method, and hence the greater the profit center manager's control over the costs that are charged to him or her. The five indices are combined here into a weighted average. We weight each term by the fraction of costs that are assigned to the profit center from other parts of the company. That is, each function's management control index is weighted by a factor representing the magnitude of assigned costs for that function relative to all costs incurred for that function.

Turning to Exhibit E−1 again, we see the management control index calculated for the hypothetical company. The fourth column of numbers lists the management control indices for all of the functions that assign costs to the profit centers. The numbers reflect the kind of cost assignment methods that the company uses. They were determined based on the definitions of Sections C and D. We multiply each index by the assigned cost (that is, the fraction of all costs that are assigned, appearing in column three) to obtain the extension in column five. Summing the extensions in this column and dividing by the sum of the weights (sum of column three), we obtain the overall management control index—the weighted sum of the management control indices for all five functions.

The management control index is calculated for all companies in this manner. The result is the distribution presented in Exhibits E−11 and E−12. These exhibits show clearly that companies differ considerably in their methods for assigning costs.

The discussion of this section arms us with a third summary measure for companies. This measure is the first to summarize the methods for charging costs of corporate-level functions to profit centers. When we apply the measure to the survey data, we obtain a distribution with a large variation revealing that the accuracy of cost assignment methods varies widely from one company to the next.

DEMOGRAPHIC AND SITUATIONAL ANALYSIS OF THE MANAGEMENT CONTROL INDEX

The relationships between the demographic variables and the management control index are studied here as before by means of a thorough search for significant relationships using cross-tabulation techniques. The results are summarized in Exhibit E−13. A few noteworthy correlations do exist, and we discuss these below.

First of all, we find a weak but positive relationship between the management control index and diversification strategy. There is a slight tendency for more diversified firms to use more accurate cost assignment methods. This relation, shown in Exhibit E−14, is not unexpected. The Unrelated Businesses of a diversified firm focus on their different external markets and let the market determine the value of their transactions. To evaluate intracompany transactions on a similar basis, realistic or market-like cost assignment methods are used.

The second relationship we note is a strong positive correlation between the management control index and company sales revenue. Apparently, cost assignment methods are more accurate in firms with larger sales volume. The data appear in Exhibit E−15. The relation may follow from the presence of more elaborate accounting systems in larger firms. Systems that keep thorough records of all incurred costs make it easy to report costs very accurately. Yet, these sophisticated information systems are more likely to exist in larger firms. We conclude that the accurate cost assignment methods are common in large firms, possibly because accurate figures are available with no extra effort.

The management control index also is related to the sales of the typical profit center. This relationship is similar to the relation between the management control index and companywide sales revenues discussed above. Since this new relation does not shed any additional light on the various cost assignment methods used by firms in the study, we do not include the cross-tabulation table in the exhibits.

The relationships between the management control index and the other summary measures introduced in this section are also of interest to us. Further analysis reveals that the management control index and the functional authority index are positively correlated, but the relationship is not highly significant. The management control index and the financial responsibility index are significantly correlated—

negatively—but the value of this observation is limited, given the highly skewed distribution of the financial responsibility measure. These facts imply that we have no noteworthy results linking together functional authority, financial responsibility, and features of the cost assignment system applicable to companies at a cross-functional summary level. The net result is that the management control index is unable in its current form to play any significant role in explaining profit center interdependence.

Exhibit E–1
Calculation of summary measures using data of a hypothetical company

Function	Financial Responsibility Index (total costs; percent)	Functional Authority Index (local costs; percent)	Assigned costs (percent)	Management control index	Weighted management control index (MCI × assigned costs)
Selling	100	100	—	—	—
Distribution	100	50	50	1.00	50
Manufacturing	100	71	29	.33	9.6
Research and development	50	50	—	—	—
Administrative services	100	59.2	40.8	.725	29.6
Total	450	330.2	119.8		89.2
Overall indices	90 (Total ÷ 5)	66 (Total ÷ 5)		.745	(Total weighted MCI ÷ Total assigned)

Exhibit E–2
Functional authority index with cut points defined

Range of values for functional authority index	Number of respondents	Percent
0–53	49	21%
54–68	48	20
69–79	47	20
80–90	48	21
91–99	42	18
Total	234	100%

Mean = 70   Minimum = 15
Median = 73   Maximum = 99

Exhibit E–3
Cumulative frequency distribution of the functional authority index (cumulative percent of respondents versus functional authority index)

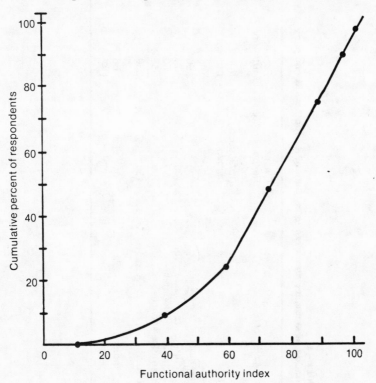

Exhibit E– 4
Correlation matrix of the seven demographic variables and the functional authority index

Demographic variable	Sign of Kendall's Tau	Significance at 1% level	Detailed exhibit
Diversification strategy	Positive	Yes	E–5
Sales revenue	Negative	No	
Profit margins	Negative	No	
EPS growth rate	Negative	No	
Return on investment	Negative	No	
Profit center sales	Negative	No	
Number of profit centers	Positive	No	

Exhibit E– 5
Functional authority index versus diversification strategy (number of respondents)

Functional authority index	Diversification strategy				
	Single business	Dominant business	Related businesses	Unrelated businesses	Total
0–51	17	12	12	3	44
52–67	9	17	6	8	40
68–78	10	13	7	17	47
79–89	7	13	18	17	55
90–100	2	11	9	26	48
Total	45	66	52	71	234

Kendall's Tau C = 0.30837   Significance = 0.0000

(distribution of functional authority index)

First quartile	44%	55%	59%	69%	58%
Mean	59	67	70	80	70
Median	62	67	78	84	73
Third quartile	75	83	85	94	87

Exhibit E – 6
Financial responsibility index with cut points defined

Range of values for financial responsibility index	Number of respondents	Percent
0–94	49	21%
95–97	32	14
98–99	27	11
100	126	54
Total	234	100%

Mean = 96   Minimum = 66
Median = 100   Maximum = 100

Exhibit E – 7
Correlation matrix of the seven demographic variables and the financial responsibility index

Demographic variable	Sign of Kendall's Tau	Significance at 1% level	Detailed exhibit
Diversification strategy	Positive	No	E–8
Sales revenue	Positive	No	
Profit margins	Negative	Yes	E–9
EPS growth rate	Positive	No	
Return on investment	Negative	No	
Profit center sales	Negative	No	
Number of profit centers	Positive	No	E–10

Exhibit E– 8
Financial responsibility index versus diversification strategy (number of respondents)

Financial responsibility index	Diversification strategy				
	Single business	Dominant business	Related businesses	Unrelated businesses	Total
0–94	12	17	8	12	49
95–97	5	8	11	8	32
98–99	3	6	7	11	27
100	25	35	26	40	126
Total	45	66	52	71	234

Kendall's Tau B = 0.04998   Significance = 0.2000

(distribution of financial responsibility index)

First quartile	94%	94%	96%	96%	95%
Mean	94	95	96	97	96
Median	100	100	99	100	100
Third quartile	100	100	100	100	100

Exhibit E– 9
Financial responsibility index versus profit margins (number of respondents)

Financial responsibility index	Profit margins (as a percent of sales)*			
	0–2.49%	2.5%–5.49%	5.5% and over	Total
0–94	7	20	17	44
95–97	6	10	14	30
98–99	6	11	5	22
100	39	43	35	117
Total	58	84	71	213

Kendall's Tau C = −0.12179   Significance = 0.0101

* The categories for profit margins are condensed here to simplify the display.

Exhibit E – 10
Financial responsibility index versus number of profit centers
(number of respondents)

Financial responsibility index	Number of profit centers*				
	5 or less	6 to 10	11 to 20	Over 20	Total
0–94	6	8	8	2	24
95–97	4	9	2	2	17
98–99	5	4	1	1	11
100	9	13	18	12	52
Total	24	34	29	17	104

Kendall's Tau C = 0.16321   Significance = 0.0187

* The categories for the number of profit centers are condensed here to simplify the display.

Exhibit E – 11
Management control index with cut points defined

Range of values for management control index	Number of respondents	Percent
0–32	47	19.7
33–47	51	21.3
48–59	48	20.1
60–72	47	19.7
72–100	46	19.2
Total	239	100.0

Mean = 53.13   Minimum = 0
Median = 53.00   Maximum = 100.00

Exhibit E– 12
Cumulative frequency distribution of the management control index

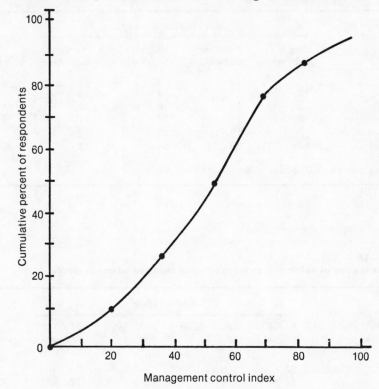

Exhibit E– 13
Correlation matrix of the seven demographic variables and the management control index

Demographic variable	Sign of Kendall's Tau	Significance at 1% level	Detailed exhibit
Diversification strategy	Positive	No	E–14
Sales revenue	Positive	Yes	E–15
Profit margins	Positive	No	
EPS growth rate	Negative	No	
Return on investment	Negative	No	
Profit center sales	Positive	No	
Number of profit centers	Negative	Yes	

Exhibit E–14
Management control index versus diversification strategy (number of respondents)

Management control index	Diversification strategy				
	Single business	Dominant business	Related businesses	Unrelated businesses	Total
0–32	15	10	9	12	46
33–47	14	13	9	15	51
48–59	6	10	14	18	48
60–72	9	14	13	11	47
73–100	4	16	9	17	46
Total	48	63	54	73	238

Kendall's Tau C = 0.09891   Significance = 0.0351

Exhibit E–15
Management control index versus sales revenue (number of respondents)

Management control index	Sales revenue*				
	$0–$199 million	$200–$399 million	$400–$999 million	$1 billion or more	Total
0–32	17	10	10	5	42
33–47	20	9	7	11	47
48–59	17	8	11	10	46
60–72	6	7	18	13	44
73–100	7	9	10	17	43
Total	67	43	56	56	222

Kendall's Tau C = 0.22903   Significance = 0.0000

* The categories for sales revenue are condensed here to simplify the display.

Perceived autonomy and fairness*

Contents	Page

Exhibits

---

* This Section was prepared by Judith Brown Kamm.

SUMMARY

This section describes the development and testing of the autonomy questionnaire. It also displays and analyzes the data that were collected. The questionnaire yielded four types of data: (1) degree of perceived autonomy (Section I); (2) length of relationship (Section II, question 21); (3) use of bonuses as incentives (Section II, question 22); and (4) perceived measurement system fairness (Section II, question 23).

The data analysis is presented in four parts in this section. The first part simply displays the data on perceived autonomy, length of relationship with the respondents' current superior, and bonus methods. The second part presents cross-tabulations of these data with the demographic data from participating companies, for those pairs of variables where we found a significant relationship. The third portion presents results from the same kind of analysis of the autonomy data and the data collected with the structural questionnaire as described in Sections B, C, D, and E. Finally, the last part presents the responses to the last question in the autonomy questionnaire about perceived fairness of the profit center measurement system.

DESIGN AND TESTING OF THE QUESTIONNAIRE

In decentralized companies, profit center managers must have a sense of their own autonomy for initiating actions in order to fulfill their responsibilities. Thus, in addition to gathering data about typical profit center managers' functional authority and financial responsibilities (reported in Sections C, D, and E), we sought to measure their perceived autonomy. Our aim was to determine whether or not autonomy is related to authority and how it is fostered by corporate management. Autonomy is a difficult concept to define and measure, however, so before we designed a questionnaire, we surveyed previous work that had been done on the subject.

In his study of diversification among large corporations, Leonard Wrigley examined the concept of autonomy and provided a conceptual approach that became instrumental in the design of our autonomy questionnaire.[1] He developed a model to explain why divisional autonomy varied directly with diversification. In the process Wrigley defined autonomy as "freedom of the divisions in respect of [*sic*] five

[1] Leonard Wrigley, *Divisional Autonomy and Diversification* (Boston: Graduate School of Business Administration, Harvard University, doctoral dissertation, 1970).

things: control over routine operations, authorship of its product strategy, freedom in supplies (seen as including research and development, engineering, marketing as well as tangible material inputs), the development of its own management, and the formulation of its own goals." (p. I–32) He assumed that autonomy and its five components are variables that can be measured.

Wrigley classified the five components into two groups, those which measure autonomy as a positive source of influence on the division itself (goal formulation and management development) and those which measure it in a negative sense as indications of the division's independence from corporate management (control over routine operations, product strategy, and supplies). For each variable he established a number of criteria for determining the degree of autonomy in a given division. For example, Wrigley stated, "Divisions have autonomy in product strategy if they are free to determine their own product line along each of four dimensions: (1) physical specification of the product, (2) prices, (3) production scheduling, and (4) markets and distribution channels. . . ." (p. IV–9) His research method was to gather enough data in the field from interviews and observations to apply these criteria and assign a degree of autonomy to each firm studied. Although Wrigley's methodology was not used in this study, his concept of autonomy in both its positive and negative senses and the criteria he applied helped us to formulate research questions.

Because we wanted to survey a large sample of profit center managers, we needed a questionnaire that could be mailed to them. Two questionnaire formats were examined in an attempt to find an already existing measurement instrument that would be suitable for our needs. One was obtained from a set of field interview schedules jointly developed by the business research divisions of three universities: Harvard Business School, the University of Western Ontario, and the University of Aston in Birmingham, England.[2] They are related to what is commonly referred to as the "Aston" questionnaire. Each schedule measures a different aspect of an organization. One set of questions is entitled "Authority." It measures a chief executive's authority to take action on a decision without waiting for confirmation from a higher organizational level such as the board of directors. Twenty-three

[2] Division of Research, Graduate School of Business Administration, Harvard University, Boston, Massachusetts, and Associates Workshop in Business Research, School of Business Administration, University of Western Ontario, London, Ontario, with the cooperation of Industrial Administration Research Unit, The University of Aston in Birmingham, *Interview Schedule of Selected Organization-Level Information* (obtainable from Chief Executive). (Third edition incorporating full technology data and selected structural configuration data.)

managerial decisions are presented, for example, "appointment of supervisory staff from outside the organization," setting the "price of the output," or establishing "buying procedures." The 23 questions fall into four categories: scope of the business, supply, operations, and personnel. These groups are similar to Wrigley's defined areas of autonomy.

Although the four types of decisions that ultimately appeared in our autonomy questionnaire are patterned after this set of questions, the actual interview schedule itself was not suitable for our purposes. Our assumption about decision making is different from that underlying the Aston questionnaire. We assume that a decision is not necessarily made by one and only one manager at a single point in time. Rather, we believe that there is a process of decision making that includes a number of people and extends over time. The Aston format seems to assume that decisions are made and acted upon by either the chief executive *or* by a higher-level person. Authority is either inside or outside of what they call "the organization circle." This instrument, as a result, measures decision-making authority and we wanted to measure the perceived degree of influence in the decision-making process.

The other questionnaire format that we investigated was created by Rensis Likert.[3] Entitled "Profile of Organizational Characteristics," its purpose is to measure attitudes, perceptions, and motivational forces in organizations. It contains 51 items, grouped into eight variables. Examples of variables are: "character of interaction-influence process," "character of decision-making process," and "character of control processes." Each item is weighted by respondents, using a four-point scale representing four types of management styles: exploitative-authoritative, benevolent-authoritative, consultative, and participative. The idea of using a scale to determine the amount of perceived influence a respondent has in the processes of the organization was useful to us. It ultimately led to our five-point scale ranging from "initiated by others" to "my decision." Likert's questionnaire format, however, was too long. We felt it would require more time than profit center managers would be willing to spend on it.

Frank Heller used a series of research instruments to measure managerial decision making, one of which is similar to the questionnaire format that we ultimately adopted.[4] Called the "Specific Deci-

[3] Rensis Likert, *The Human Organization. Its Management and Value* (New York: McGraw-Hill, 1967), Appendix II, pp. 197–211.

[4] Frank A. Heller, *Managerial Decision Making* (London: Tavistock, 1971), pp. 51–54 and Appendix, p. 121.

sion Questionnaire," it asks managers at the corporate vice president or division president level to estimate on a five-point cumulative percentage scale how they make 12 types of decisions pertaining to their immediate subordinates. The five points on the scale extend from no delegation to consultation to delegation. Respondents use a percentage to express the frequency with which they use each method for making each of the 12 specific questions. Of the 12 decisions measured, a number of them were similar to what we eventually classified as "personnel decisions."

We were unaware of Heller's work, however, until after our questionnaire had been sent out and we had collected our data. In any event, his questionnaire's range of questions, though quite similar, is narrower than ours, and his emphasis is on division managers' relations to subordinates. We wanted to measure their relations to their superiors. Therefore a format tailored to our unique needs was clearly necessary. We began with questions about the amount of influence respondents have on the four types of decision making included in the Aston group's interview schedule: product/market, supply, operations, and personnel. In order to determine whether incentive systems and perceived autonomy are related, we also included questions about bonus practices. We believed, in addition, that the length of the profit center manager's relationship with his or her current supervisor might be related to perceived autonomy, so we asked for it in terms of months. Finally, we wanted to know whether or not these managers feel that the system measuring their performance is fair. Consequently, we included questions to gauge the nature and "perceived fairness" of their firm's measurement systems.

Testing the questionnaire

We field-tested the initial questionnaire with at least one profit center manager in several corporations that had participated in the structural study. We sat with the managers while they filled out the form, then asked them their opinion of its structure and design. After some modifications, the questionnaire was tested again. We received a total of 42 questionnaires from 17 participating companies. The managers' comments and questions about the format led us to further refine and shorten it.

The actual questionnaire finally used is in Appendix H. We sent three copies of it to the chief financial officers of the 291 corporations that had returned the structural questionnaire to us. We wanted to survey more than one profit center manager from each company in order to get data representative of the entire organization. We sent a total of 873 autonomy questionnaires. At the same time, a request for follow-up information on typical profit center size and corporate financial performance was mailed to the same financial executives. Of the 291 executives contacted, 117 answered this follow-up request. Of the 873 autonomy questionnaires sent, 317 were returned to us, resulting in a 36 percent response rate for individual participants. Of the 291 companies that were contacted, 124 responded, for a response rate of 43 percent. It is possible that many of the 174 financial executives who did not return the follow-up information also did not distribute the autonomy questionnaire to three profit center managers. If this speculation is true, then only 351 autonomy questionnaires may have been distributed, of which 317 were returned, resulting in a 90 percent response rate. Only 12 firms were represented by a single respondent, although some companies were represented by two profit center managers.

The cover letter transmitting the autonomy questionnaire, included in Appendix H, specifically asked financial executives to distribute them only to profit center managers who had been in their current positions for at least two years. We felt that experienced profit center managers would have had enough time to develop clearer perceptions of their influence on the actions of their divisions, as well as more trusting relationships with their superiors, than inexperienced managers would have.

DATA PROVIDED BY PROFIT CENTER MANAGERS

Perceived autonomy

The instructions for answering the first portion of the autonomy questionnaire are reproduced below. The labels for the points along the autonomy scale are included. Not all questionnaires presented the six options in this order, however, because we wanted to avoid bias in our sample due to the possible influence of the measurement instrument itself on respondents. Two versions of the questionnaire were sent out: Type A, in which the "initiated by others" option appeared first, and Type B, which is the form reproduced here. We sent each company three copies of the same type of forms. The type of form a company received depended upon its company code number, although form types were arbitrarily assigned to blocks of code numbers. Of the 124 firms whose profit center managers responded, ap-

proximately one half filled out Type A and one half filled out Type B
forms. We prepared the data for analysis, however, by recoding the
Type B forms so that all "my decision" responses were scored as five
and all "initiated by others" responses were scored as one.

INSTRUCTIONS FOR COMPLETING THE
AUTONOMY QUESTIONNAIRE

I. *Major Actions Affecting the Performance of Your Profit Center*

Listed below are actions which could have an impact on the
performance of your profit center. We are interested in the
extent of your influence in determining what action is taken.
Please read the six categories carefully. Then, for each action,
check the category which most closely describes the way that the
decision is "typically" determined.

MY INITIATIVE.   I identify an issue on which action appears
necessary, and proceed as follows:

1. MY DECISION.   I decide what action to take.

2. TWO-PERSON DECISION.   My superior and I discuss
    the issue and decide what action to take.

3. MULTI-PERSON DECISION.   My superior and I, and
    other operating or administrative managers who need
    to be involved, discuss the issue and decide what action
    to take.

4. CORPORATE DECISION.   The action to take is decided
    at the corporate level because it (1) requires a change in
    existing corporate policy, or (2) is the responsibility of a
    corporate-level department or committee.

INITIATED BY OTHERS.   The need for an action of this sort is
usually initiated by a higher level administrative department, but
I may be consulted before the decision is made.

NOT APPLICABLE.   Actions of this sort do not occur in this
business or do not affect the performance of my profit center.

	MY INITIATIVE				
MY DECI-SION	TWO-PERSON DECI-SION	MULTI-PERSON DECI-SION	COR-PORATE DECI-SION	INITI-ATED BY OTHERS	NOT APPLI-CABLE

We tested for bias by using the company code number as a variable to represent the type of questionnaire form that a respondent returned to us. A new dummy variable was created with values corresponding to either a Type A or Type B questionnaire. Then we cross-tabulated this variable with a sample of four questions taken from the first section of the questionnaire where the bias might exist: perceived autonomy to discontinue a product or product line; to buy from an outside vendor when the items could be supplied by another unit of the company; to increase the planned level of advertising and promotion expenditures; and to promote a lower-level manager in the profit center. The cross-tabulations revealed only one relationship that could be considered strong enough to raise a suspicion of bias, and that was the relationship between Type A questionnaires and the very first question, about autonomy to discontinue a major product or product line. The Kendall's Tau C was .14. We did not consider the bias to be serious enough to prohibit us from using data about the first question.

The first section of the questionnaire was subdivided into four categories, each related to a different type of decision: product/market, sourcing, operating, and personnel. Within each category, respondents were asked to scale five decisions according to the amount of influence they felt they had over them. The "my decision" option, scored with a five as previously mentioned, represented the highest degree of perceived autonomy. The "initiated by others," scored with a one, represented the lowest degree of perceived autonomy. Each respondent was asked to scale 20 decisions, but because we recognized that not all of them would be applicable to some profit center managers, we also offered a "not applicable" option. If checked, this response was coded as a missing value, as were responses in which more than one option was checked for a given question or no options were checked. Exhibit F−1 displays the means and medians of the responses to the first section of the questionnaire.

In Exhibit F−1 all the respondent data appear. They are also grouped and averaged over two samples: One sample is individual profit center managers, while the other consists of 112 corporations. In order to obtain data for the corporate sample, the two or three individuals' responses from each firm were averaged. These data were necessary to provide typical responses from each company, as well as to allow comparisons between the data from the autonomy and the structural questionnaires. The size of the individual respondents' sample differs among decisions because not all decisions were applicable to all respondents. Of the 124 firms that participated in our study, 112 appear in our corporation sample because more than one profit center manager responded, allowing us to calculate an average response.

Exhibit F−1 displays autonomy indices that summarize the data. There is one index for each of the four types of decisions we included in the questionnaire, and an overall index derived from these four subindices. We determined these indices by calculating an index for each profit center manager for each type of decision. The calculation consisted of averaging the scores given to each decision within a particular class, say the product/market decisions. If a respondent did not score three or more decisions in a group, the case was considered to be missing and an index was not calculated. As a result, when each of the four subindices for the entire sample were calculated, the denominator used to average the responses (the number of cases) differed among classes of decisions.

The "total perceived autonomy index" was calculated for each respondent by averaging all subindices. At this level of summarization there were no missing cases because all respondents found a majority of the four types of decisions applicable to their situation. Therefore in calculating the average for the entire sample, all 317 or 112 cases were used in the denominator. To create corporate data, all individual responses from each company were averaged, using the number of respondents from the firm as the denominator. Indices were calculated in the same manner as they were for individuals. The resulting corporate data are averages of averages.

Exhibit F−2 presents the distribution of the five autonomy indices for participating corporations. Product/market decisions show the second greatest dispersion across all companies in the sample, and 25 percent of the respondents scored these decisions with a three or less, indicating the least amount of perceived autonomy for all decisions. This finding is not surprising, however, given the highly strategic nature of many product/market decisions. The greatest amount of dispersion across the sample, as well as the greatest average degree of autonomy, is found in sourcing decisions. It is to be expected that profit center managers would have more influence over these decisions because they develop from tasks that are often unique to the profit centers themselves. Similarly, the third type of decision, called "other operating," shows high dispersion and high autonomy. Average perceived autonomy for personnel decisions, however, is lowest and varies least in our sample. Care must be exercised in interpreting this average for personnel decisions, though, because for most personnel decisions profit center managers have a high degree of influence. Only bonus awards and fringe benefit decisions are not likely to be strongly influenced by profit center managers; for promotion, hiring, and firing decisions they typically have a high degree of influence.

With a few exceptions, then, profit center managers initiate the decision-making process on the issues we included in our survey, and they most frequently make the decisions by themselves or in consultation with their superior.

Length of relationship

We asked respondents to specify the length of time during which they had been reporting to their current superiors because we wanted to test whether or not trust between profit center managers and their superiors could affect perceived autonomy. We assumed that a very rough measure of trust is the length of time during which they have worked together. At least it seemed that sufficient time to get to know one another would be a condition of developing a trusting relationship. We also wanted to identify cases in which the respondent's superior was new to his or her position. Exhibit F−3 displays the distribution of the responses we received.

Both individual responses and the average responses for each company appear in Exhibit F−3. The distribution of corporate responses was split into equal groups to facilitate cross-tabulation. Because of the averaging done to create the corporate data, decimals resulted. The data with decimals had to be transformed into integers, thus five equal brackets (scored from one to five) were created. The cut points evenly dividing the distribution are as follows: 20.50, 30.35, 41.10 and 61.50 months. Using the same cut points, the distribution of individual respondents was subdivided. The range of individual responses was from 1 to 300 months, with a median of 36 months.

We cross-tabulated the length of relationship with the total perceived autonomy index, as well as with the four subindices and with each of the 20 individual autonomy questions. We discovered no significant relationships. Professor John Gabarro has hypothesized, however, that trust is built up in stages during the first year or two of the superior-subordinate relationship.[5] One of the earliest stages is

---

[5] John J. Gabarro, "Stages in the Development of Working Relationships," unpublished working paper, Harvard Business School, 1976.

the development of expectations about performance roles, and the relationship itself. In his research findings, issues of autonomy and influence seem to surface at this early stage. With Professor Gabarro's work in mind, we divided our sample according to varying lengths of relationship and discovered that as the length of relationship became shorter, it became more closely related to total perceived autonomy (Exhibit F−6). The strongest relationship, with a Kendall's Tau of .15, occurred in the sample with a length of relationship of 12 months or less. This subsample consisted of 62 profit center managers, or 20 percent of the 314 usable responses. When the individual responses were averaged to produce corporate data, only 9 of the 112 companies had an average length of relationship of 12 months or less.

We reasoned that within the 20 percent subgroup of individual respondents, the longer the profit center managers spent in working with their bosses, the more trust developed and the more autonomy they perceived that they had. After a year or so the effect of time tended to diminish. Because of the relationship between the length of time during which profit center managers had worked with their superiors and total perceived autonomy for this subgroup of the sample, we concluded that we might be seeing the effects of intervening variables. To test for this possibility, when we cross-tabulated total perceived autonomy and the variables that measured incentive compensation practices, we did so for three samples: the entire sample, the sample from which the 20 percent of respondents having a length of relationship of 12 months or less had been dropped, and the sample of 62 managers having a short relationship with their superiors. The results of this test are discussed in the next section.

Incentive compensation practices

We included questions about incentive compensation in our study of managerial autonomy because we wanted to know whether or not this type of structural factor has an effect on perceived autonomy. We were also curious about the nature of bonuses themselves: how they are commonly allocated, how important is financial performance in allocating them, and how large they are.

As Exhibit F−4 indicates, almost 90 percent of the profit center managers responding to this questionnaire do receive an annual cash bonus. In over 80 percent of the usable responses, a formula exists for determining a total corporate bonus pool based on corporate financial performance. In addition, for 65 percent of the respondents the method of determining their individual bonus was another formula based at least partially on financial performance. Even if no formula was used for individual bonuses, financial performance was an important determinant. In fact, in only 3.9 percent of all cases did respondents perceive that financial performance was *not* important. The method of awarding bonuses was scaled from one to five to capture the importance of financial criteria.

Exhibit F−5, Part A, presents the amount of bonus received as a three-year average percentage of annual salary. The responses were divided into five equal groups to facilitate cross-tabulation in the same way that the length of relationship data were grouped. The cut points in the distribution are: 14.82 percent, 20.40 percent, 26.30 percent, and 38.00 percent. The same cut points were used to group individual responses. The range of individual bonuses was from 2 percent to 99 percent. (Two respondents reported an average bonus in excess of 99 percent, but we had only provided for a two-digit response in our computer file, so these respondents were scored as 99 percent.) The median individual bonus was close to 25 percent.

Part B of Exhibit F−5 presents the distribution of the composite variable called "bonus index." This index was created in order to combine the impact of financial performance (as scored in Part C of Exhibit F−4) with the size of the bonus. For each respondent the reported average bonus percent was multiplied by the bonus method score of from one to five. A sample calculation appears at the bottom of Exhibit F−5. The highest possible index score is 495, indicating a bonus equal to 99 percent of the annual salary over the past three years, determined solely by the profit center's financial performance. The lowest possible score is two, since the lowest bonus amount reported was 2 percent and the lowest score is one. The lowest actual index value reported was 7 and the highest was 495. The median value was 90. There are some important objections that could be raised over the use of this index since it attempts to combine into one measure several discernible features of the bonus system. For example, an index of 90 could mean either a 30 percent bonus with a score of 3 or a 45 percent bonus with a score of 2. For our data, though, the measure proved useful for distinguishing individuals according to key attributes of their recent bonuses.

The bonus index for corporations was derived by averaging the bonus method scores reported by the two or three respondents in each company, and then multiplying that average score by the average bonus amount received by those respondents. In other words, two averages were multiplied to determine the index for each corporation. In this way a truly "typical" index for each corporation was obtained. The corporate bonus index values were then ordered and divided into five equal groups, as had been done with length of relationship and bonus percentage data in order to facilitate crosstabulation. The cut points used are 53.70, 75.12, 97.00, and 138.00. These cut points were also used to group individual responses, as displayed in the exhibit.

Exhibit F−6 presents the Kendall's Tau statistic obtained by crosstabulating total perceived autonomy and each one of the incentive compensation variables. The exhibit displays the differences between the entire sample of individual profit center managers, a subsample from which "short-duration" managers had been dropped, and the subsample of "short-duration" managers. We believe that the differences between the first two samples are insignificant, meaning that the effect of short-duration respondents in the entire sample is too small to warrant dropping them from the rest of the analysis.

As Exhibit F−6 suggests, none of the incentive compensation measures was strongly related to perceived autonomy in our total sample of individual profit center managers. Of all the compensation variables, a variable telling whether or not the firm used bonuses as incentives and the bonus index showed the strongest relationships, with Kendall's Taus of .10 and .09, respectively. Exhibit F−7, Parts A and B, presents the contigency tables for these relationships. It could be that using bonuses is a form of signal to profit center managers of their autonomy. The connection between high autonomy companies and the explicit linkage between the bonus and financial performance suggests that the use of financial performance criteria may be particularly common in firms where top management is too removed from each profit center manager's business to judge him or her upon more specific criteria.

DEMOGRAPHIC ANALYSIS

Perceived autonomy and financial performance

Each of the seven demographic variables described in Section A was cross-tabulated with the perceived autonomy indices for 112 corporations. Except for two weak relationships between perceived autonomy for personnel decisions and profit margins and return on investment, there were no other relationships between perceived autonomy and financial performance. We did find, however, that the more autonomy that profit center managers perceived they had in making personnel decisions, the lower both profit margins and return on investment tended to be. The Kendall's Tau B statistics for these relationships were $-.146$ and $-.157$ respectively; both were significant at less than the 5 percent level. We are not sure what this relationship means.

Perceived autonomy and diversification strategy

Exhibit F–8 presents the cross-tabulation of total perceived autonomy and diversification strategy. As the exhibit indicates, the patterns of perceived autonomy are similar for single and dominant business firms. Related and unrelated business firms also have a similar pattern of responses. The Kendall's Tau statistic is .342 at close to the nil level of significance. It appears, then, that diversification strategy is strongly related to the perceived autonomy of profit center managers.

Exhibit F–9 displays the pattern of median values of perceived autonomy for each type of decision (product/market, etc.) across each type of diversification. Again, single and dominant business firms' responses were similar. The split between these two subgroups reflects the fact that single and dominant business companies tend to make more frequent use of a multiperson decision-making process while related and unrelated business firms generally rely on two-person decision making. If, in a highly diversified company, each profit center manager is equivalent to the president of a small- to medium-sized company, it follows that corporate management will not be able to intervene very much in the profit center managers' affairs due to time and expertise constraints. Therefore the profit center manager is highly influential in decisions made about his or her unit. In a single or dominant business firm, on the other hand, corporate management is likely to have gained experience in the business and to have the necessary knowledge to become more involved in the units' decision-making processes. As a result, the profit center manager perceives his or her degree of autonomy to be lower than what it might be in a conglomerate. The relationships between classes of decisions and diversification strategy are significant at less than the 1% level except for personnel decisions. These decisions tend to involve corporate management regardless of the firm's diversification strategy.

There were no significant relationships between the length of time during which profit center managers and their current superiors had been working together and any of the demographic variables.

Incentive compensation practices and diversification strategy

Whether or not a firm uses a bonus as an incentive for profit center managers is related to the firm's diversification strategy in our sample. Please see Exhibit F−10, Part A. Over 90 percent of the more diversified firms use bonuses, whereas single and dominant business firms make less use of this kind of incentive. In more diversified organizations there may be a greater need for bonuses to reinforce profit center managers' attention to corporate interests, as well as to those of his or her own unit. In less diversified firms, on the other hand, bonuses may not be as necessary because there may be more opportunity for interpersonal recognition by corporate management. Furthermore, some firms may attempt to maintain an "egalitarian" culture and so avoid the potentially large compensation differentials that bonuses can produce.

Exhibit F−10, Part B, presents the mean and median bonus amounts reported, classified by diversification strategy. It is apparent from the similarity of mean percentage figures across all diversification categories that the amount of bonus received has no relationship to diversification strategy.

The diversification strategy of a firm and the method it uses to calculate the amount of bonus awards are, however, related to each other. The Kendall's Tau C is .211, significant at less than the 5 percent level. Exhibit F−11 displays the contingency table of this relationship. It suggests that few single, dominant, or related business firms in our sample use a formula to determine the amount of bonus that profit center managers receive, but that more unrelated business firms do. Financial performance is a more important criterion in awarding bonuses in highly diversified companies than in single or dominant business firms. The reason for this finding may be that, in more highly diversified companies, corporate management is forced to rely upon gross, financial measures of performance because it lacks enough detailed knowledge to judge all of its businesses and their managers with more refined measures. Also, financial performance, expressed in the common denominator of dollars, permits comparative evaluation of different businesses' activities. Another possible reason for this relationship could be that there tends to be greater interdependency among profit center managers in less diversified companies. More resources may be shared and more goods may be transferred between profit centers. Such interdependency clouds responsibility for financial performance. Thus it might not be considered fair to use the financial performance of individual profit centers as a criterion for awarding bonuses.

Because the bonus index consists of both the amount of bonuses and the method of awarding them, it is reasonable that a relationship exists between the bonus index and diversification strategy. Exhibit F−10, Part C, presents the mean and median indices for each type of diversification strategy. The Kendall's Tau *C* is .158, significant at less than the 5 percent level.

Incentive compensation practices and financial performance

Whether or not companies use a formula to determine the total corporate bonus pool based on corporate financial performance is related to the sales revenue of the firms in our sample. A cross-tabulation of these variables produced a Kendall's Tau *C* of .157, significant at less than the 5 percent level. As sales revenue increases, the tendency to use a financial formula to allocate the total corporate bonus pool also increases. It may just be that increased complexity necessitates the use of formulas.

Whether or not a formula is used to determine the amount of *individual* profit center managers' bonuses in our sample of 112 companies is also related to sales revenue. Exhibit F−12 provides a contingency table displaying a relationship of −0.159. It appears that just because firms with high sales revenue tend to use a financially based formula to determine the size of their total corporate bonus pool does not mean that individual bonuses will be determined using a similar kind of formula in such firms. In fact, it seems that firms with the highest sales revenues tend to use formulas infrequently, whereas firms with the lowest sales revenues use them more frequently. Financial performance seems to be as important a criterion to firms with high sales revenue as it does to those firms with low sales revenue, however. Great reliance upon financial measures of performance is reasonable in firms that are trying to grow as well as in firms that have grown so large that such general criteria are necessary. Some of the firms with high sales in our sample are integrated, and as Exhibit F−11 suggests, these firms tend not to use formulas. Diversification strategy may be interacting with sales to produce this effect.

The average size of the bonuses that corporations awarded to profit center managers appears to be weakly related to return on investment. The Kendall's Tau *B* was .143, significant at the 5 percent level. If return on investment is a common criterion used by companies that do award bonuses based on financial performance, then this finding is not surprising.

SITUATIONAL ANALYSIS

One of the major reasons for gathering data on profit center managers' autonomy was to learn if it is significantly affected by their companies' structuring of the authority over physical resources and their accounting for the responsibility for utilizing those resources. In addition to constructing summary measures of functional authority as described in Chapter 3 and of financial responsibility as described in Chapter 5, and cross-tabulating these with our summary measure of perceived autonomy, we also looked for relationships between the components of these indices. We wanted to know for which specific decisions did functional authority, financial responsibility, and control affect perceived autonomy.

We did not select the types of decisions we included in the autonomy questionnaire to match precisely with the types of functions and services included in the structural questionnaire, and this limited our ability to observe a large number of specific relationships. We did find that in general, however, decisions about sourcing materials and services were most frequently affected by functional authority and financial responsibility. In fact, the only decision that seemed to be affected by how corporate administrative service costs are assigned to profit centers, a measure of managers' control, was a sourcing matter: hiring a consultant for assistance in developing or modifying operating systems. A discussion of this relationship appears in Chapter 5. Many other specific decisions that we included, nonetheless, were affected by the functional authority structure or the financial responsibility structure.

Only perceived autonomy for the following decisions was unaffected: major capacity expansion investment; major new product line development; increase beyond the budgeted number of exempt and nonexempt personnel employed in the profit centers; and all of the decisions in the managerial personnel category (see Section H). Exhibit F−1 reveals that respondents had least autonomy for capacity expansion and new product line development decisions of all product/market decisions in our questionnaire. Within the managerial personnel decisions category, respondents had the least autonomy in setting bonuses and changing fringe benefits of all decisions in our questionnaire. It could be that decisions made primarily at the corporate level are unaffected by authority or responsibility indicators. There is little need to signal or to reinforce a sense of autonomy when in fact managers have restricted influence over these decisions.

The other five decisions unaffected by functional authority and financial responsibility are increasing the budgeted number of exempt and nonexempt personnel, and promoting, firing, and hiring managers. These decisions, however, do show fairly high autonomy scores in Exhibit F−1. Perhaps how extensively physical resources are shared within the corporation or who pays for them is not relevant to autonomy for such decisions in a particular profit center. If a job needs to be done and the best person must be obtained or kept to do it, the size of the personnel department or whether or not the corporate sales force is shared among several profit centers does not necessarily signal to profit center managers the extent of their autonomy to perform these tasks.

Perceived autonomy and functional authority

The summary measure of functional authority is related to the total perceived autonomy index, as discussed in Chapter 3. The greater the proportion of functional resources that are under the physical custody of profit center managers, the greater the autonomy perceived by those managers. Exhibit F−13 presents the contingency table for this relationship, which has a Kendall's Tau B of .301, significant at less than the 1 percent level.

As described in Section E, this summary measure of functional authority consists of five subindices for sales, distribution, manufacturing, research and development, and a composite of 12 administrative services. We examined these individual elements of functional authority, mapping them against the 20 decisions in the autonomy questionnaire, in order to identify specific relationships. Given the strong correlation between the total functional authority index and the total perceived autonomy index, we believed that many specific relationships existed. We wanted to identify those relationships to see if they made sense. Exhibit F−14 is a summary of our findings of the relationships that were significant at the .05 level or better. Each of the relationships shown in Exhibit F−14 are discussed briefly below, and contingency tables are presented for the relationships that are significant at the .01 level.

Functional authority for sales. We found relationships significant at less than the 5 percent level between perceived autonomy for discontinuing major existing products or product lines and functional authority for sales, and between autonomy for taking existing products into new marketing territories and functional authority for sales. The Kendall's Tau B's are .166 and .204, respectively. Perceived autonomy for changing the selling price on a major product or product line was also strongly related to functional authority with a Kendall's Tau B of .272. The contingency table for this relationship appears in Exhibit F—15. It appears that even though profit center managers typically perceive themselves to have less autonomy for product/market decisions than for, say, sourcing decisions, what autonomy they do sense is reinforced by the volume of domestic sales made by their own sales forces in relation to sales made by corporate-level sales forces. The higher the proportion of sales made by their own people, the more autonomy they feel they have to change selling prices, enter new markets, or discontinue products or product lines.

Perceived autonomy to change the policy governing the level of investment in inventories was also related to functional authority for sales. The Kendall's Tau B is .175, significant at less than the 5 percent level. In companies for which prompt and reliable delivery is key to making sales, inventory levels are critical. The sales function within the profit center may be held responsible for inventory levels. Hence it is reasonable that in companies where most sales are made by profit center sales forces, profit center managers would have more influence in policies on inventory levels.

Functional authority for R&D. We found a relationship between perceived autonomy to redesign products for a major existing product line and functional authority for research and development. The Kendall's Tau B was .165, significant at less than the 5 percent level. This relationship indicates that the more R&D that is performed in the profit center, as compared to the corporate R&D facility, the more autonomy the profit center manager feels he or she has to redesign a product. This relationship is a good example for how authority over resources can foster taking initiatives to use those resources.

Functional authority for manufacturing. Functional authority over manufacturing processes rather weakly affected profit center managers' perceived autonomy to buy from outside vendors when another unit in the corporation could supply the needed item. The Kendall's Tau B was .149, significant at less than the 5 percent level. A much stronger relationship existed between perceived autonomy to select the outside vendor to supply an important raw material or component used in operations and functional authority for manufacturing. The Kendall's Tau B was .260, significant at less than the .001 level. The contingency table for this relationship appears in Exhibit F−16. Again, it is reasonable that managers in whose profit centers a high proportion of their manufacturing activities are performed feel more autonomy in sourcing decisions. Sourcing of raw materials is directly related to manufacturing. Companies in our sample seem to believe that it is best done by people closest to that task, who know best what they need and how to get it most efficiently.

The same sourcing decisions were also significantly affected by the volume of goods transferred between profit centers in those cases where the transfer price included a profit for the seller. In such cases, autonomy for buying from an outside source when an internal source existed was negatively related to the extent of such intracompany transfers. The Kendall's Tau B was −.20, significant at less than the 5 percent level. Autonomy to select outside vendors to supply important raw materials or components was also significantly affected by the extent of transfers that included a profit for the seller. The Kendall's Tau B was −.23, significant at the 1 percent level. Exhibit F−17 displays the results of the latter cross-tabulation. Finally, autonomy to choose between internal or external vendors was related to the total dollar amount of goods transferred as a percentage of total goods produced and sold by the companies in our sample. The Kendall's Tau was −.15, significant at less than the 5 percent level. We also cross-tabulated the measures of goods transferred against autonomy to change inventory policies, but found no significant relationship.

We have found that profit center managers' perceived autonomy to initiate and make sourcing decisions decreases as the amount of manufacturing performed outside of his or her profit center increases. The location of the manufacturing function and dependence upon other profit centers for resources are strong indicators to profit center managers of how much autonomy they have in the decisions most closely related to manufacturing.

Functional authority for administrative services. Perceived autonomy to hire consultants, either to assist in developing or in modifying operating systems or to make special studies, is related to functional authority for administrative services. The Kendall's Tau B's are .225 and .170, respectively. The contingency table for the stronger relationship, significant at less than the 1 percent level appears in

Exhibit F—18. These relationships indicate that profit center managers whose own staff rather than corporate staff provide most of their administrative services feel that they can take more initiative in bringing consultants into their units to bolster the staff they currently have.

The functional authority index for administrative services is a composite of 12 services, listed under question 7 of the questionnaire in Section H and discussed in Section D. We cross-tabulated the cost of each of these services performed at the corporate level as a percentage of the total cost of domestic companywide services performed at all levels with perceived autonomy for each of the 20 decisions in the autonomy questionnaire. Because we were measuring the percentage of services *not* performed in the profit center, we found some significant negative relationships. In other words, the higher the percentage of a service such as purchasing that was performed by corporate staff, the less autonomy profit center managers perceived themselves to have in decisions involving such services.

We found that the more general marketing services that corporate headquarters provided, the less autonomy profit center managers felt they had in expanding into new marketing territories (Kendall's Tau $B = -.208$, significance $= .005$) and in product/market decisions in general (Kendall's Tau $B = -.228$, significance $= .002$). Exhibit F—19 displays the cross-tabulations of these relationships. The more market *research* services performed by corporate staff, the less influence profit center managers felt they had in decisions to enter new markets. The Kendall's Tau B was $-.146$, significant at less than the 5 percent level. Autonomy to hire a consultant for special studies such as market research was also negatively related to the proportion of market research done by corporate as opposed to profit center staff. The Kendall's Tau B was $-.128$, significant at less than the 5 percent level.

The amount of market research performed by corporate staff negatively affected profit center managers' perceived autonomy to increase the planned level of expenditures for advertising and promotion (Kendall's Tau $B = .176$, significance $= .012$). Autonomy for this decision was also negatively affected by the amount of advertising services performed by corporate staff (Kendall's Tau $B = -.222$, significance $= .002$) and by the proportion of general marketing services performed at the corporate level (Kendall's Tau $B = -.268$, significance $= .000$). Exhibit F—20 provides contingency tables of the latter two relationships. Autonomy to change selling prices was also weakly related to the location of general marketing services. The Kendall's Tau B was $-.134$, significant at the 5 percent level. It appears that of all corporate administrative services provided to profit centers in our sample, those dealing with marketing most frequently affect perceived autonomy.

The extent of purchasing services provided by corporate headquarters had a particularly strong negative impact upon profit center managerial autonomy in decisions about sourcing of materials. Exhibit F−21 displays the results of cross-tabulating perceived autonomy to select outside vendors to supply raw materials with extent of corporate purchasing services (Kendall's Tau $B = -.280$, significance $= .000$) and perceived autonomy to select a vendor to supply major components for an approved capital expenditure project with extent of corporate purchasing services (Kendall's Tau $B = -.380$, significance $= .000$). The location of purchasing services seems to be an especially clear signal to profit center managers about how much influence they have in making purchasing decisions.

The extent of operations research services provided by corporate headquarters was related to profit center managers' perceived autonomy to hire consultants to help develop or modify such operating systems as production scheduling or accounting. The Kendall's Tau B was $-.177$, significant at the 1 percent level. Autonomy for this decision was also affected by the extent to which finance and accounting services are provided at the corporate level. The Kendall's Tau B was $-.187$, significant at less than the 5 percent level.

Perceived autonomy and financial responsibility

As discussed in Chapter 5, profit center managers' financial responsibility for the five operating functions is significantly related to their total perceived autonomy. The higher the proportion of the total cost of these functions that is either incurred within the profit center or assigned to it (if incurred outside the profit center), the higher is the profit center managers' perceived autonomy. The contingency table for this relationship appears in Exhibit F−22. The Kendall's Tau B is .325, significant at less than the 1 percent level.

The inclusion of certain corporate administrative service costs in a profit center income statement indicates to profit center managers that they must use these services as effectively as possible in order to maximize their profits. The need to use services effectively encourages profit center managers to take initiatives and to use as much influence as possible to ensure that corporate services do benefit their profit center. In other words, profit center managers perceive that their autonomy is greater if they have to pay for the cost of corporate resources than if they do not have to pay for them. Of course, if they have functional authority for their own resources, their perceived autonomy is greatest. In addition to measuring the overall effects of financial responsibility on autonomy, however, we wanted to gauge how important being charged for the costs of specific administrative services performed outside of profit centers was to profit center managers' perceived autonomy to influence decisions related to these services. We wanted to see in more detail which services and decisions were causing the relationship between the two summary variables.

We found that if no corporate general marketing services exist, perceived autonomy for the decision to expand into new marketing territories is high. If corporate marketing services exist and profit center managers are charged for them, perceived autonomy for this decision is moderately high, and if profit centers are not charged, profit center managers tend to perceive low autonomy in this area. The Kendall's Tau C was .226, significant at the 1 percent level. In fact, the summary index for all product/market decisions was significantly related to whether profit centers are charged for general marketing services at the corporate level. The Kendall's Tau C was .278, significant at the 1 percent level. Both contingency tables appear in Exhibit F−23.

Perceived autonomy for the decision to change the selling price on a major product or product line was also significantly related to whether or not a corporate general marketing service is available and whether or not its cost is charged to profit centers. The Kendall's Tau C was .213, significant at less than the 1 percent level. Autonomy for increasing planned levels of advertising and promotion expenditure were related to whether corporate advertising services existed or were charged to profit centers. The Kendall's Tau C was .258, significant at less than the 5 percent level.

Perceived autonomy for various kinds of marketing decisions, then, in general seems to be particularly sensitive to whether or not profit center managers are charged for corporate marketing-related services. Product/market decisions individually and as a group in our survey tended to permit less initiative and influence to profit center managers than did all other types of decisions. But when they must pay for services related to these decisions, profit center managers are

signalled that they need to take the initiative and interact with peers
and superiors outside of their profit centers.

Whether or not profit centers are charged for corporate purchasing services is related to perceived autonomy for selecting vendors to
supply major components for an approved capital expenditure project. The Kendall's Tau C was .230, significant at less than the 1 percent level. Autonomy for decisions to bring in outside consultants to
develop or modify operating systems is also related to whether or not
corporate operations research service expenses are charged to profit
centers. The Kendall's Tau C was .222, significant at less than the 1
percent level. And, autonomy for this same decision is also affected by
whether or not corporate electronic data processing services exist and
are charged to profit centers. The Kendall's Tau C was .212, significant
at less than the 1 percent level. In general, perceived autonomy for
sourcing decisions also seems to be sensitive to whether or not profit
center managers have financial responsibility for corporate administrative services.

Of all the decisions and corporate services that are cross-tabulated,
only autonomy for product/market and sourcing decisions were related to financial responsibility. Autonomy for personnel decisions
was unaffected by assigning the costs of a corporate personnel
department. It may be that the same reasoning applies here as it did
in our previous discussion of the impact of functional authority on
personnel decisions. How costs are accounted for is irrelevant to getting and keeping the best people to perform critical tasks. Other
factors, such as the corporate policy-making process, climate and
managerial style, not captured in our study, may be more relevant to
personnel decisions.

Perceived autonomy and control of corporate assigned costs

In addition to examining the effect of financial responsibility on
perceived autonomy for specific decisions, we also examined the
methods used to charge profit centers for these services. We interpreted the methods used as indicators of profit center managers'
control over the expenses charged to them. A manager has least control over assigned costs when they are prorated on the basis of profit
center sales, costs, profits or assets. Managers have more control
when charges are based on estimated usage or negotiation. They have
most control when expenses are assigned as a function of services

actually used. We believed that the amount of control over expenses that a profit center manager had could affect his or her perceived autonomy, and we cross-tabulated our measure of the method used to assign corporate costs against perceived autonomy for a number of decisions. We found one significant relationship. The method of charging for EDP services affects perceived autonomy for bringing in outside consultants to develop or modify operating systems. The Kendall's Tau B is .34, significant at less than the 1 percent level. The contingency table for this relationship appears in Exhibit F−24. A discussion of the implications of this relationship appears in Chapter 5. In general we believe that it does support our hypothesis that the method used to assign costs to profit centers does affect profit center managers' perception of their influence in decisions involving the utilization of the underlying resources.

Incentive compensation practices

We have already seen (Exhibit F−7A) that there is a relationship between incentive compensation practices and the perceived autonomy of profit center managers. Further, we wanted to examine the relationship between incentive compensation practices and the two summary structural variables—functional authority and financial responsibility—that we had calculated for each firm. In order to perform this analysis we used corporate bonus data, created by averaging individual bonus responses from each company. We found several significant relationships.

Whether or not corporations in our sample award annual bonuses is related to the functional authority index, with a Kendall's Tau C of .202, significant at less than the 1 percent level. The method of awarding bonuses is also related to functional authority. The Kendall's Tau B is .22, significant at less than the 1 percent level. This relationship suggests that the more functional authority profit center managers have the more likely that financial performance will be an important criterion for awarding bonuses. The contingency table for this relationship appears in Exhibit F−25. Finally, the bonus index was related to functional authority with a Kendall's Tau B of .186, significant at less than the 5 percent level. Our findings suggest that in our sample of corporations the functional authority structure and the reward system are consistent with each other.

The financial responsibility index (see Section E) is composed of both local costs (incurred within the profit center) and assigned costs (incurred elsewhere). Because local costs are measured by the functional authority index, it is natural to expect that bonus compensation practices would also be related to the financial responsibility index. We did find a significant relationship between whether bonuses are awarded and the financial responsibility index (Kendall's Tau C = .217, significance = .01). Although the size of the bonus awarded was not significantly related to functional authority, however, it *was* related to financial responsibility, with a Kendall's Tau B of .166, significant at less than the 5 percent level. This finding means that the more financial responsibility profit center managers tend to have, the higher the average bonus. It could be that larger bonuses are necessary to motivate profit center managers to take responsibility for more functions and services within their profit center, or conversely, the more responsibilities that they have the more bonus corporate management feels that they deserve.

The bonus method was related to financial responsibility, with a Kendall's Tau B of .251, significant at less than the 1 percent level. Because the bonus index consists of both the bonus percentage and the method used to award it, it is not surprising that the bonus index was also related to financial responsibility, with a Kendall's Tau B of .236, significant at less than the 1 percent level. Exhibit F−26 displays the contingency table for this relationship. Companies giving high levels of financial responsibility to their profit center managers also tend to award them large bonuses based at least partially upon financial performance. Many of the companies in our sample, then, tend to use a financial incentive system based on financial performance to reward the successful fulfillment of financial responsibilities.

We wanted to learn what the effect of both diversification strategy and financial responsibility is upon perceived autonomy in our sample of firms. Consequently, we cross-tabulated perceived autonomy and financial responsibility for each type of diversification strategy. As Exhibit F−27 suggests, we found that the relationship is strong and significant only in single and dominant business firms. This result may mean that in more diversified firms profit center managers expect to have a high ratio of financial responsibility, hence its measurable effect upon perceived autonomy is less than it is in less diversified companies. Other factors, such as managerial style or corporate culture, not measured by our instruments, may be more important in how a profit center manager perceives his or her autonomy in diversified firms. In single and dominant business firms, on the other hand, the degree to which profit center managers are financially responsible for functional operating costs is a major signal from corporate headquarters about how autonomous they are. Perhaps such signals are needed to foster initiative—one of the purposes of profit centers—against what may frequently be a background of centralized decision making.

PERCEIVED FAIRNESS OF THE PROFIT CENTER MEASUREMENT SYSTEM

The last question in the autonomy questionnaire read as follows: "Do you believe that profit, as it is routinely calculated for your profit center, fairly reflects the effectiveness of your performance as a manager, to the extent that such performance can be measured in financial terms?" Three response options were offered: "Yes, it is a fair measurement of my performance," "A few imperfections, but still a useful measurement," and "Serious flaws. I don't think it is a fair measurement." The distribution of responses is in Exhibit F—28, Part A. This exhibit suggests that the first and second categories received a total of 90.4 percent of the responses. In general, most profit center managers in our sample believe that their measurement systems are useful, if not completely fair.

Nonetheless, we asked respondents in the second as well as the third categories of response to comment on the most important imperfections and flaws that they perceived in their measurement systems. Many respondents with unfavorable opinions about profit as a measure of managerial performance, however, interpreted the question to mean that it applied to profit measurement *in general,* and not to the particular profit center measurement system used in their company. We were looking for opinions about the profit center measurement system itself. That there was misinterpretation among respondents was signaled by the following comment made by one profit center manager:

> I assume the underlined clause [to the extent that such performance can be measured in financial terms] is intended to confirm that in some cases or to some degree managerial performance does not come out on the bottom line—e.g., in times of recession or strong markets, and that the thrust of the question is whether our divisional profit calculations are as fair and representative as they can inherently be—I think they are.

Consequently, a number of the comments in the second and third categories of response seem to represent discomfort with the inherent limitations of profit as a performance measure.

For example, profit reflects environmental conditions, such as a recession, over which managers have no control. Also, a profit figure that measures only one year's performance does not adequately indicate the state of the company's long-term health. Our question tried to avoid eliciting comments on such inadequacies of profit as a performance measure by adding the conditional phrase "to the extent that such performance can be measured in financial terms." We felt that little could be done to remedy these inadequacies. We were unsuccessful in avoiding comments on the inherent problems with using profit as a measure, however, so we decided not to search for relationships between these data and other data such as perceived autonomy or incentive compensation practices.

We did, however, investigate the nature of all comments to determine which ones provided usable data. We classified the 178 comments from 148 managers into four major categories, as follows:

1. *Incomplete measure.* Managers commented that current profit neither completely measures the health of the business nor reflects the short- versus long-term trade-offs necessary to maintain that health. For example, one respondent wrote: "Current profitability is always influenced by current investments in capital equipment and R&D for future profits, therefore current performance does not necessarily reflect the long-term contributions or abilities of the manager."

2. *Environmental conditions.* Comments in this category reflected managers' inability to control environmental forces. One representative comment was, "Profit performance reflects managerial performance fairly to the extent that the supervisor considers noncontrollable factors such as: market fluctuations, extraordinary material or service cost increases, acts of God, high start-up costs for a new product or cost center, labor unrest not attributable to poor management, and supplier problems outside the control of management. If the profit center performance compares favorably with competitor performance during a business downturn, management should be given high marks despite a profit drop-off below plan."

3. *Structural interdependencies.* In this category, which contains the type of comments we had intended to elicit, respondents indicated that their performance measurement system was flawed because it did not consider uncontrollable forces within the corporation. For instance, a respondent noted, "Sales volume, the responsibility of the sales manager, is the single, strongest factor on our plant operating profit. Lack of sales or frequent inconsis-

tency directly causes percentages of most plant accounting line items to appear (and be) unsatisfactory in spite of local operating performance 'truths'."

4. *Measurement system design.*   The original survey question also attempted to elicit this type of remark. For instance, one manager said, "Corporate allocations can be made somewhat unilaterally. This area needs better feedback measurement systems and work must be done on establishing fair projected charges for a coming (budget) year."

One other category of comments was about the fairness of the reward system in relation to the performance measurement system. One respondent wrote, for example: "The one very serious flaw is that too high a percentage of the bonus is based on total earnings of the corporation. My division has exceeded its profit plan in the past with zero bonus because it was the only division in the corporation that made a plan. . . . This has a decided negative impact on our key people." We did not pursue comments of this sort, however, because we had not intended to elicit them.

Analysis of comments

Part B of Exhibit F−28 indicates that measurement system design and structural interdependency comments made up 34 percent of the total number of remarks we received. Exhibits F−29 and F−30 contain representative samples of comments made about each of these two kinds of measurement systems inadequacy. We also cross-tabulated the subjects of the comments made by whether the measurement system was considered to be imperfect but useful or seriously flawed. The contingency table appears in Exhibit F−31. It seems that a slightly higher percentage of the authors of comments on structural interdependency perceived their measurement system to be seriously flawed than did the authors of other types of comments. It may be that when managers feel that they are held responsible for and are measured by financial performance over which they do not have control, they become uncomfortable enough to see the measurement system as seriously flawed. Conditions of high interdependency in a firm may be said to reduce the appropriateness of using profitability as the major measure of managerial performance. For 80 percent of our sample that commented, however, respondents did find their performance measurement system to be useful, if not perfect. And of all the types of comments made, more than 65 percent were addressed to problems *other* than structural interdependencies and measurement system design problems.

Because the 34 percent subsample of comments that did address these issues represented the data we had originally hoped to obtain, we decided to use it to determine whether any relationships existed between them and such variables as total perceived autonomy, the functional authority index, the financial responsibility index, and diversification strategy. We believed that structural interdependencies and measurement system design imperfections could be caused by poor "fit" between their authority and responsibility, on the one hand, and their perceived autonomy on the other. We also wanted to learn if there was any relationship between the incidence of such problems and the diversification strategy of a firm. In order to look for relationships between perceived autonomy and structural interdependencies or system design problems, we used our sample of individual profit center managers. In order to look for the other relationships, however, we needed to identify each comment with the company about which it was made. Therefore we regrouped them according to company identification number.

We expressed structural interdependency comments with a dummy variable. A value of one represented the incidence of such a comment. We also used a dummy variable in the same way to represent measurement system design comments. A third dummy variable represented the incidence of either or both kinds of comments made by the same respondent. By using these dummy variables we were able to avoid having to create a new data file with a subsample of respondents who made these types of comments.

Our expectation that interdependency complaints and perceived autonomy would be related was confirmed. The more influence in decision making that profit center managers felt they had, the less likely they were to complain about structural interdependencies. When the incidence of this kind of comment was added to that of measurement system design flaws, the relationship between the combination of complaints and perceived autonomy was slightly strengthened. Measurement system design complaints by themselves, however, were not significantly related to perceived autonomy.

In addition, a weak relationship was found between both structural interdependency and measurement system design flaw comments and the length of time during which profit center managers and their superiors had been working together. The Kendall's Tau statistic was −.11, significant at the 5 percent level. This negative relationship suggests that the longer a respondent had worked with his or her current superior, the less likely was a comment on interdependency or measurement system design problems. It could be that *who* uses the profit measurement as well as how one is measured can make a difference in how fair the appraisal system appears to be. If a profit center manager trusts his or her superior there may be less likelihood that the measurement system will seem unfair.

Structural interdependency complaints were negatively related to the functional authority index. The Kendall's Tau C was −.184, significant at less than the 5 percent level. Both this kind of complaint and/or measurement system design flaw complaints were also negatively related to functional authority. The Kendall's Tau was −.22, significant at less than the 5 percent level. The more functional resources over which profit center managers have physical control, the less likely they are to feel that they are not being measured fairly due to faulty systems. Our functional authority index roughly measures the degree of structural interdependency, hence it is reasonable that comments about this condition and the index are related.

Profit center managers' responsibility for functions and services performed in their own profit center as a percentage of total functions and services for which they are responsible, as measured by the financial responsibility index, and their tendency to comment upon interdependency and measurement systems problems were related. The more financial responsibility profit center managers have in a corporation, the less likely they are to complain about structural interdependency. This finding confirms what we expected, given the relationship of functional authority and this type of comment. The finding also held when interdependency and measurement system design complaints were combined into a single variable and cross-tabulated with the financial responsibility index. Exhibit F−32 contains contingency tables of these relationships. Again, measurement system design comments alone were not significantly related to the financial responsibility index.

We did not find any relationship between the tendency to make structural interdependency and/or measurement system design complaints and diversification strategy. The other relationships that we found, however, lead us to conclude that the degree of perceived autonomy and the amount of authority and responsibility profit center managers have affects their perception of the fairness of their company's measurement systems. The measurement system, in turn, can be an important signal to profit center managers about how they should think about their position and role in the company. Measurement systems are generally intended to motivate and control behavior. Our findings suggest that one way in which they achieve this goal is by affecting managers' perceptions about their roles in their organizations.

Exhibit F– 1
Perceived autonomy of profit center managers

| | Degree of perceived autonomy (number of respondents) | | | | | | Summary statistics | | | |
| | Individual decision 5 | Two-person decision 4 | Multiperson decision 3 | Corporate decision 2 | Initiated by others 1 | Total number of applicable responses | Individual respondents | | 112 corporations | |
							Mean	Median	Mean	Median
A. Product/market decisions										
1. Discontinue a product	70	79	79	54	21	303	3.41	3.47	3.42	3.50
2. Redesign a product	165	26	71	14	17	293	4.05	4.61	4.06	4.30
3. Expand into new markets	177	35	39	27	27	305	4.01	4.64	3.96	4.31
4. Expand capacity	16	40	94	145	10	305	2.70	2.48	2.70	2.64
5. Develop new products	51	57	104	69	18	299	3.18	3.10	3.21	3.06
Autonomy index for group A						314	3.45	3.60	3.46	3.60
B. Sourcing materials and services										
6. Buy outside not inside	112	67	53	30	22	284	3.76	4.05	3.82	3.99
7. Select vendor-materials	189	25	42	13	35	304	4.05	4.70	4.05	4.38
8. Select vendor-equipment	164	25	52	23	41	305	3.81	4.57	3.85	4.03
9. Hire consultant-operations	121	87	51	28	19	306	3.86	4.13	3.81	4.01
10. Hire consultant-studies	140	67	49	32	20	308	3.89	4.29	3.88	4.04
Autonomy index for group B						315	3.87	4.02	3.87	3.98
C. Other operating decisions										
11. Increase advertising	132	71	37	32	30	302	3.81	4.23	3.85	4.03
12. Change selling price	169	59	44	22	18	312	4.09	4.58	4.09	4.38
13. Change inventory policy	84	86	71	54	14	309	3.56	3.68	3.57	3.66
14. Increase personnel-exempt	95	147	41	29	1	313	3.98	4.08	4.00	4.04
15. Increase personnel-nonexempt	170	87	31	20	3	311	4.29	4.59	4.31	4.53
Autonomy index for group C						315	3.95	4.02	3.96	4.07
D. Personnel decisions										
16. Promote a manager	236	57	16	5	1	315	4.66	4.83	4.67	4.93
17. Fire a manager	138	148	22	8	0	316	4.32	4.37	4.31	4.35
18. Hire new manager	121	141	41	9	0	312	4.20	4.25	4.19	4.30
19. Set bonuses	55	113	44	53	19	284	3.47	3.73	3.49	3.66
20. Change fringe benefits	3	12	26	189	82	312	1.93	1.89	1.94	1.96
Autonomy index for group D						317	3.72	3.80	3.72	3.79
Total perceived autonomy index						317	3.75	3.83	3.71	3.81

Exhibit F− 2
Perceived autonomy by type of decision (112 corporate respondents)

Type of decision	Median	First quartile	Third quartile
Product/market decisions	3.60	3.06	4.00
Sourcing decisions	3.98	3.40	4.53
Other operating decisions	4.07	3.53	4.46
Personnel decisions	3.79	3.53	3.93
All decisions	3.81	3.40	4.00

Exhibit F− 3
Length of relationship between profit center manager and his/her current superior

Number of months of relationship	Individual respondents		Corporate respondents	
	Number	Percent	Number	Percent
12 or less	62	19.7%	8	7.1%
13 to 24	59	18.8	24	21.4
25 to 36	69	22.0	24	21.4
37 to 48	30	9.6	20	17.9
49 to 72	48	15.3	18	16.1
73 or more	46	14.6	18	16.1
Totals	314	100.0%	112	100.0%
Minimum	1.0 month		3.0 months	
Median	35.5		35.8	
Mean	45.9		45.4	
Maximum	300.0		185.3	

Exhibit F– 4
Incentive compensation practices (reported by individual profit center managers)

A. Receive annual bonus	Number of respondents	Percent
Yes	285	89.9
No	32	10.1
Total	317	100.0

B. Corporate formula (for total bonus pool)		
Yes	242	80.7
No	58	19.3
Total	300	100.0

C. *Method of determining bonus award (recoded from original)*

Bonus method score	Importance of financial performance		
1	Not important	11	3.9
2	No formula—some importance	37	13.1
3	No formula—very important	50	17.7
4	Formula—partly on financial performance	100	35.5
5	Formula—solely on financial performance	84	29.8
	Total	282	100.0

Exhibit F- 5
Bonus awards and bonus performance index

		Individual respondents		*Corporate respondents*	
		Number	*Percent*	*Number*	*Percent*
A.	*Bonus percent of annual salary, three-year average*				
1.	Less than 14.8	48	17.9	19	19.8
2.	14.8 to 20.4	66	24.6	19	19.8
3.	20.4 to 26.3	48	17.9	20	20.8
4.	26.3 to 38.0	51	19.0	19	19.8
5.	38.0 or more	55	20.5	19	19.8
	Totals	268	100.0	96	100.0
	Minimum	2%			
	Median	24.8%		22.9%	
	Maximum	99%			
B.	*Bonus index (Bonus percent multiplied by bonus method score)*				
1.	Less than 53.7	68	26.4%	19	19.8%
2.	53.7 to 75.1	30	11.6	19	19.8
3.	75.1 to 97.0	35	13.6	20	20.8
4.	97.0 to 138.0	66	25.6	19	19.8
5.	138.0 or more	59	22.9	19	19.8
	Totals	258	100.0%	96	100.0%
	Median	90.3		87.5	

Sample calculation of bonus index:
An individual profit center manager received annual bonuses recently amounting to 20 percent of annual salary. The company does not use a formula for determining size of the bonus, but financial information is very important in such decisions.
Bonus index = (Bonus percent 20%) (Bonus method score 2) = 40

Exhibit F– 6
Total perceived autonomy versus incentive compensation practices as a function of length of working relationship (for individual profit center managers)

Relationship	Length of time profit center manager and superior have been working together (months)	Sample size	Kendall's Tau
Total perceived autonomy versus length of relationships	0–300	317	.083
	≥ 13	252	.093
	≤ 12	62	.150
Total perceived autonomy versus incentive (yes/no)	0–300	317	.104
	≥ 13	252	.104
	≤ 12	62	.064
Total perceived autonomy versus corporate bonus pool (yes/no)	0–300	300	.005
	≥ 13	240	.003
	≤ 12	59	.030
Total perceived autonomy versus bonus method	0–300	282	.050
	≥ 13	223	.005
	≤ 12	56	.201
Total perceived autonomy versus bonus percentage	0–300	272	.077
	≥ 13	215	.095
	≤ 12	51	.027
Total perceived autonomy versus bonus index	0–300	258	.094
	≥ 13	207	.084
	≤ 12	49	.124

Exhibit F– 7A
Total perceived autonomy versus bonus index (number of individuals)

Total perceived autonomy score	Bonus index score					Total
	1	2	3	4	5	
1	12	4	8	13	6	43
2	23	3	11	13	11	61
3	12	6	4	8	10	40
4	7	6	1	10	16	40
5	14	11	11	22	16	74
Total	68	30	35	66	59	258

Kendall's Tau B = 0.094   Significance = 0.03

Exhibit F– 7B
Total perceived autonomy versus use of incentives
(number of individuals)

Total perceived autonomy score	1 (yes)	0 (no)	Total
1	53	14	67
2	67	3	70
3	40	10	50
4	45	0	45
5	80	5	85
Total	285	32	317

Kendall's Tau C = 0.1039   Significance = 0.012

Exhibit F– 8
Total perceived autonomy versus diversification strategy (number of companies)

Perceived autonomy index	Diversification strategy				
	Single business	Dominant business	Related businesses	Unrelated businesses	Totals
Low	12	14	4	8	38
Medium	8	13	9	7	37
High	3	4	12	18	37
Totals	23	31	25	33	112

Kendall's Tau C = 0.342   Significance = 0.0000

Distribution of perceived autonomy index					
First quartile	3.10	3.20	3.70	3.70	3.40
Median	3.58	3.64	3.96	4.04	3.81
Third quartile	3.90	3.90	4.30	4.20	4.00

Exhibit F– 9
Perceived autonomy for types of decisions versus diversification strategy
(median index for corporations)

	Diversification strategy				
Type of decision	Single business n = 23	Dominant business n = 31	Related businesses n = 25	Unrelated businesses n = 33	Total n = 112
Product/market	3.25	3.25	3.83	3.71	3.60
Sourcing	3.39	3.92	4.26	4.32	3.98
Other operating	3.89	3.85	4.21	4.31	4.07
Personnel	3.72	3.60	3.86	3.86	3.79
Total perceived autonomy index	3.58	3.64	3.96	4.04	3.81

Statistics for cross-tabulation

Kendall's Tau C

Product/market	0.22 (0.003)
Sourcing	0.34 (0.000)
Other	0.22 (0.003)
Personnel	0.15 (0.034)
Total index	0.33 (0.000)

Exhibit F– 10
Bonus practices versus diversification strategy (numbers of companies)

	Diversification strategy				
	Single business	Dominant business	Related businesses	Unrelated businesses	Total
A. *Receive annual bonus*					
Number of respondents	23	31	25	33	112
Percent "yes"	65%	87%	92%	91%	85%
Kendall's Tau *C* = 0.183	Significance = 0.008				
B. *Bonus percent*					
Number of respondents	17	25	23	31	96
Mean percent	27%	27%	25%	27%	27%
Median percent	22%	21%	20%	25%	23%
First quartile	16	10	15	20	15
Third quartile	38	37	28	35	33
Kendall's Tau *C* = 0.074	Significance = 0.196				
C. *Bonus index*					
Number of respondents	17	25	23	31	96
Mean index	95	89	82	115	97
Median index	91	75	78	101	88
First quartile	55	33	58	69	62
Third quartile	100	106	104	155	122
Kendall's Tau *C* = 0.158	Significance = 0.033				

Exhibit F– 11
Method used to award bonuses versus diversification strategy (number of companies)

	Diversification strategy				
Bonus method	Single business	Dominant business	Related business	Unrelated business	Total
1. Financial performance not important	4	6	5	4	19
2. No formula—some importance to financial performance	3	9	6	2	20
3. No formula—financial performance very important	6	7	7	10	30
4. Formula based partly on financial performance	0	3	4	2	9
5. Formula based solely on financial performance	4	2	1	13	20
Total	17	27	23	31	98

Kendall's Tau C = 0.211   Significance = 0.006

Exhibit F– 12
Method used to award bonuses versus sales revenue (number of companies)

	1974 sales revenue (in millions)					
Bonus method	$0–200	$201–400	$401–600	$601–800	$801–1,000 (and more)	Total
1. Financial performance not important	2	3	5	2	7	19
2. No formula—some importance to financial performance	4	2	3	3	7	19
3. No formula—financial performance very important	10	2	5	2	10	29
4. Formula based partly on financial performance	2	0	3	1	2	8
5. Formula based solely on financial performance	5	6	4	1	3	19
Total	23	13	20	9	29	94

Kendall's Tau B = −0.159   Significance = 0.030

Exhibit F- 13
Total perceived autonomy versus functional authority (number of companies)

Total perceived autonomy index	Total functional authority index					Total
	1 (low)	2	3	4	5 (high)	
1 (low)	10	3	2	2	3	20
2	2	7	1	3	2	15
3	3	3	6	6	1	19
4	1	3	5	2	7	18
5 (high)	1	2	4	5	4	16
Total	17	18	18	18	17	88

Kendall's Tau B = 0.301   Significance = 0.000

Exhibit F- 14
Summary of specific relationships between individual elements of functional authority and perceived autonomy for individual decisions (decisions under each category are related to that category with significance of .05 or better)

Functional authority for sales
A1   Discontinue a product
A3   Expand into new markets
C12 Change selling price
C13 Change inventory policy

Functional authority for total administrative services
B9   Hire consultant—operations
B10 Hire consultant—studies

Functional authority for market research
A3   Expand into new markets
B10 Hire consultant—studies
C11 Increase advertising

Functional authority for purchasing
B7   Select vendor—materials
B8   Select vendor—equipment

Functional authority for finance and accounting
B9   Hire consultant—operations

Functional authority for R&D
A2   Redesign a product

Functional authority for manufacturing
B6   Buy outside not inside
B7   Select vendor—materials

Functional authority for general marketing services
A3   Expand into new markets
C11 Increase advertising
C12 Change selling price

Functional authority for advertising
C11 Increase advertising

Functional authority for operations research
B9   Hire consultant—operations

Exhibit F– 15
Perceived autonomy to change selling prices on major product or product line versus functional authority for sales (number of companies)

Perceived autonomy for decision C12	*Functional authority for sales*					
	Less than 15%	*15%*	*50%*	*85%*	*100%*	*Total*
1 (low)	6	3	2	2	10	23
2......................	0	2	2	2	16	22
3......................	0	2	2	2	13	19
4......................	0	0	0	1	11	12
5 (high)	0	2	3	1	26	32
Total	6	9	9	8	76	108

Kendall's Tau *B* = 0.272   Significance = 0.001

Exhibit F– 16
Perceived autonomy to select the outside vendor to supply an important raw material or component versus functional authority index for manufacturing (number of companies)

Perceived autonomy for decision B7	*Functional authority index for manufacturing*					
	1 (low)	*2*	*3*	*4*	*5 (high)*	*Total*
1 (low)	10	7	4	3	4	28
2	5	3	4	3	3	18
3	3	3	7	3	2	18
4	0	0	0	0	0	0
5 (high)	4	8	7	14	12	45
Total	22	21	22	23	21	109

Kendall's Tau *B* = 0.260   Significance = 0.001

Exhibit F– 17
Perceived autonomy to select the outside vendor to supply an important raw material or component versus extent of transferred goods including intracompany profit (number of companies)

Perceived autonomy for decision B7	Extent of transferred goods					
	1 (low)	2	3	4	5 (high)	Total
1 (low)	0	2	2	2	5	11
2	2	2	3	2	3	12
3	4	1	2	4	0	11
4	0	0	0	0	0	0
5 (high)	9	7	8	4	5	33
Total	15	12	15	12	13	67

Kendall's Tau $B = -0.231$ Significance $= 0.012$

Exhibit F– 18
Perceived autonomy to hire a consultant to assist in developing or modifying operating systems versus functional authority index for administrative services (number of companies)

Perceived autonomy for decision B9	Total functional authority index for administrative services					
	1 (low)	2	3	4	5 (high)	Total
1 (low)	7	5	5	2	2	21
2	5	4	4	6	2	21
3	3	4	5	4	4	20
4	3	5	6	7	9	30
5 (high)	1	4	3	5	4	17
Total	19	22	23	24	21	109

Kendall's Tau $B = 0.225$ Significance $= 0.002$

Exhibit F– 19

A. Perceived autonomy to expand into new marketing territories for existing products versus extent of corporate general marketing services (number of companies)

Perceived autonomy for decision A3	Extent of corporate general marketing services					Total
	None	1%–30%	30%–70%	70%–99%	All	
1 (low)	7	5	2	5	5	24
2.....................	11	10	3	2	1	27
3.....................	5	5	2	3	1	16
4.....................	5	3	0	0	0	8
5 (high)	20	7	0	4	3	34
Total	48	30	7	14	10	109

Kendall's Tau $B = -0.208$ Significance $= 0.005$

B. Perceived autonomy for product/market decisions versus extent of corporate general marketing services (number of companies)

Perceived autonomy for type A decisions	Extent of corporate general marketing services					Total
	None	1%–30%	30%–70%	70%–99%	All	
1 (low)	7	6	3	3	3	22
2.....................	6	7	2	5	1	21
3.....................	9	9	0	3	3	24
4.....................	11	5	2	1	2	21
5 (high)	15	3	0	2	1	21
Total	48	30	7	14	10	109

Kendall's Tau $B = -0.228$ Significance $= 0.002$

Exhibit F– 20

A. Perceived autonomy to increase the planned level of advertising and promotion expenditures versus extent of corporate advertising services (number of companies)

Perceived autonomy for decision C11	Extent of corporate advertising services					Total
	None	1%–30%	30%–70%	70%–99%	All	
1 (low)	4	3	4	4	9	24
2	5	5	1	3	5	19
3	10	6	5	2	2	25
4	9	3	3	3	2	20
5 (high)	8	6	2	3	2	21
Total	36	23	15	15	20	109

Kendall's Tau $B = -0.222$ Significance $= 0.002$

B. Perceived autonomy to increase the planned level of advertising and promotion expenditures versus extent of corporate general marketing services (number of companies)

Perceived autonomy for decision C11	Extent of corporate general marketing services					Total
	None	1%–30%	30%–70%	70%–99%	All	
1 (low)	3	7	4	6	4	24
2	7	9	0	1	2	19
3	13	8	1	2	1	25
4	13	2	2	2	1	20
5 (high)	12	4	0	3	2	21
Total	48	30	7	14	10	109

Kendall's Tau $B = -0.268$ Significance $= 0.000$

Exhibit F- 21

A. Perceived autonomy to select the outside vendor to supply an important raw material or component versus extent of corporate purchasing services (number of companies)

Perceived autonomy for decision B7	Extent of corporate purchasing service					
	None	1–30%	30–70%	70–99%	All	Total
1 (low)	5	6	5	7	3	26
2	1	10	4	3	1	19
3	5	7	3	2	1	18
4	0	0	0	0	0	0
5 (high)	17	17	8	3	0	45
Total	28	40	20	15	5	108

Kendall's Tau $B = -0.280$ Significance $= 0.000$

B. Perceived autonomy to select the vendor to supply major components for an approved capital expenditure project versus extent of corporate purchasing services (number of companies)

Perceived autonomy for decision B8	Extent of corporate purchasing service					
	None	1–30%	30–70%	70–99%	All	Total
1 (low)	1	3	4	8	3	19
2	3	14	4	2	2	25
3	5	8	5	2	0	20
4	3	3	1	0	0	7
5 (high)	16	12	5	3	0	36
Total	28	40	19	15	5	107

Kendall's Tau $B = -0.380$ Significance $= 0.000$

Exhibit F- 22
Total perceived autonomy versus financial responsibility (number of companies)

Total perceived autonomy	Financial responsibility index					
	1 (low)	2	3	4	5 (high)	Total
1 (low)	11	1	3	3	2	20
2	2	6	3	3	1	15
3	3	6	5	1	4	19
4	1	2	3	5	7	18
5 (high)	1	2	4	5	4	16
Total	18	17	18	17	18	88

Kendall's Tau $B = 0.325$ Significance $= 0.000$

Exhibit F– 23

A. Perceived autonomy to expand into new marketing territories for existing products versus assignment of corporate general marketing costs (number of companies)

Perceived autonomy for decision A3	Corporate-level general marketing services			
	Not assigned	Assigned	All local	Total
1 (low)	9	9	6	24
2	3	14	10	27
3	1	10	5	16
4	2	3	4	9
5 (high)	4	12	19	35
Total	19	48	44	111

Kendall's Tau C = 0.226   Significance = 0.004

B. Perceived autonomy for all product/market decisions versus assignment of corporate general marketing costs (number of companies)

Perceived autonomy for type A decisions	Corporate-level general marketing services			
	Not assigned	Assigned	All local	Total
1 (low)	7	9	6	22
2	3	15	4	22
3	2	12	9	23
4	5	8	10	23
5 (high)	2	4	15	21
Total	19	48	44	111

Kendall's Tau C = 0.278   Significance = 0.001

Exhibit F– 24
Perceived autonomy to hire a consultant to assist in developing or modifying operating systems versus management control index for corporate EDP services (number of companies)

Perceived autonomy decision B9	Management control index for corporate EDP services			Total
	Prorated	Estimated usage	Actual usage	
1 (low)	7	4	6	17
2	6	3	3	12
3	2	5	7	14
4	1	6	14	21
5 (high)	2	3	8	13
Total	18	21	38	77

Kendall's Tau C = 0.295   Significance = 0.002

Exhibit F– 25
Method of awarding bonuses versus functional authority index (number of companies)

Bonus method	Functional authority index					Total
	1 (low)	2	3	4	5 (high)	
1. Financial performance not important	4	2	2	3	2	13
2. No formula—some importance to financial performance	5	4	1	1	2	13
3. No formula— financial performance very important	3	4	5	6	5	23
4. Formula based partly on financial performance	0	3	3	1	2	9
5. Formula based solely on financial performance	1	2	6	4	6	19
Total	13	15	17	15	17	77

Kendall's Tau B = 0.222   Significance = 0.008

Exhibit F– 26
Bonus index versus financial responsibility index (number of companies)

Bonus index	Financial responsibility index					Total
	1 (low)	2	3	4	5 (high)	
1 (low)	5	2	3	1	5	16
2	4	4	2	5	1	16
3	2	3	3	4	0	12
4	3	4	3	3	3	16
5 (high)	0	0	4	3	8	15
Total	14	13	15	16	17	75

Kendall's Tau B = 0.236   Significance = 0.006

Exhibit F– 27
Perceived autonomy versus financial responsibility index for each type of diversification strategy

Category	n	Perceived autonomy versus financial responsibility	
		Kendall's Tau C	Significance
Single business firms	16	0.542	0.005
Dominant business firms	24	0.306	0.04
Related business firms	20	0.244	0.09
Unrelated business firms	28	0.128	0.196

Exhibit F– 28
Perceived measurement fairness

A. *Distribution of responses*

Response	Number	Percent
A fair measure	131	42.0
Imperfect but useful	151	48.4
Flawed, not fair	30	9.6
Total	312	100.0

B. *Classification of comments on imperfections and flaws*

Category	Number	Percent All categories	Nonbonus categories
1. Incomplete measure	58	32.6	34.9
2. Uncontrollable environmental conditions	47	26.4	28.3
3. Structural interdependencies*	31	17.4	18.7
4. Measurement system design*	30	16.9	18.1
5. Bonus method inadequacies	12	6.7	—
Total	178	100.0	100.0

* Subsample used in analysis.

Exhibit F– 29
Comments on structural interdependencies perceived by profit center managers to cause imperfections in the measurement system

Division performance dependent to a degree on purchases by other divisions not under our control.

Sales, service, and distribution under control of another division. Dependent on them in large measure.

Required to use goods and services available from other divisions within the company.

Very limited control of material cost due to corporate level decisions primarily related to internal sourcing/transfer pricing/engineering standards.

No control of price or market decisions.

Minor control of methods due to capital investment guidelines and constraints.

Cannot measure effectiveness of managers working on interdivisional problems.

Sales volume, the responsibility of the sales manager, is the single, strongest factor on our plant operating profit. Lack of sales or frequent inconsistancy directly causes percentages of most plant accounting line items to appear (and be) unsatisfactory in spite of local operating performance "truths."

Dollar of margin, determined by sales division, frequently incompatible with profit requirements.

Profit highly impacted by other departments over which I have *NO direct* control, that is, purchasing/subcontracts, manufacturing, other corporate groups. It is also obviously impacted by burdening rates, such as overhead, G&A, material handling, and so forth. Again, I have *some,* but only a small amount of *direct* control over these.

Corporate decisions totally outside control of profit center management significantly affect profit. Far too much impact by corporate staff personnel, who do not have to take responsibility for decisions.

Current approach leads to "sandbagging" of goals and overemphasis on short-term profits.

Exhibit F– 30
Comments on measurement system designs flaws perceived by profit center managers

Corporate level expenses are assigned by some very arbitrary accounting decisions and the resulting values do not relate closely enough to "true" expenses for my profit center. In our corporation this does result in significant distortion of the "true" profits being produced by different profit centers. Improvements are being made and must be made so that proper motivation is produced and also that correct business judgments can be made.

We use an internal transfer price mechanism between raw material supplying units and conversion units. Adjusted quarterly, using as a basis the highest possible price that an outsider would pay for a small volume of raw material. This motivates careful and thoughtful use of raw material. Problem side is that competition pays less on a volume basis—hence our performance vs. competition appears to be poorer.

Since all accounting, credit, and computer functions are performed at the home office—our profit center is charged a percentage of the total cost and we don't get our money's worth.

Inter-divisional sales are at much lower margins than direct customer sales. As inter-divisional sales vary significantly from one year to the next, the *relevant* performance in "profit" terms can be very significant.

Divisions transfer products at cost to other divisions, thus have no sales credit or profit on products transferred. Many times the lowest cost plant facility does the transferring, thus the highest profit potential to the transferring division is lost and must be substituted by a higher cost plant facility to meet service requirements, thereby lowering the transferring division's profitability.

Current system utilized to determine interdepartmental transfer prices has no relationship to marketplace and is extremely crude.

The accounting system books large utility bills as expense when occurred but does not recognize as accrued income delayed recovery of utility costs above a certain base established in long-term contracts. Therefore, profits are seriously understated.

Exhibit F– 31
Type of comment made about the measurement system versus questionnaire response (number of respondents)

	Questionnaire response—measurement system perceived to be:		
Subject of comment	Imperfect but useful	Seriously flawed	Total
1. Incomplete measure	49 (.85%)	9 (.15%)	58 (100%)
2. Environmental conditions	40 (.85)	7 (.15)	47 (100)
3. Structural interdependencies	22 (.71)	9 (.29)	31 (100)
4. Measurement system design	25 (.83)	5 (.17)	30 (100)
5. Bonus method inadequacies	7 (.58)	5 (.42)	12 (100)
Total	143 (.80%)	35 (.20%)	178 (100%)

Exhibit F– 32

A. Incidence of structural interdependency comments versus financial responsibility index (number of companies)

Structural interdependency comment made	Financial responsibility index					Total
	1	2	3	4	5	
No	9	12	15	14	15	65
Yes	9	5	3	3	3	23
Total	18	17	18	17	18	88

Kendall's Tau $C = -0.253$ Significance $= 0.008$

B. Incidence of structural interdependency and/or measurement system design comments versus financial responsibility index (number of companies)

Structural interdependency and/or measurement system design comments made	Financial responsibility index					Total
	1	2	3	4	5	
No	5	10	11	11	14	51
Yes	13	7	7	6	4	37
Total	18	17	18	17	18	88

Kendall's Tau $C = -0.344$ Significance $= 0.002$

Section G

Profit center investment base measurement*

---

* This Section was prepared by Paul C. Browne.

SUMMARY

Throughout this volume we have used the term "profit center" to denote the decentralized organizational units of the large manufacturing corporations that have served as the object of our study. Sometimes a distinction is drawn between profit centers and investment centers, with the latter being a special case in which the unit's performance is measured in terms of its profit in relation to the investment required to generate that profit. While such a differentiation is not central to the underlying theme of this study, we did collect data during the survey about the measurement practices used to calculate the "investment base" for a "typical" profit center by the companies in our sample. Section G explores this aspect of the study.

The material and analysis presented is exploratory and tentative, with the aim of suggesting possible relationships of interest and lines of investigation for future studies. The practicing manager may wish to reflect upon the issues appearing here as an aid in thinking about his or her own organization's design of profit center measurement systems, but should recognize the preliminary nature of our inquiry and rely heavily on his or her own judgment in assessing their usefulness for a particular situation.

The section consists of three parts. The first presents the data as they were gathered through the questionnaire and then summarized. The second examines the relationships between these data and the demographic variables reported in Section A. The third part looks at the interplay of the investment base data and the summary measures of a profit center manager's authority and autonomy, as presented in Sections E and F. A final note reports the survey results of a question on external and internal accounting practices.

MEASURING PROFIT CENTER INVESTMENT

Question 14 of the structural questionnaire (see Section H) begins by asking whether companies calculate the corporate investment in each typical profit center. All but five companies answered this question, and of those that did, 84 percent responded affirmatively, as shown in Exhibit G−1. It is interesting to compare this finding with the results of surveys conducted by Mauriel and Anthony in 1966, and

Reece and Cool in 1977.[1] Mauriel and Anthony investigated investment center performance evaluation practices among large U.S. corporations. Of the manufacturing firms reporting the use of profit centers, 76 percent reported treating their profit centers as investment centers.[2] Our survey's figure of 84 percent would suggest a slight growth in the pervasiveness of the use of investment centers during the eight intervening years. We should be cautious in this interpretation, however, because a positive response does not necessarily imply the treatment of decentralized units as investment centers. The measurement of the investment associated with a profit center could be for purposes other than performance evaluation. Such caution is further suggested by the results of the Reece and Cool survey. In their sample, only 74 percent of the firms reported having investment centers. It does seem safe to conclude, nonetheless, that of the large majority of manufacturing firms using profit centers, about three out of four use some form of return-on-investment criterion in evaluating divisional performance.

The second part of Question 14 sought information about the practices of the various responding companies in calculating the investment base of their profit centers. To our knowledge this was the first time information of this type was collected for a large number of companies.[3]

We asked that those companies responding positively to the first question indicate what assets from the corporate balance sheet were typically included in the profit center investment base. The results are presented in Exhibit G−2. A cursory examination of that table shows that virtually all responding companies include external receivables, inventories, and fixed assets used exclusively by the profit center in

---

[1] John J. Mauriel and Robert N. Anthony, "Misevaluation of Investment Center Performance," *Harvard Business Review,* March−April 1966 pp. 98−105; and James S. Reece and William R. Cool, "Measuring Investment Center Performance," *Harvard Business Review,* May−June 1978, pp. 28−35.

[2] There were 1,302 manufacturing companies which answered the questionnaire. Of those, 90 percent reported having profit centers, a finding in line with the suggestion in Section A of this study that a substantial majority of large manufacturing firms in the United States have profit centers.

[3] Gerald Johnson designed a questionnaire to gather such information, but did not carry out his survey. His questionnaire contributed to the design of Question 14 of our survey instrument. Mauriel and Anthony in the article previously cited gathered information on practices relating to fixed asset valuation, but not on the other items treated here. More recently, Reece and Cool, as reported in the article cited previously, gathered similar information from 620 companies. The results they obtained are strikingly similar to those reported here.

their profit centers' investment base. Cash and other current assets are also included by many but not all companies.

Looking at those items related to transactions between profit centers within the same company, we find that nine out of ten firms report having intracompany receivables, but only 52 percent of those include such receivables in the investment base of their profit centers. On the other hand, while only two out of three companies report having fixed assets that are shared by two or more profit centers, about 80 percent of those having such assets do include them in the profit center investment base.

Assets of central headquarters units are generally not included in the investment base of the profit centers, with only 30 percent of the respondents for which this item is applicable reporting affirmatively. This finding is somewhat surprising in light of the data on cost assignment practices for corporate level support presented in previous sections of Part Two of this book.

Section C reports that the cost of corporate support in manufacturing, distribution, and sales is always assigned to the profit center but that in 27 percent of the cases the cost of corporate R&D support is not. In Section D we saw that roughly two thirds of the companies assign administrative service costs to their profit centers, with some variation depending on the service performed. Electronic data processing is the category having the lowest proportion of companies, 12 percent, assigning no cost to the profit centers. The category top corporate management tops the list with 40 percent not assigning any cost. (See Exhibit D−2.)

A partial explanation of this apparent discrepancy may be that the questionnaire, as phrased, specifically mentions research units as illustrative of central headquarter support units. It is possible, therefore, that many of the responses reflect company practice with regard to assigning headquarters R&D investments to the profit center's investment base. This may not, however, be an accurate description of practice on the assignment of other support unit investments.

The responses concerning items in the other assets category (investments and goodwill) show no strong pattern. About half the companies include such items in the investment base for their profit centers.

The questionnaire also requested information on the basis for measuring the value of each asset item used in the investment base. Exhibit G−3 provides a summary of the responses. In general, the companies report that they directly identify the value of each asset to be assigned to a profit center. There are two major and two minor exceptions. Fixed assets shared by two or more profit centers are not generally identified directly with the profit center but are prorated on the basis of a utilization criterion. Only one of four companies that include the assets of headquarters research or other such units in the profit center investment base use a direct measure in determining the value of the assigned assets. Seventy-six percent use some form of proration. Cash and other current assets provide the minor exceptions with 28 percent and 12 percent of the companies, respectively, reporting the use of some form of proration in determining the asset value.

We also asked how each company determined the value of its fixed assets in calculating profit center investment. Of the companies that answered this part of the question, practically all reported either gross or net book value. Exhibit G−4 shows that 85 percent of them used net book value. This is somewhat more than the 80 percent reported by Mauriel and Anthony in their 1966 report but coincides exactly with the finding of Reece and Cool in 1977.[4] This method clearly continues to be predominant for the valuation of fixed assets in ROI calculations.[5]

The final part of Question 14 dealt with liabilities that might be deducted from the investment base of each profit center. A summary of the responses is presented in Exhibit G−5.

Investment base indices

It would be difficult and cumbersome to compare the various companies with each other as to their investment measurement practices using all of the variables presented so far. Some way of summarizing the data into a more succinct representation is desirable. After considering several possible ways of building an index number

---

[4] Mauriel and Anthony, *"Misevaluation of Investment Center Performance"*, p. 102, and Reece and Cool, *"Measuring Investment Center Performance"* p. 33.

[5] For a critical review of the pros and cons of different methods of fixed asset valuation see Mauriel and Anthony (see footnote 4); John Dearden, "The Case Against ROI Control," *Harvard Business Review,* May−June 1969, pp. 124−35; and Reece and Cool (see footnote 4).

for each company based on its reported practices, we opted for a "responsibility" measure and a "control" measure, both of which are described below. Another scheme based on a classification according to clusters of assets might also allow a useful categorization of investment measurement practices, but we will not attempt to present such an index here.

The Asset Responsibility Index (ARI) shows the proportion of applicable asset items that are included in the profit center investment base for each company. This index is analogous to the cost responsibility indices for operating functions and administrative services presented in Sections C, D, and E. It reflects the degree to which the profit center manager is held responsible for the assets used in his business. Our first task in computing the ARI was to exclude from the analysis those questionnaires that contained insufficiently detailed or contradictory responses. It was necessary in this phase to reduce the sample to 220 companies. As a second step we reduced to ten the number of asset items in the list included with Question 14 of Section H, eliminating those which duplicated other items on the list. Thus, raw materials and work-in-process inventories were dropped, with finished goods inventories standing in for all three (see list below). Similarly, equipment used by a single profit center was excluded while land and buildings used by a single profit center was retained. Equipment shared by two or more profit centers remained and shared land and buildings was dropped. The ten items used in calculating the ARI are shown below with their relationship to the items

Reduced list	*Original list*
1. Cash	Cash
2. External receivables	External receivables
3. Intracompany receivables	Intracompany receivables
4. Inventories	{ Finished goods inventory / Raw materials inventory / Work-in-process inventory
5. Other current assets	Other current assets
6. Fixed assets used by one profit center	{ Land and buildings—One profit center / Equipment—One profit center
7. Shared fixed assets	{ Equipment—Two or more profit centers / Land and buildings—Two or more profit centers
8. Headquarters support unit assets	Headquarters research or other such unit
9. Investments	Investments
10. Goodwill	Goodwill

on the questionnaire. The denominator of the index was determined by the number of asset items that were reported as applicable for each company; items checked as not applicable were excluded from the denominator. The numerator was simply the number of applicable asset items actually used in calculating the investment base. Companies not using an investment base calculation were assigned an index value of zero. The resulting index values range from 0 to 1.0.

Exhibit G−6 outlines the procedure for deriving the *ARI,* and Exhibit G−7 presents a numerical example.

The Asset Control Index (*ACI*) is analogous to the cost control indices developed in Sections C, D, and E. It reflects the ability of a profit center manager to affect the magnitude of the assets assigned to his or her unit. When assets are assigned based on direct identification, more control is possible than when the assignment is a proration. The approach for computing the index is the same as for the *ARI* except for a final step in which those items directly identified with the profit center are scored as 1.0, while those that are prorated are scored 0.5. The resulting index also ranges from 0 to 1.0, but has a lower value for many of the companies than the *ARI.* Exhibits G−6 and G−7 also illustrate how the *ACI* is computed.

Exhibit G−8 shows how the two asset indices are distributed for the 220 companies providing usable data.

DEMOGRAPHIC ANALYSIS

Given the substantial variation in a profit center manager's responsibility for and control over the assets used in his or her business, we attempted to identify the characteristics of the companies that would help us understand the reasons underlying these variations. As a first, rudimentary, attempt at looking for informative relationships, we took the investment base data described above and examined them in relation to the demographic variables presented in Section A. Using two-way cross-tabulation, we examined the pattern of absolute frequency distributions, the Kendall's Tau statistic (especially its sign) and the significance level associated with it. Using an arbitrary cutoff point of .05 for the significance level, we proceeded to look more closely at a few of the relationships to see what they might suggest for our understanding of the issues at hand.

Exhibit G—9 highlights the relationships selected for further examination between the demographic variables and the four major investment base indicators: (1) whether the investment base for profit centers is calculated, (2) the asset responsibility index, (3) the asset control index, and (4) the fixed asset valuation procedure.

As has been the case in similar analyses in previous sections, the diversification strategy of the companies in our sample shows a marked association with the investment base measurement practices. Exhibit G—10 indicates that as we move along the diversification continuum from Single Business to Unrelated Businesses firms, the proportion of companies using investment base measurement for their profit centers increases from 67 percent to 85 percent.[6] This would seem to indicate that while the use of investment centers is prevalent throughout all of the companies in our study it is more pronounced among those with a greater degree of diversification.

The asset responsibility index (ARI) is also associated with diversification strategy. Exhibit G—11 shows that the more diversified companies tend to cluster in the higher brackets of the ARI while the less diversified companies tend to cluster in the lower brackets. Examining the asset control index (ACI), we see that the basic pattern remains the same, as shown in Exhibit G—12.

The decision to use gross book or net book value for fixed assets included in the investment base is not related in any visible way to diversification strategy in our sample of companies.

A relationship also emerged between sales volume and the two asset indices. Exhibits G—13 and G—14 show how the index scores tend to rise as sales revenue increases. Similar relationships have shown up in previous sections between sales revenue and other indices of profit center management practices. As we designed our study, we did not believe that such relationships would manifest themselves. Their persistent emergence, however, leads us to believe that further research in this area is warranted. It may simply be that sales volume is standing in as a proxy for some other structural or

---

[6] The proportions discussed here are not easily compared with those in Exhibit G—1 because of the need to drop observations in the present analysis due to incomplete or contradictory answers. The need to use different parts of the sample at different stages of the analysis throughout this study, because of missing, incomplete, partial or contradictory answers, requires special caution on the part of the reader in thinking about the results of the analysis.

strategic variables which we have not yet identified clearly. On the other hand, it is possible that as companies get larger there is a qualitative shift in the nature of their management practices.

The remaining relationships shown in Exhibit G−9 as strong enough to deserve reporting will not be examined further in this appendix. We leave it to the reader to think through their possible meanings. We limit ourselves to reporting that the signs on the Kendall's Tau statistic and an eyeball examination of the cross-tabulation tables show that (1) as EPS growth increases, the proportion of companies using investment base measurement and the *ARI* also increase; (2) as profit margins increase the proportion of companies using investment base measurement decreases; (3) as ROI increases, so does the proportion of companies using gross rather than net book value for fixed assets in the investment base;[7] and (4) as the number of profit centers increases, the *ARI* and the tendency to use net book value also increase.

We also looked at the cross-tabulation of certain individual asset items and the demographic variables. External receivables, inventories, and nonshared fixed assets are included by almost all the companies in our sample which calculate an investment base, and there is nothing to be learned from their cross-tabulation with other variables.

Exhibit G−15 presents the relationships of interest between the remaining seven asset categories and the demographic variables. All but goodwill showed a marked association with sales volume. It appears that the same relationship which emerged between sales volume and the asset responsibility index is appearing again at a lower level of detail. Exhibit G−16 illustrates these relationships, showing the cross-tabulation of investments and sales volume. Intracompany receivables, other current assets, shared fixed assets, and investments show the same relationship with diversification strategy as reported earlier for the *ARI*. Headquarters support unit assets, however, show an opposite sign on the Kendall's Tau statistic, further strengthening our supposition that the responses reflect a different treatment for corporate R&D in the measurement of profit centers than for other facets of headquarters support.[8]

---

[7] This is not contradictory since the ROI figure used in our analysis is computed on a uniform (net book) basis for all companies.

[8] We report this deviation from an otherwise uniform pattern, even though the significance level on the Tau statistic of .08 is somewhat below our cutoff point, because we find it thought-provoking.

We also observed a relationship between (1) the inclusion of cash in the investment base and the number of profit centers, and (2) the inclusion of shared fixed assets and EPS growth rate.

INVESTMENT BASE INDICES AND PROFIT CENTER MANAGER AUTHORITY AND AUTONOMY

Section E developed the "functional authority index" as a measure of the extent to which a typical profit center manager has physical custody of the corporate resources needed in his or her business. We were interested in observing whether the variation among companies along this dimension was related to the differences in the profit center manager's responsibility for and control over corporate resources when those resources are measured in financial terms as "assets." To this end we cross-tabulated the various investment base variables against the functional authority index (see Section E).

Both the *ARI* and the *ACI* showed a relationship whereby as their scores increased so did the functional authority index, suggesting that as the functional authority of profit center managers goes up, their responsibility and control of assets does also. Exhibit G−17 displays the cross-tabulation for the *ACI* and the functional authority index. The only specific asset categories that showed a relationship with the functional authority index were investments and goodwill, as shown in Exhibit G−18 for investments. This observation is puzzling until one realizes that these two asset items are among the least frequently used in investment base measurement, and, hence, are associated with higher values of the asset indices.

It also seemed likely that the asset indices would be related to the profit center manager's perceived autonomy (see Section F). It was disappointing, therefore, to find that in cross-tabulating the asset indices against the perceived autonomy index no relationships were observed. A similar absence of relationship is reported in Section F between the cost control index and the perceived autonomy index. In spite of this, it still seems reasonable to postulate such a relationship. While the investment base measurement system does carry implications about the responsibility for and control over assets, it represents only one of several signals that can be given to profit center managers as to the degree of autonomy they are to exercise. The absence of a discernible pattern in the current analysis could be the result of inadequate measurement of the autonomy index or of the asset indices. Or, perhaps, there is an intervening variable or variables masking the relationship and for which it is impossible to control in a two-way cross-tabulation analysis. These reflections suggest several avenues of further inquiry which are appropriate not only for the matters covered in this section but also for several other aspects of this study.

EXTERNAL AND INTERNAL ACCOUNTING PRACTICES

As a final note to this section, we report the survey results on the extent to which external and internal accounting practices differ. (See Question 16 of the structural questionnaire, Section H.) Exhibit G – 19 summarizes the findings. An overwhelming proportion of the companies in the sample report that they use the same accounting practices for internal and external reporting purposes with regard to such items as research and development (98 percent), amortization of goodwill (95 percent), leases (93 percent) and depreciation (92 percent). The exception is inventory accounting for which 21 percent of the companies report using LIFO (last in – first out) for public reporting but FIFO (first in – first out) for internal reporting.

Exhibit G–1
Calculation of investment for each profit center
(286 responses)

	Number of responses	Percent
Yes	239	84%
No	47	16
Total	286	100%

Exhibit G–2
Assets used in measuring investment base (239 respondents)

Item	Yes Freq.	Yes Per-cent	No Freq.	No Per-cent	Not applicable Freq.	Not applicable Per-cent	Number of valid responses
Current assets							
Cash	149	.64	77	.33	8	.03	234
External receivables	230	.98	3	.01	2	.01	235
Intracompany receivables	105	.46	95	.42	27	.12	227
Raw materials inventory	228	.98	3	.01	3	.01	234
Work-in-process inventory	228	.98	3	.01	3	.01	234
Finished goods inventory	229	.98	1	—	4	.02	234
Other current assets	179	.78	47	.20	5	.02	231
Fixed assets							
Land and buildings used solely by profit center	222	.96	9	.04	0	—	231
Equipment used solely by profit center	227	.98	5	.02	0	—	232
Land and buildings used by two or more profit centers	125	.56	31	.14	67	.30	223
Equipment used by two or more profit centers	102	.46	32	.15	87	.39	221
Assets of headquarters central research or similar unit	54	.25	129	.58	38	.17	221
Other assets							
Investments	107	.49	79	.36	34	.15	220
Goodwill	87	.40	84	.38	48	.22	219
Capitalized rent charge	11	.92	0	—	1	.08	12

Exhibit G—3

Basis for measuring the value of each asset in calculating profit center investment

Item	Directly identified with profit center	Prorated on the basis of								Number of respondents reporting basis of measurement	Number of respondents reporting use of asset in investment base
		Profit center sales	Profit center costs	Profit center assets	Other methods	Square feet	Estimated use	Principal user	Profit center liabilities		
Current assets											
Cash	102	13	7	12	3	1		1	2	141	149
External receivables	209	9					1			219	230
Intracompany receivables	98	2								100	105
Raw materials inventory	210		7	1	1					219	228
Work-in-process inventory	212		6	1	1					219	228
Finished goods inventory	218		2							220	229
Other current assets	150	6	2	8	4	1				171	179
Fixed assets											
Land and buildings used solely by profit center	209	1			2					212	222
Equipment used solely by profit center	213	1			2					216	227
Land and buildings used by two or more profit centers	46	8	15	8	6	17	11	6		117	125
Equipment used by two or more profit centers	36	9	14	7	7	3	14	3	1	94	102
Assets of headquarters central research or similar unit	12	11	9	7	5	2	4	1		51	54
Other assets											
Investment	92	1	1	4	1					99	107
Goodwill	76	1	1	1	1					80	87
Capitalized rent charge	9		1							10	11

Exhibit G– 4
Method for determining the value of fixed assets in calculating profit center investment (227 responses)

	Number of respondents	Percent
Gross book value (original cost)	35	15%
Net book value (cost less accumulated depreciation)	192	85
Total	227	100%

Exhibit G– 5
Liabilities deducted in measuring investment base

Item	Yes		No		Number of responses
	Freq.	Percent	Freq.	Percent	
Current external payables	100	.49	103	.51	203
Current payables to other corporate units	58	.29	144	.71	202
Other current liabilities	85	.42	118	.58	203
Deferred taxes	38	.19	158	.81	196
Other noncurrent liabilities	151	.77	46	.23	197

Exhibit G–6
How the investment base indices are computed

Is investment in each profit center computed?

For how many of the ten asset items in the analysis is the questionnaire scored?

How many of the ten asset items appear on the balance sheet?

How many of them are included in the investment base?

Is the method of value assignment specified for all asset items in the investment base?

How many asset items in the investment base have values assigned by each method?

Method weight

Definition of indices:
ARI: If S_y, $ARI = U/T$; If S_n, $ARI = 0$.
ACI: If S_y, $ACI = (1*V + .5*W)/T$; If S_n, $ACI = 0$.

Exhibit G-7
Investment base indices—a numerical example

Asset	Is asset applicable to respondent?		Is asset used in profit center investment base?		Method of assigning value to asset		Weighted value
					Direct	Prorated	
Cash	Yes	1	No	0			0
External receivables	Yes	1	Yes	1		.5	.5
Intracompany receivables	No	0	///				
Inventories	Yes	1	Yes	1	1		1
Other current assets	Yes	1	Yes	1		.5	.5
Nonshared fixed assets	Yes	1	Yes	1	1		1
Shared fixed assets	Yes	1	Yes	1		.5	.5
Assets of headquarters units	Yes	1	No	0			0
Investments	No	0	///				
Goodwill	Yes	1	Yes	1	1		1
Total		8		6			4.5

$ARI = 6/8 = .750$

$ACI = 4.5/8 = .562$

Exhibit G– 8
Distribution of the investment base indices (220 companies)

Descriptive statistics	Asset responsibility index	Asset control
Range	0 to 1.0	0 to 1.0
Mean	.563	.528
Standard deviation	.348	.332
Median	.666	.600
Interquartile range	.332 to .874	.299 to .778

Graphical representation

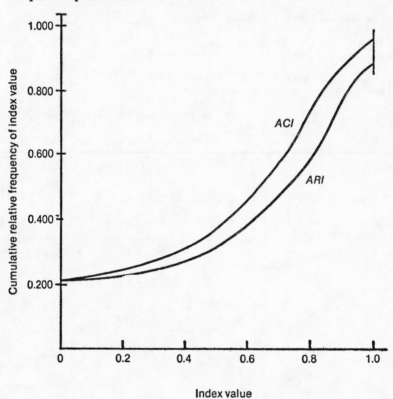

Exhibit G—9
Selected investment base measurement practice indicators versus demographic variables

Selected investment base measurement practice indicators	Seven demographic variables						
	Diversification strategy	Sales	EPS growth	Profit after tax/sales	Return on investment	Number of profit centers	Profit center sales
Investment base calculated or not (yes or no)	Kendall's Tau = -.13 Sig. .018		Kendall's Tau = -.13 Sig. .032	Kendall's Tau = .12 Sig. .031			
Asset responsibility index (ARI)	Kendall's Tau = .16 Sig. .003	Kendall's Tau = .16 Sig. .002	Kendall's Tau = .12 Sig. .036			Kendall's Tau = .17 Sig. .019	
Asset control index (ACI)	Kendall's Tau = .18 Sig. .001	Kendall's Tau = .13 Sig. .009					
Fixed asset valuation procedure (gross or net book value)					Kendall's Tau = -.14 Sig. .038	Kendall's Tau = .21 Sig. .016	

Exhibit G– 10
Use of investment base measurement versus diversification strategy (220 companies)

Investment base computed for each profit center	Diversification strategy				
	Single business	Dominant business	Related businesses	Unrelated businesses	Total
Yes	29	47	43	55	174
No	14	13	9	10	46
Total	43	60	52	65	220

Kendall's Tau = −0.12793
Significance level = 0.0185 (two-tail test)

Exhibit G– 11
Asset responsibility index versus diversification strategy (220 companies)

Asset responsibility index (with cut points)	Diversification strategy				
	Single business	Dominant business	Related businesses	Unrelated businesses	Total
1	14	13	9	10	46
2	13	9	8	11	41
3	7	15	13	10	45
4	3	7	13	20	43
5	6	16	9	14	45
Total	43	60	52	65	220

Kendall's Tau = 0.15609
Significance level = 0.0030 (two-tail test)

Exhibit G– 12
Asset control index versus diversification strategy (220 companies)

Asset control index (with cut points)	Diversification strategy				
	Single business	Dominant business	Related businesses	Unrelated businesses	Total
1	14	13	9	10	46
2	15	10	10	12	47
3	4	15	12	11	42
4	6	8	13	14	41
5	4	14	8	18	44
Total	43	60	52	65	220

Kendall's Tau = 0.17570
Significance level = 0.0010 (two-tail test)

Exhibit G– 13
Asset responsibility index versus 1974 sales revenue (205 companies)

Asset responsibility index (with cut points)	1974 sales revenue ($ million)				
	0–99	100–299	300–599	600 or more	Total
1..................	13	5	9	14	41
2..................	3	18	12	5	38
3..................	7	12	9	16	44
4..................	1	15	6	19	41
5..................	3	11	7	20	41
Total	27	61	43	74	205

Kendall's Tau based on nine levels of sales revenue = 0.15486
Significance level = 0.0024

Exhibit G– 14
Asset control index versus 1974 sales revenue (205 companies)

Asset control index (with cut points)	1974 sales revenue ($ million)				
	0–99	100–299	300–599	600 or more	Total
1..................	13	5	9	14	41
2..................	4	19	14	8	45
3..................	5	12	6	15	38
4..................	2	13	7	19	41
5..................	3	12	7	18	40
Total	27	61	43	74	205

Kendall's Tau based on nine levels of sales revenue = 0.13427
Significance level = 0.0085

Exhibit G– 15
Use of selected asset items in investment base versus demographic variables

Asset items	Seven demographic variables						
	Diversi-fication strategy	Sales	EPS growth	Profit after tax/sales	Return on investment	Number of profit centers	Profit center sales
Cash		Tau = –.17 Sig. .022				Tau = –.19 Sig. .050	
Intracompany receivables	Tau = –.23 Sig. .005	Tau = –.21 Sig. .016					
Other current assets	Tau = –.13 Sig. .033	Tau = –.16 Sig. .019					
Shared fixed assets	Tau = –.21 Sig. .013	Tau = –.28 Sig. .002	Tau = –.28 Sig. .006				
Headquarters support unit assets	[Tau = .11 Sig. .083]	Tau = .15 Sig. .039					
Investments	Tau = –.17 Sig. .030	Tau = –.25 Sig. .005					
Goodwill							

Exhibit G– 16
Use of "investments" in profit center investment base versus 1974 sales revenue (137 companies)

"Investments" used in profit center investment base	1974 sales revenue ($ millions)				
	0–199	200–399	400–999	1,000 or more	Total
Yes	15	12	20	28	75
No	21	15	14	12	62
Total	36	27	34	40	137

Kendall's Tau based on nine categories of sales revenue = −0.25169
Significance level = 0.0046

Exhibit G– 17
Asset control index versus functional authority index (178 companies)

Asset control index	Functional authority index					
	1	2	3	4	5	Total
1.....................	12	4	4	3	9	32
2.....................	13	4	11	7	5	40
3.....................	4	14	7	4	5	34
4.....................	4	5	8	10	6	33
5.....................	3	8	8	8	12	39
Total	36	35	38	32	37	178

Kendall's Tau = 0.16776
Significance level = 0.0027 (two-tail test)

Exhibit G– 18
Use of "investments" in profit center investment base versus functional authority index (123 companies)

"Investments" used in profit center investment base	Functional authority index					
	1	2	3	4	5	Total
Yes	7	13	13	18	16	67
No	14	13	13	7	9	56
Total	21	26	26	25	25	123

Kendall's Tau = −0.25487
Significance level = 0.0062 (two-tail test)

Exhibit G– 19
External and internal accounting practices

| Category | External and internal accounting | | | | |
| | Is the same | | Is different | | |
	Freq.	Percent	Freq.	Percent	N
Inventory accounting	230	79.2	59	20.4	289
Depreciation accounting	266	92.4	22	7.6	288
Research & Development accounting	280	98.2	5	1.8	285
Lease accounting	261	93.5	18	6.5	279
Accounting for amortization of goodwill	258	94.9	14	5.1	272

Section H

Questionnaires; partial list of participants*

Contents — **Page**

* This Section was prepared by Lee E. Buddrus.

FINANCIAL EXECUTIVES RESEARCH FOUNDATION
633 THIRD AVENUE NEW YORK N Y 10017 · 212 953 0900

May 20, 1975

Mr. John Jones
Vice President-Finance
XYZ Company
745 Concord Avenue
Cambridge, Massachusetts 02138

Dear Mr. Jones:

We would like you to participate in a new research project recently approved
by the Financial Executives Research Foundation. The working title is
"Profit Measurement and Decentralization," and the project will focus on the
use of profit centers for management control in large corporations.

The study will result in a published book. In addition to a description of
how various companies measure profit in profit centers, a relationship between method of profit measurement and decentralization will be sought.

The study is being conducted by Professor Richard F. Vancil of Harvard
Business School, assisted by the staff of Management Analysis Center, a
national general management consulting and research firm. Professor Vancil,
author of many books and articles on planning and control, was also editor of
the Financial Executives Handbook.

It is important that information be gathered from responsible financial executives. That is why you are being asked to help. We are asking that you
fill out a questionnaire that will be sent to you shortly. The questionnaire
has taken others between thirty to forty-five minutes to complete.

By participating you will not only be contributing to your profession but
other benefits will accrue to you.

Prior to publication of the book we will send you a computer generated
analysis that summarizes the responses of all participants together with a
restatement of your responses. You will be able to compare your company to
tabulations developed from our research. Of course, the data will be in
summarized form and no individual company data other than your own will
be made available to you.

We intend to list in the book, with your permission, the names and companies
of participants as contributors to the research.

THE RESEARCH ARM OF FINANCIAL EXECUTIVES INSTITUTE

Mr. John Jones
May 20, 1975
Page Two

Of course the information provided will be treated in strict confidence.
All responses will be entered in the data bank in coded form with company
identities known only to the project director and his assistant. Companies
will not be identified as participants in any reports used either within or
outside FERF without written consent. And, in no instance, will a company
ever be identified as having given a particular response.

We will send you the questionnaire within one week. Thank you in advance
for your participation.

Sincerely,

Ben Makela
Research Director

FINANCIAL EXECUTIVES RESEARCH FOUNDATION

PROFIT MEASUREMENT AND DECENTRALIZATION

QUESTIONNAIRE

(This is the cover sheet for a 16
page booklet. The inside front
cover and the outside back cover
were blank.)

We hope you are willing to participate in this research study by completing this questionnaire. Field tests indicated that it takes 30 minutes to an hour to complete.

We desire responses from companies with two or more DOMESTIC profit centers. A profit center is defined as any fairly independent organizational unit, accountable separately for its performance, for which some measure of profit is determined periodically. (Examples include decentralized divisions or departments, and product groups.) This questionnaire requests information only for your DOMESTIC profit centers which are not separate legal entities (subsidiaries).

Does your company have two or more domestic profit centers?

Yes ☐ ⁷/₁

No ☐ ²

If you checked Yes, please complete the questionnaire.

If you checked No, please return this questionnaire along with your latest annual report in the enclosed self-addressed envelope.

This questionnaire requests specific information on:

- How you TYPICALLY calculate profit and assets employed for your profit centers

- The diversity of your corporation

and proceeds as follows:

- Common functions serving two or more profit centers

- Transfers of goods between domestic profit centers

- Charges for corporation level services

- Allocation of common facilities costs

- Transfers of services between domestic profit centers

- Miscellaneous corporate income

- Corporate interest and questions on assets employed by profit centers, fixed asset valuation, and liabilities

- Allocation of taxes

- Corporate financial accounting versus profit center accounting

- Questions on corporate diversity

We would like you to send us:

1) Your latest annual report

2) An organization chart which illustrates the relationship between your top management organization at the corporate level and your profit centers. Please circle a typical profit center on the chart. If you wish, delete names of personnel on the chart. If a published organization chart illustrating the relationship between top management at the corporate level and your profit centers is not readily available, please sketch a simple chart illustrating the organizational relationship.

This information will help us to better understand the context of your answers given in the questionnaire.

Since the information is confidential, we assure you that precautions are taken to protect you and your company. All responses are entered in the data bank in coded form with company identities known only to the Project Director and his assistant. Companies are not identified as participants in any reports used either within or outside FERF without written consent. And, in no instance is a company ever identified as having given a particular response.

Please Note:

1) If you use different practices for different profit centers, please describe only the method for the MOST TYPICAL DOMESTIC profit center.

2) We are requesting information only on how you calculate profit center profit, not how calculations are used to measure managerial performance.

3) If you use a calculation procedure different than any method described in a question, please explain your procedure in the margin next to the question, or on the back of the questionnaire.

COMMON FUNCTIONS SERVING TWO OR MORE PROFIT CENTERS

1. Manufacturing Costs — Are some or all of your profit centers served by a common manufacturing function (or several manufacturing functions) which is not contained within the profit centers?
(Note: Transfers of goods between profit centers will be covered in Question 5.)

Yes ☐ ⁸/₁

No ☐ ²

If you checked NO, please go on to Question 2. If you checked YES, please answer the following.

3

The common manufacturing function(s) typically manufacture(s) what percentage of the entire value of goods and services utilized by the profit centers which the common manufacturing function(s) serves. (check one)

9

1-30% □ **1**

30-70% □ **2**

70-99% □ **3**

All □ **4**

What is the most common method you use for transferring costs from your common manufacturing function to your profit centers?

10-11

A. Variable (or Direct) Manufacturing Cost

At Standard (or Contracted) Cost □ **1**

or

At Actual Cost (or Standard Cost plus

Variances at Year End) □ **2**

B. Full Manufacturing Cost (Variable Cost plus Manufacturing Overhead)

At Standard Cost □ **3**

or

At Actual Cost □ **4**

C. Full Manufacturing Cost plus a Defined Profit

At a Profit Based on Corporate Return on Sales □ **5**

or

At a Profit Based on Corporate Return on

Investment □ **6**

or

At a Profit Based on External Market Prices □ **7**

or

Some Other Defined Profit. Please Explain: □

4

D. Negotiation Between Profit Center Managers and Manufacturing Manager □ **8**

E. Some Other Method. Please Explain: □

2. Research and Development — Are some or all of your profit centers served by a common research and development function (or several common R & D functions) which is not contained within the profit centers?

12

Yes □ **1**

No □ **2**

If you checked No, please go on to Question 3. If you checked Yes, please tell us what percent of total research and development is performed at the corporate level (rather than at the profit center level). You may either check column A for all research or if your corporation distinguishes between basic and applied research please give us separate answers for basic and applied research in columns B and C and ignore column A.

Corporate Level Performs	A All Research	B Basic Research	C Applied Research
	13	**14**	
1-30%	□ **1**	□ **1**	□ **5**
30-70%	□ **2**	□ **2**	□ **6**
70-99%	□ **3**	□ **3**	□ **7**
All	□ **4**	□ **4**	□ **8**

Please tell us if you charge your profit centers for research costs. You may either check column A for all research or if your corporation distinguishes between basic and applied research please give us separate answers for basic and applied research in columns B and C and ignore column A.

A All Research	B Basic Research	C Applied Research
15		
Yes □ **1**	Yes □ **2**	Yes □ **3**
No □ **4**	No □ **5**	No □ **6**

If you checked No for all research (or for both basic and applied research), go on to Question 3. If you checked Yes, please tell us how you charge your profit centers for the research costs.

	A All Research 16	B Basic Research 17	C Applied Research 18-19
A. Project Research Cost Based on Actual Usage	1 ☐	1 ☐	1 ☐
B. Prorated Across Profit Centers on the Basis of:			
Sales Revenue	2 ☐	2 ☐	2 ☐
Operating Costs (or a Subset of Costs Defined by You)	3 ☐	3 ☐	3 ☐
Profit	4 ☐	4 ☐	4 ☐
C. Prorate Some Costs; Actual Usage Charge for Other Costs	5 ☐	5 ☐	5 ☐
D. Negotiation Between Profit Center and Research and Development Function	6 ☐	6 ☐	6 ☐
E. Some Other Method. Please Explain:	☐	☐	☐

Is your research and development department(s) treated as a profit center?

20

Yes   1 ☐

For Some But Not All Projects   2 ☐

No   3 ☐

3. **Selling Costs — Do you have a common domestic sales force (or several common domestic sales forces) which sells products for more than one profit center?**

21

Yes   1 ☐

No   2 ☐

If you answered No, please go on to Question 4. If you answered Yes, please tell us what percent of <u>total</u> domestic corporate sales is handled by the common sales force(s).

22

1-30%   1 ☐

30-70%   2 ☐

70-99%   3 ☐

All   4 ☐

Please tell us how sales force costs are typically charged to profit centers.

23-24

A. Charge Based on Actual Usage of Time Spent in Selling Product   1 ☐

B. Charge Based on Budgeted Usage of Time Spent in Selling Product   2 ☐

C. Prorated Across Profit Centers on the Basis of:

   Sales Revenue   3 ☐

   Operating Costs (or a Subset of Costs Defined by You)   4 ☐

   Profit   5 ☐

D. Negotiation Between Profit Center Manager and Sales Force Manager   6 ☐

E. Some Other Method. Please Explain: ☐

4. **Distribution Costs — Do you have a common domestic physical distribution function (or several distribution functions) which distributes and/or transports goods for more than one profit center?**

25

Yes   1 ☐

No   2 ☐

If you answered No, please go on to Question 5. If you answered Yes, please tell us the percent of the <u>total</u> value of domestic goods distributed by the common physical distribution function(s).

26

1-30%   1 ☐

30-70%   2 ☐

70-99%   3 ☐

All   4 ☐

5

How are physical distribution costs typically charged to profit centers?

27-28

A. Charge Based on Actual Usage of Physical Distribution Resources in Handling Profit Centers' Goods ☐ 1

B. Charge Based on Budgeted Usage of Time Spent in Handling Profit Centers' Goods ☐ 2

C. Prorated Across Profit Centers on the Basis of:

    Sales Revenue ☐ 3

    Operating Costs (or a Subset of Costs as Defined by You) ☐ 4

    Profit ☐ 5

D. Prorate Management Costs of Distribution Function to Profit Center Based on Profit Center Proportion of Sales, or Number of Orders, or Inventory Value; Charge Direct Labor Hours to Profit Center Based on Actual Usage ☐ 6

E. Negotiation Between Profit Center Manager and Physical Distribution Manager ☐ 7

F. Some Other Method. Please Explain: ☐

TRANSFER OF GOODS BETWEEN DOMESTIC PROFIT CENTERS

5. Do you transfer goods among profit centers?

29

Yes ☐ 1

No ☐ 2

If you answered No, please go to Question 7. If you answered Yes, please tell us how you most commonly set transfer prices at year end for the goods which flow between your profit centers? Please check the appropriate answer.

A. Variable (or Direct) Manufacturing Cost

30-31

    At Stardard (or Contracted) Cost ☐ 1

    or

    At Actual Cost (or Standard Cost plus Variances at Year End) ☐ 2

B. Full Manufacturing Cost (Variable Cost plus Manufacturing Overhead)

    At Standard Cost ☐ 3

    or

    At Actual Cost ☐ 4

C. Full Manufacturing Cost Plus a Defined Profit

    At Profit Based on Corporate Return on Sales ☐ 5

    or

    At Profit Based on Corporate Return on Investment ☐ 6

    or

    Some Other Defined Profit. Please Explain: ☐

D. Market Price

    Based on Competitor's Price ☐ 7

    or

    Based on Your List Price ☐ 8

    or

    Based on Most Recent Bid Price Received ☐ 9

    or

    Some Other Market Price. Please Explain: ☐

E. Negotiated Price Between Profit Center Managers ☐ 1

F. Some Other Method. Please Explain: ☐

6. We would like to have some measure of the amount of goods transferred among domestic profit centers. If you treat transfers of goods as a purchase and sale including a profit in the transfer price, please answer Section A. If you transfer goods on a cost basis, please answer Section B. Note: Transfers of services between profit centers will be covered in Question 9.

Section A

In transferring goods between profit centers, companies frequently employ an intracompany eliminations account to compute total external sales and cost of sales. Please estimate the percent of the intracompany cost of _sales_ elimination to total external cost of _sales_ which most closely approximates your corporation's ratio in 1974: _____% (32, 33, 34)

Section B

Please estimate the percent of the total "value of goods" transferred between profit centers as a percent of the corporate total "value of goods" manufactured. "Value of goods" is defined by the cost basis of your method of transferring goods. _____% (35, 36, 37)

6

CHARGES FOR CORPORATE LEVEL SERVICES

7. Listed below are service departments which are often located at the corporate level and which many times perform services for profit centers.

Estimate the cost of the service performed at the corporate level as a percent of total domestic company-wide service costs performed at all levels including profit center levels.

Corporate Level Service Center	1 None	2 1-30%	3 30-70%	4 70-99%	5 All	
1. Finance & accounting						38
2. Legal						39
3. Electronic data processing						40
4. General Marketing Services						41
5. Advertising						42
6. Market Research Services						43
7. Public Relations						44
8. Industrial Relations						45
9. Personnel						46
10. Top Corporate Management Overhead (i.e., president's office)	///////	///////	///////	///////	✔	
11. Real Estate						47
12. Operation Research Dept						48
13. Corporate Planning Dept	///////	///////	///////	///////	✔	
14. Purchasing Dept						49
	1	2	3	4	5	

Estimate the percent of corporate level service cost allocated to profit centers.

Corporate Level Service Center	1 None	2 1-30%	3 30-70%	4 70-99%	5 All	
1. Finance & accounting						50
2. Legal						51
3. Electronic data processing						52
4. General Marketing Services						53
5. Advertising						54
6. Market Research Services						55
7. Public Relations						56
8. Industrial Relations						57
9. Personnel						58
10. Top Corporate Management Overhead (i.e., president's office)						59
11. Real Estate						60
12. Operation Research Dept						61
13. Corporate Planning Dept						62
14. Purchasing Dept						63
	1	2	3	4	5	

7

Please fill in the following table, according to the instructions below.

In Section I you are asked if you charge the profit center for the service center's costs. If you check No or N/A (not applicable, which means you do not have such a corporate level department), please go on to the next service center.

If you answer Yes, please go on to Section II which asks you to check Column A, B, or C, depending on whether or not you charge the profit center for the service center's activities based on:

A. Budgeted or Standard cost of service center (Contracted Costs)
   or

B. Actual cost of service center
   or

C. Market price of services (or cost plus a defined profit)

Then in Section III, for each service center for which you checked A or B, check the most common method of allocating costs at year end:

a) Charge based on actual usage of service center's resources

b) Charge based on estimated usage of service center's resources

c) Negotiations between profit center manager and service center manager

d) Prorated across profit centers on the basis of sales revenue

e) Prorated across profit centers on the basis of operating costs (or a subset of costs defined by you)

f) Prorated across profit centers on the basis of profit

g) Some other method.

If you have any other significant corporate level service centers which service your profit centers, list these service centers after the last corporate service given below (14. Purchasing Dept.). Then complete the row using the instructions given above.

	I — Is Profit Center Charged?			II — Basis of Charges			III — The Most Common Method of Charging for Service Center's Cost							
	Yes	No	N/A	Budgeted or Standard Cost A	Actual Cost B	Market Price or Cost plus Defined Profit C	Actual Usage (a)	Estimated Usage (b)	Negotiations (c)	Prorated on Sales Revenues (d)	Prorated on Some Cost Basis (e)	Prorated on Profit (f)	Other Method (g)	
Corporate Level Service Center														
1. Finance and accounting														64, 65, 66
2. Legal														67, 68, 69
3. Electronic data processing														70, 71, 72
4. General Marketing Services														73, 74, 75
5. Advertising														76, 77, 78
6. Market Research Services														7, 8, 9
7. Public Relations														10, 11, 12
8. Industrial Relations														13, 14, 15
9. Personnel														16, 17, 18
10. Top Corporate Overhead (i.e., president's office)														19, 20, 21
11. Real Estate														22, 23, 24
12. Operation Research Dept														25, 26, 27
13. Corporate Planning Dept														28, 29, 30
14. Purchasing Dept														31, 32, 33
Other Significant Service Centers 15.														34, 35, 36
16.														37, 38, 39
17.														40, 41, 42
18.														43, 44, 45
19.														46, 47, 48
	1	2	3	1	2	3	1	2	3	4	5	6		

If you checked "(g) Other Method", Please Explain:

8

8. Is your Electronic Data Processing Department a profit center?

49

Yes ☐ 1

No ☐ 2

Please list any other significant corporate level service centers you may have which are profit centers.

1. _____

2. _____

3. _____   (50)

4. _____

ALLOCATION OF COMMON FACILITIES COSTS

9. Do you have any common facilities (plants, offices, etc.) which are used jointly by two or more profit centers?

51

Yes ☐ 1

No ☐ 2

If No, please go to Question 10. If Yes, how do you typically allocate joint occupancy costs such as depreciation, heat, light, air conditioning, janitorial services, rent, etc.?

52-53

Square Feet used by Each Profit Center ☐ 1

Personnel Employed by Each Profit Center ☐ 2

Negotiation Among Profit Centers ☐ 3

Prorated Across Profit Centers on the Basis of:

Sales Revenue ☐ 4

Operating Costs (or a Subset of Costs as Defined by You) ☐ 5

Profit ☐ 6

Some Other Method. Please Explain: ☐

TRANSFER OF SERVICES BETWEEN PROFIT CENTERS

10. In some companies, one profit center may perform services for itself and one or more other profit centers (services such as finance and accounting, EDP, engineering, purchasing, etc.). Do you have any such transfers of services between profit centers?

54

Yes ☐ 1

No ☐ 2

If No, go on to Question II. If Yes, please tell us how you charge for the transfer price of these services.

55-56

Do Not Charge ☐ 1

Direct Usage Charge ☐ 2

Prorated Across Profit Centers on the Basis of:

Sales Revenue ☐ 3

Operating Costs (or a Subset of Costs as Defined by You) ☐ 4

Profit ☐ 5

Negotiation Between Profit Center Managers ☐ 6

Some Other Method. Please Explain: ☐

MISCELLANEOUS ("OTHER") CORPORATE INCOME

11. Does your company have material amounts of miscellaneous ("other") corporate income, say 2% of net profit or more?

57

Yes ☐ 1

No ☐ 2

If No, go to Question 12. If Yes, tell us how you allocate this income to profit centers.

58-59

Do Not Allocate ☐ 1

All Income is Directly Identifiable with Profit Center and Accounted for by Profit Center ☐ 2

Prorated Across Profit Centers on the Basis of:

Sales Revenue ☐ 3

Operating Costs (or a Subset of Costs as Defined by You) ☐ 4

Profit ☐ 5

Some Other Method. Please Explain: ☐

9

CORPORATE INTEREST AND QUESTIONS ON ASSETS EMPLOYED

12. Do you allocate corporate interest expense and/or charge your profit centers for the use of capital invested in the profit centers? (Check both (a) and (b) if you perform both calculations for different purposes.)

60

a) Allocate Actual Corporate Interest ☐ 1

b) Assign a Charge for the Use of Capital Invested in the Profit Center ☐ 2

c) Profit Centers Are Not Charged for Interest Expense or the Use of Capital Employed ☐ 3

If you answered (c) above, please go on to Question 14. If you answered (b) and did not also check (a), please go on to Question 13. If you answered (a), please tell us the basis for charging profit centers for corporate interest expense.

61

I. Prorate Based on Profit Center Sales ☐ 1

II. Prorate Based on Profit Center Profits ☐ 2

III. Prorate Based on Percent of Capital Employed by the Profit Center (Investment Base as Defined in Question 14 below) ☐ 3

IV. Calculated Using a Simulated Capital Structure for the Profit Center (Breaking the Total Investment into Debt and Equity Components) and Multiplying the Debt Component by an Interest Rate. ☐ 4

Go on to Question 14 if you checked I, II, or III and do not have a capital charge (i.e., you did not check (b) in Question 12). Otherwise, answer Question 13.

13. What interest rate do you use (see Table)?

Answer Section I if you have indicated you charge for corporate interest. Answer Section II if you have indicated you charge for the use of capital invested in the profit center. Answer both Sections if you have indicated you both allocate an interest expense (using a simulated capital structure, i.e., answered IV above in Question 12), and charge for the use of capital employed.

Note: If you distinguish between "short" and "long" term debt please give us answers for both types of

debt and ignore the box labeled "Total Debt". If you do not distinguished between "short" and "long" term debt just answer for total debt.

Check appropriate boxes.

	Section I			Section II
	For allocation of actual corporate interest expense			For assigning a charge for the use of capital employed in the profit center
	If debt is split by maturity date		Total Debt	
	Short Term Debt	Long Term Debt		
Historial average rate					62
Current corporate rate					63
Prime rate					64
Corporate cost of capital					65
Some other computed rate					66-67
	1	2	3	4	

If some other computed rate, please explain: _____

_____

14. Do you calculate the corporation investment in each typical profit center?

68

Yes ☐ 1

No ☐ 2

If you answered No, please go to Question 15. If you answered Yes, please follow the instructions below.

Listed on the following page are asset items commonly used in calculating the corporate investment in a profit center. Please indicate if you include the item in the asset base for such a calculation by checking YES or NO in the appropriate column. If YES, please check the basis for measuring the value of that asset (identifiable with the profit center or prorated in some manner). If we have missed any items please fill them in at the bottom and complete the columns. Answer N/A (not applicable) if you do not have such items on the corporate balance sheet.

10

BASIS OF ASSET MEASUREMENT

ASSET ITEMS	N/A	Is Item Included In Asset Base YES	Is Item Included In Asset Base NO	Asset is directly ident. with profit center	Prorated based on profit center sales	Prorated based on profit center costs	Prorated based on other profit center assets	Some other method	If Other Explain	
Current Assets										
1. Cash										69, 70
2. External Receivables										71, 72
3. Intracompany receivables										73, 74
4. Raw material inv.										75, 76
5. Work-in-process inv.										77, 78
6. Finished goods inv.										79, 80
7. Other current assets										7, 8
Fixed Assets										
6. Land & bldgs. used solely by profit centers										9, 10
7. Equip. used solely by profit centers										11, 12
8. Land & bldg. used by two or more profit centers										13, 14
9. Equip. used by two or more profit centers										15, 16
10. Assets of hdqtrs. central research or similar units										17, 18
Other Assets										
11. Investments										19, 20
12. Goodwill										21, 22
Assets Not Listed Above										
13.										23, 24
14.										25, 26
15.										27, 28
	1	2	3	1	2	3	4	5		

11

(Question 14 — cont'd)
For fixed assets (land, buildings and equipment), at what amounts are they included in the asset base? (Check one)

		29
Not Applicable Because Not in Asset Base		☐ 1
Gross Book Value (i.e., Original Cost)		☐ 2
Net Book Value (i.e., Cost Less Accumulated Depreciation)		☐ 3
Some Measure That Departs From Cost, Such as Insurance Value, Appraisal Value, or Replacement Value (Please Explain How you Calculate)_____		☐

Do you deduct any of the following in arriving at the investment base for calculation of interest and/or a capital charge?

		30-31
Current Payables (External)	Yes ☐ 1	No ☐ 6
Current Payables to Other Corporate Units	Yes ☐ 2	No ☐ 7
Other Current Liabilities	Yes ☐ 3	No ☐ 8
Deferred Taxes	Yes ☐ 4	No ☐ 9
Other Non-current Liabilities	Yes ☐ 5	No ☐ 1

Other Deductions Please List: _____

_____

_____

ALLOCATION OF TAXES

15. Do you calculate profits after tax for your profit centers?

	32
Yes	☐ 1
No	☐ 2

12

If No, please go to question 16. If Yes, how do you determine the profit center share of corporate taxes? Please check one:

33-34

Actual Calculation — (Treating the Profit Center as if It Were a Separate Company)   ☐ 1

Nominal Rate — Profit Before Tax of Profit Center Times Nominal Corporate Tax Rate to Get the Profit Center Tax. The Nominal Rate Equals the U.S. Statutory Rate on Corporations in Year of Tax Calculations.   ☐ 2

Effective Rate — Profit Before Tax of Profit Center Times Effective Corporate Tax Rate to Get Profit Center Tax. The Effective Corporate Tax Rate Equals Total Corporate Taxes Divided by Profits Before Tax.   ☐ 3

Prorated Across Profit Centers on the Basis of:

Sales Revenue	☐ 4
Operating Costs (or a Subset of Costs as Defined by You)	☐ 5
Profit	☐ 6
Some Other Method. Please Explain:	☐

Do you include as an expense for your profit center profit calculation any special taxes a profit center might incur which other profit centers would not incur? (For example, as a result of a profit center's operation in a high tax state, its taxes would be higher than other profit centers.)

	35
Yes	☐ 1
No	☐ 2

If you receive an investment tax credit, do you reflect the investment tax credit in the profit center's tax calculation?

	36
Yes	☐ 1
No	☐ 2
Not Applicable	☐ 3

CORPORATE FINANCIAL ACCOUNTING VERSUS PROFIT CENTER ACCOUNTING

16. Do you typically calculate profit center profit differently from the accounting principles followed in your annual report with respect to:

a) Inventory Accounting

37, 38, 39

Yes ☐[1] No ☐[2]

If Yes, please briefly explain why difference exists: _____

_____

_____

_____

b) Depreciation

Yes ☐[3] No ☐[4]

If Yes, please briefly explain why difference exists: _____

_____

_____

_____

c) Research and Development Costs

Yes ☐[5] No ☐[6]

If Yes, please briefly explain why difference exists: _____

_____

_____

_____

d) Lease Accounting (e.g. noncapitalized financing leases, off balance sheet financing)

Yes ☐[7] No ☐[8]

If Yes, please briefly explain why difference exists: _____

_____

_____

_____

e) Amortization of Goodwill

Yes ☐[9] No ☐[1]

If Yes, please briefly explain why difference exists: _____

_____

_____

_____

f) Would you please list any other areas where your profit center accounting principles will differ from corporate external reporting accounting principles for those items included in both corporate and profit center calculations:

_____

_____

_____

QUESTIONS ON CORPORATE DIVERSITY

The questions in this section are designed to help us understand the amount of diversity present in your company's activities and the underlying logic behind this diversity. You need not answer all the questions in this section — as you check each box you will be guided to the next appropriate question.

17. DEGREE OF VERTICAL INTEGRATION — Many firms that produce a wide variety of end products are vertically integrated companies that process a single material through a number of stages before finally fabricating a variety of finished goods. For example, an aluminum company may produce and sell ingot, structural aluminum, cookware, wire and cable, auto parts, and containers all as outputs of a single integrated chain of aluminum processing operations. Similar patterns frequently occur in the forest products, steel, oil, rubber, and meat packing industries.

What percentage of corporate revenues is attributable to all sales of final products, by-products, and intermediate products associated with a vertically integrated raw materials processing sequence?

40

More Than 95%, please go to Question 24 ☐[1]

Between 70% and 95%, please go to Question 24 ☐[2]

Less Than 70%, please answer Question 18. ☐[3]

13

18. SIZE OF LARGEST SINGLE BUSINESS UNIT —
In this study a single business unit is the set of
activities associated with the production and
marketing of a single product/service or a line of
closely related products/services. Included within
a business unit are all products or product lines
that require close coordination or which share
important resources. The organization's profit
centers do not necessarily correspond to business
units — a large division may include several business units while a smaller profit center may
actually be part of a larger business unit. In deciding whether two product-market activities are
part of the same business unit or not, it is helpful
to ask this question: "Would a major change in
pricing, manufacturing processes, technology, materials used, etc., in one of these areas have a
strong effect on the operations in the other area?"
If not, the two product-market activities are
separate and not part of the same business unit.
Some corporate examples of single business units
are:

Company	Largest Single Business Unit
Ford Motor	Automobiles
Eastman Kodak	Photographic supplies
Gillette	Shaving supplies
Proctor and Gamble	Soaps, detergents, and cleansers
General Electric	Electric power generating equip.

**What percentage of corporate revenues are attributable
to your company's largest single business unit?**

41

More Than 95%, please go to Question 24 ☐ 1

Between 70% and 95%, please answer ☐ 2
Question 19

Less Than 70%, please answer Question 20 ☐ 3

19. You have indicated that 70 to 95% of corporate
revenues are derived from a single dominant
business activity. Check the statement below
which best describes the relationship between
the company's minor business activities and this
dominant business.

COMMON SKILL OR RESOURCE — most of the
minor businesses are related to the firm's dominant
business and to one another by some central skill,

concept, or resource. Corporate examples are IBM
(EDP technology) and Outboard Marine (in which chain
saws, snowmobiles and lawnmowers are closely related
to the engine used in its dominant outboard motor
business).

42

☐ 1

LINKED RELATEDNESS — not all of the minor businesses are closely related to the dominant business,
but most have at least some relationship to other
corporate activities. For example, a company's dominant farm equipment business might be related to a
smaller fertilizer business which is, in turn, related to
a petrochemical plastics business.

☐ 2

UNRELATED — most of the minor business activities are unrelated to the company's dominant business. For example, Phillip Morris' beer, hospital supplies, razor blade, and gum businesses are unrelated
to its dominant cigarette business.

☐ 3

After completing this question, please go to Question 24.

20. RELATED BUSINESSES — A business is part of
a group of "somehow related businesses" as long
as it is tangibly related to at least one other business in the group. Thus, photographic film,
cameras, dyes, pigments, and textile chemicals
form a group of related businesses. While textile
chemicals is not obviously related to cameras, in
this firm the links are clear; cameras — film —
dyes — textile chemicals. Examples of firms
whose preponderance of businesses are somehow
related are 3M (Tape, adhesives, coated paper,
film, microfilm equipment, projectors, etc.) and
Miles Laboratories (pharmaceuticals, lab supplies, medical electronics). Examples of firms
engaging in unrelated businesses are Ford (automobiles and trucks, electronics), Xerox (copiers,
digital computers), and OLIN (aluminum, plastics,
publishing, arms and ammunition).

**What percentage of corporate revenues is attributable
to the largest group of somehow related businesses?
(Note: You may wish to read all of Question 20 before
answering this specfic question.)**

43

Less Than 70%, please go to Question 21 ☐ 1

70% or More, please answer question ☐ 2
below

Which statement best describes the logic underlying the relationships among the businesses within the "largest group of somehow related businesses?"

COMMON SKILL OR RESOURCE — the businesses in this group are mostly related through some common central skill or resource so that <u>each is related to most of the others</u>. For example, industrial chemicals, specialty chemicals, fibers, plastics, and drugs are related by a common skill in chemical technology.

₄₄

[1] □

LINKED RELATEDNESS — the businesses in this group are not all interrelated but each is related tangibly to at least one other business in the group. For example, while General Electric is active in businesses as disparate as jet engines and TV broadcasting, it has always linked new businesses to old when expanding. Jet engines are linked to turbines, which are linked to electric power equipment. Electric power equipment is linked to electric appliances, electronic appliances to electronics and electronics finally to TV broadcasting.

Please go to Question 24.

[2] □

21. You have indicated that your company is active in a number of unrelated business areas. Which statement best describes the process by which the company became active in unrelated businesses?

MAJOR MERGER — the firm merged with another firm of comparable size, producing a combined company that is active in unrelated businesses. Corporate examples are Rockwell International (North American Aviation and Rockwell-Standard) and Martin-Marietta (Martin Company and American Marietta).

[1] □

ACQUISITION — the firm acquired a number of companies that were active in areas unrelated to the original firm's businesses. Corporate examples are Litton Industries, LTV, and Lear Siegler.

[2] □

INTERNAL DEVELOPMENT — the firm became active in unrelated businesses through internal investment and development.

[3] □

Please go on to question 22.

22. Has the corporation made five or more acquisitions in the past five years, each of which added at least 5% to corporate revenues?

Yes, please answer Question 23   [1] □

No, please go to Question 24   [2] □

23. Of the five acquisitions referred to in Question 22, were at least three diversification moves into businesses unrelated to previous activities?

Yes [1] □

No [2] □

Please go to Question 24.

24. Please tell us who you are?

Name _____

Title _____

Mailing Address _____

_____

_____

Telephone _____

25. May we list the name of your company as a participant in this research (although we will not disclose your specific response)?

Yes □

No □

Please return the questionnaire, your latest annual report, and the requested organization chart in the enclosed self-addressed envelope.

Thank you for completing the questionnaire.

15

FINANCIAL EXECUTIVES RESEARCH FOUNDATION

633 THIRD AVENUE
NEW YORK. N.Y. 10017
TEL 212 953 0500

Dear FEI Member:

Last summer you completed a questionnaire for a research study entitled "Profit Measurement and Decentralization" sponsored by the Financial Executives Research Foundation and conducted by Professor Richard F. Vancil of Harvard Business School, assisted by the staff of Management Analysis Center, a national management consulting and research firm. In return for your participation we promised to send you a computer generated analysis that summarizes the responses of all participants. We have enclosed this summary along with a copy of your original questionnaire response, so that you will be able to compare your company to tabulations developed in our research.

As a result of our data analysis we think it essential to extend the scope of the study to include a measurement of the responsibilities of profit center managers. We have enclosed three additional question- naires designed and carefully field tested to gather this information. We would like you to forward these questionnaires to three operating profit center managers who manage profit centers typical of the ones you had in mind in completing the first questionnaire. It is important that these respondents have at least two years experience in their current position. Field tests indicate that it takes less than ten minutes to complete this questionnaire.

Please remember that a profit center is defined as any fairly independent organizational unit, accountable separately for its performance, for which some measure of profit is determined periodically. Examples include decentralized divisions or departments, and product groups. This questionnaire requests information only for your **DOMESTIC** profit centers which are not separate legal entities (subsidiaries).

Also, we have enclosed a short questionnaire containing a few demographic questions. Would **you** please complete this questionnaire and return it in the attached envelope.

Since the information is confidential, we again assure you that precautions are taken to protect you and your company. All responses are entered in the data bank in coded form with company identities known only to the project director and his assistant. You will be identified as a participant in the research only if specifically requested in the first questionnaire. In no instance will your company ever be identified as giving a particular response.

Your cooperation is vital if we are to obtain full value from the information already submitted by your corporate officer. Please take a few minutes to forward the Profit Center Manager questionnaires and to complete the demographic questionnaire.

Sincerely,

Ben Makela

Ben Makela
Research Director

```
┌──┬──┬──┬──┐   ┌──┐
│  │  │  │  │   │  │
└──┴──┴──┴──┘   └──┘
 1  2  3  4      5
```

Demographic Questionnaire
(to be completed by FEI participant)

1. 1975 Percentage Income Statement for Corporation:

   Note: This question is very important for our data analysis. It requests information that may not be readily available at the corporate level and, even if available, is highly confidential. We do not need precise answers — your estimates will suffice. For two-digit percentages, you may round to the nearest five percent. For one-digit percentages, you may alter the real number by one percent in either direction. Please make sure the column adds to 100%.

   Revenue 100%

   Cost of Goods Sold .... _____ 10 11

   Research and Development Expense .... _____ 12 13

   Sales and Marketing Expense .... _____ 14 15

   Distribution Expense .... _____ 16 17

   Administration Expense .... _____ 18 19

   Interest Expense .... _____ 20 21

   Other Income and Expense (Net) .... _____ 22 23

   Taxes .... _____ 24 25

   Profits After Tax .... _____ 26 27
                                                                              100%

2. Average Size of Typical Profit Center as a Percent of Total Corporate Revenues:

0- 5%	☐	1 28
5-10%	☐	2
10-20%	☐	3
20-30%	☐	4
30-40%	☐	5
40-50%	☐	6

4. 1975 Sales Revenue .... $ 0 - 24 million ☐   1   7
                                                            25 - 49 million ☐   2
                                                            50 - 99 million ☐   3
                                           100 - 199 million ☑   4
                                         200 - 299 million ☐   5
                                         300 - 399 million ☐   6
                                         400 - 599 million ☐   7
                                         600 - 999 million ☐   8
                                         1 billion or more ☐   9

5. 1975 Profit After Tax / Sales ....   0% - 2.49% ☐   1   8
                                            2.5% - 5.49% ☐   2
                                            5.5% - 9.49% ☐   3
                                           9.5% - 15.49% ☐   4
                                        15.5% or more ☐   5

6. 1975/1965 EPS Ratio .... 0.   - 1.28 ☐   1   9
    (divide your 1975 earnings per share by your 1965 E.P.S.,   1.29 - 1.71 ☐   2
    adjusted for stock splits):   1.72 - 2.48 ☐   3
                                           2.49 - 4.22 ☐   4
                                             Over 4.23 ☐   5

[Note: From these figures we automatically derive the 10-year compounded growth rate. For example, over 4.23 ratio implies over 15.5% growth compounded growth rate.]

PLEASE COMPLETE BOTH SIDES

QUESTIONNAIRE

Responsibilities of Profit Center Managers

Dear Sir:

Last Fall the central financial office of your corporation agreed to cooperate with the Financial Executives Research Foundation on a research project entitled "Profit Measurement and Decentralization." At that time, your corporate office provided us with detailed information about the accounting policies used to calculate profit for a "typical" profit center such as yours.

To help us analyze the data we have already received, we would now like to learn something about the nature of your responsibilities as a profit center manager. This questionnaire has been carefully field tested and can be completed in ten minutes or less. Your answers will be treated as strictly confidential. We will not transmit them to anyone in your corporation, and in the final report on this project they will be an anonymous portion of the data provided by other profit center managers in the 300 participating corporations.

Your cooperation is vital if we are to obtain full value from the information already submitted by your corporate office. Please take a few minutes to complete the questionnaire and return it directly to me in the attached envelope.

Your assistance is greatly appreciated.

Sincerely yours,

R F Vancil

Richard F. Vancil
M.A.C. Inc.
10 Moulton Street
Cambridge, Ma. 02138

I. Major Actions Affecting the Performance of Your Profit Center

Listed below are actions which could have an impact on the performance of your profit center. We are interested in the extent of your influence in determining what action is taken. Please read the six categories carefully. Then, for each action, check the category which most closely describes the way that the decision is "typically" determined.

MY INITIATIVE. I identify an issue on which action appears necessary, and proceed as follows:

MY DECISION. I (or one of my subordinates) decide what action to take.

Note: We are not asking whether you have the authority to decide, but whether you usually do make the decision without first discussing it with others outside your profit center.

TWO-PERSON DECISION. My superior and I discuss the issue and decide what action to take.

MULTI-PERSON DECISION. My superior and I, and other operating or administrative managers outside my profit center who need to be involved, discuss the issue and decide what action to take.

CORPORATE DECISION. The action to take is decided at the corporate level because it (1) requires a change in existing corporate policy, or (2) is the responsibility of a corporate-level department or committee.

INITIATED BY OTHERS. The need for an action of this sort is usually initiated by a higher level administrative department, but I may be consulted before the decision is made.

NOT APPLICABLE. Actions of this sort do not occur in this business or do not affect the performance of my profit center.

	My Initiative					
	My Decision	Two-Person Decision	Multi-Person Decision	Corporate Decision	Initiated By Others	Not Applicable
A. Product/Market Decisions 1. Discontinuing a major existing product or product line.							7
2. Redesigning products for a major existing product line.							8
3. Expanding into new marketing territories for existing products.							9
4. Investing in major plant and equipment to expand capacity for existing products.							10
5. Developing a major new product line.							11
B. Sourcing of Materials and Services 6. Buying from an outside vendor when the items required could be supplied by another unit in your corporation.							12
7. Selecting the outside vendor to supply an important raw material or component used in operations.							13

	My Initiative				Initiated By Others	Not Applicable	
	My Decision	Two-Person Decision	Multi-Person Decision	Corporate Decision			
8. Selecting the vendor to supply major components for an approved capital expenditure project.							14
9. Hiring a consultant for assistance in developing or modifying operating systems (such as production scheduling or accounting).							15
10. Hiring a consultant for special studies (such as market research or technological surveys).							6
C. Other Operating Decisions 11. Increasing the planned level of expenditures for advertising and promotion.							17
12. Changing the selling price on a major product or product line.							18
13. Changing the policy governing the level of investment in inventories.							19
14. Increasing (beyond budget) the number of exempt personnel employed in your profit center.							20
15. Increasing (beyond budget) the number of non-exempt personnel employed in your profit center.							21
D. Personnel Decisions 16. Promoting one of your lower-level managers to a higher position in your profit center.							22
17. Firing one of your direct subordinates (a manager at the next level below you).							23
18. Hiring a new person from outside your corporation to become one of your direct subordinates.							24
19. Determining the size of a bonus to be paid to a direct subordinate.							25
20. Changing the fringe benefits (pension plan, medical insurance, etc.) provided to salaried personnel in your profit center.							26
	1	2	3	4	5	6	

II. Other Questions

21. How many months have you reported to your current superior? Length of relationship_____ months.

22. Do you normally receive incentive compensation in the form of an annual cash bonus?   Yes
                                                                                                  No

   If yes, what is the approximate amount of the bonus, stated as a percentage of your annual salary?
   (Please use a rough average of the percentages over the last three years.)   Bonus percentage _____ %

   Does your corporation have a formula for determining a total corporate bonus pool based on   Yes
   corporate financial performance?   No

   How, if at all, is **your** bonus (or share of a corporate pool) related to the current financial performance of **your**
   profit center? (Check one)
   a. Bonus is determined by a formula:
      (1) Based solely on financial performance
      (2) Based partly on financial performance
   b. No formula, but financial performance is clearly a factor in determining the size of the bonus:
      (1) A very important factor
      (2) A reasonably important factor
   c. Financial performance is not an important factor in determining my bonus.

23. Do you believe that profit, as it is routinely calculated for your profit center, fairly reflects the
    effectiveness of your performance as a manager, to the extent that such performance can be
    measured in financial terms?
   a. Yes, it is a fair measurement of my performance.
   b. A few imperfections, but still a useful measurement.
   c. Serious flaws. I don't think it is a fair measurement.
   If you checked (b) or (c) above, please comment on the most important imperfections or flaws.

Partial list of corporations responding to the structural questionnaire (261 out of 291 in the sample)

Abbott Laboratories
Addressograph Multigraph Corp.
A. E. Stanley Mfg. Co.
Agway Inc.
A. H. Robins Co., Inc.
Air Products and Chemicals, Inc.
Akzona Inc.
Albany International Corp.
Allied Chemical Corp.
Allis-Chalmers Corp.
Aluminum Company of America
American Cyanamid Co.
Anchor Hocking Glass Corp.
Ashland Oil Inc.
Atlantic Richfield Co.
ATO, Inc.
Automation Industries, Inc.
AVM Corp.
Avon Products, Inc.
Avondale Shipyards, Inc.

Balfour Guthrie & Co. Ltd.
Banner Industries, Inc.
BASF Wyandotte, Corp.
Bath Industries, Inc.
Bay State Milling Co.
Beckman Instruments, Inc.
Becton Dickenson & Co.
Belden Corporation
Bemis Co., Inc.
Bergen Brunswick Corp.
Bird & Son, Inc.
Blue Bell Inc.
Bobbie Brooks, Inc.
Boise Cascade Corp.
Borg-Warner Corp.
Brown Co.
Brush Wellman, Inc.
Bunker Ramo Corp.
Burlington Industries, Inc.

Burlington Northern, Inc.
Burroughs Corp.
Burroughs Wellcome Co.
Butler Mfg. Co.

California Portland Cement Co.
Cameron Iron Works, Inc.
Campbell Taggert, Inc.
Carlisle Corp.
Caron International, Inc.
Carpenter Technology Corp.
Carrier Corp.
Castle & Cooke, Inc.
CBS, Inc.
Celanese Corp. of America
Certain-Teed Products Corp.
Champion International Corp.
Chemed Corp.
Chemetron Corp.
Chicopee Mfg. Co.
Chromalloy Nat. Res. Co.
Ciba-Geigy Ltd.
Clark Oil and Refining Corp.
Clopay Corp.
Clow Corp.
Coats & Clark, Inc.
Cole National Corp.
Colgate Palmolive Co.
Cone Mills Corp.
Consolidated Food Corp.
Consolidated Paper, Inc.
Container Corp. of America
Continental Can Co., Inc.
Continental Oil Co.
Cordis Corp.
Cortland Corp.
Cott Corp.
Crompton & Knowles Corp.
C. R. Bard, Inc.
Cummins Engine Co., Inc.

Curtice-Burns Inc.
Cyclops Corp.

Dan River Inc.
Dayco Corp.
Dayton-Walther Corp.
DeSoto Inc.
Diamond Shamrock Corp.
DiGiorgio Corp.
Digital Equipment Corp.
Dover Corp.
Dravo Corp.
Dresser Industries, Inc.
Du Pont (E.I.) de Nemours & Co.
Dymo Industries Inc.
Dynalectron Corp.
Dyson-Kissner Corp.

Earle M. Jorgensen Co.
EG & G, Inc.
Endicott Johnson Corp.
Esterline Corp.

Fairchild Camera & Instrument Corp.
Falcon Products, Inc.
Fansteel Inc.
Federal Mogul Corp.
Fieldcrest Mills, Inc.
Filtrol Corp.
Firestone Tire & Rubber Co.
Fisher Scientific Co.
Flintkote Co.
Florida Steel Co.
Flowers Industries, Inc.
FMC Corp.
Foremost-McKesson, Inc.
Foster Grant Co., Inc.
Foster Wheeler Corp.
Freeport Minerals Co.
Fruehauf Corp.

Garlock Inc.
General Cable Corp.
General Foods Corp.
General Host Corp.
General Mills, Inc.
General Portland Inc.
General Signal Corp.

Genesco Inc.
Gerber Products Co.
Getty Oil Co.
Giddings and Lewis, Inc.
Gifford-Hill & Co., Inc.
Gillette Co.
Globe-Union, Inc.
Grumman Allied Industries, Inc.

Halliburton Co.
Hallmark Cards, Inc.
Hammermill Paper Co.
Hanes Corp.
Harnischfeger Corp.
Harsco Corp.
Heublein, Inc.
H. H. Robertson Co.
Hitco
Hoerner Waldorf Corp.
Honeywell Inc.
Hooker Chemicals
Houghton Mifflin Co.
The Huffman Manufacturing Co.
Huyck Corp.
Hyster Co.

IBM Corp.
Indian Head, Inc.
Inland-Ryerson Construction
    Products Co.
Inland Steel Co.
Interlake, Inc.
International Basic Economy Corp.
International Multifoods Corp.
Interpace Corp.
Iowa Beef Processors, Inc.
Itek Corp.
ITT Corp.

Jantzen, Inc.
Johns-Manville Corp.
Jones & Laughlin Steel Corp.
Joslyn Mfg. & Supply Co.
J. P. Stevens & Co., Inc.

Kaiser Aluminum & Chemical Corp.
Katy Industries, Inc.
Keller Industries, Inc.

Koehring Co.
Kroehler Mfg. Co.

The Lamson & Sessions Co.
Land O'Lakes, Inc.
L. B. Foster Co.
Lehigh Portland Cement Co.
Lennox Industries Inc.

Lenox, Inc.
Levi Strauss & Co.
LFE Corp.
Libby, McNeil & Libby
Liggett & Myers Inc.
Lipton (Thomas J.) Inc.
Lone Star Gas Co.
Louisiana-Pacific Corp.
LTV Corp.
Ludlow Corp.

The Magnavox Co.
Mapco Inc.
Marathon Steel Co.
Maremont Corp.
Martin Marietta Corp.
McGraw-Edison Co.
Medusa Corp.
Midland Company
Midland Cooperatives, Inc.
Miles Laboratories, Inc.
Mobil Oil Corp.
Monsanto Co.
MTS Systems Corp
Munsingwear Inc.

Nabisco, Inc.
National Homes Corp.
NCR Corp.
Northrop Corp.
Norton Company

Olin Corp.
Omark Industries, Inc.
Otis Elevator Co.
Owens-Illinois, Inc.

Perkin Elmer Corp.
Pfizer, Inc.

Pillsbury Co.
Procter & Gamble Co.

Quaker Oats Co.

Rath Packing Co.
Regal Textile
The Richardson Co.
Riker Maxson Corp.
The Riley Co.
Riverside Manufacturing Industries,
    Inc.
Robert Shaw Controls Co.
RTE Corporation
The Rucker Company
Russell Corp.
Ryan Homes Inc.

Sanders Associates, Inc.
SCM Corp.
The Seagrave Corp.
Sherwin Williams Co.
Singer Co.
Smith & Wesson
The Southland Corp.
Standard Products Co.

The Tanner Companies
The Tappan Co.
Thiokol Corp.
Tillie Lewis Foods
Toro Co.
Total Petroleum Ltd.
The Tournal Co.
Triangle Pacific Corp.
Turbodyne Corp.
Twentieth Century Fox Film Corp.

Union Camp Corp.
Union Oil Co.
United States Gypsum Co.
United States Shoe Corp.
United States Steel Corp.
UOP Inc.
USM Corp.
Utah International, Inc.

Vulcan Materials Co.

Warner-Lambert Co.
The Warner & Swasey Co.
Weyerhaeuser
Whirlpool Co.
White Castle System, Inc.
Whittaker Corp.
Willamette Industries, Inc.
W.T.C. Air Freight

Wurlitzer
Wyman-Gordon Co.

Xerox Corp.

Zapata Corp.
Zurn Industries

Index